WAR BREAD

WAR BREAD

A PERSONAL NARRATIVE OF THE WAR AND RELIEF IN BELGIUM

BY
EDWARD EYRE HUNT

American Delegate of the Commission for Relief in Belgium in charge of the Province of Antwerp

(*With Illustrations*)

WILDSIDE PRESS

Aan
Zyne Eminentie
DÉSIRÉ JOSEPH KARDINAAL MERCIER
Aartsbisschop van Mechelen

aan
DEN HEER LOUIS FRANCK
*Gemeenteraadslid, Schepen, en Volksvertegenwoordiger,
Voorzitter van het Nationaal Komiteit voor
Hulp en Voeding der Provincie
Antwerpen*

aan
DEN HEER EDOUARD BUNGE
*Onder-Voorzitter van het Nationaal Komiteit voor
Hulp en Voeding der Provincie Antwerpen*

To
HERBERT CLARK HOOVER, of California
Chairman of the Commission for Relief in Belgium

and to
BENNETT H. BRANSCOMB, of Alabama
OLIVER C. CARMICHAEL, of Alabama
RICHARD H. SIMPSON, of Indiana
W. W. FLINT, of New Hampshire
W. W. STRATTON, of Utah
THOMAS O. CONNETT, of New York
GARDNER RICHARDSON, of Connecticut
GILCHRIST H. STOCKTON, of Florida
J. B. VAN SCHAICK, of New York

—*Loyal friends, Americans all, fellow-members of the
Antwerp delegation of the Commission for
Relief in Belgium*

Thanks are due the *Metropolitan Magazine,* the *Outlook, Leslie's Weekly,* the *New Republic,* and *Collier's Weekly* for permission to republish portions of this book which have appeared in their pages.

CONTENTS

CHAPTER	PAGE
I. A Voyage in Wartime	1
Off to the Wars	1
Mutiny	4
Captured at Sea	13
Floating Mines	19
Interned	23
A Night on Devil's Island	27
II. Berlin the Terrible	34
Osnabrück to Berlin	34
Prussia Enthroned	38
How the Poor Fared	44
War Worship	50
German "Preparedness"	53
Three Famous Socialists	59
The Attack	67
III. The Fall of Antwerp	71
Berlin Versus Antwerp	71
An American Spy	74
England Aids Belgium	78
War Correspondents	82
The Bombardment of Antwerp	87
What a Shrapnel Shell Did	91
A Bath and a Forced March	95
Blowing up the Bridge	100
Enter: the Germans	104
The Army of Occupation	107
First Aid to Antwerp	110

CONTENTS

CHAPTER		PAGE
	On the Road to Holland	114
	'Vluchtelingen	118
	At the Frontier	121
	Dutch Hospitality	127
	Atrocities	133
	Relief Work in Holland	138
	Cities of Refuge	144
	A Story of King Albert	148
IV.	BELGIUM AS A GERMAN PROVINCE	152
	Antwerp Again	152
	The Conquerors	156
	Humorous Herr Baedeker	162
	German Government	169
V.	STARVING BELGIUM	175
	The Catastrophe	175
	The Cry for Help	180
	Brand Whitlock	185
	Herbert C. Hoover	191
	The Commission for Relief in Belgium	198
	A Dead City	202
	American Delegate for Antwerp	206
	Misery in the Campine	210
	Communications	216
	A Visit from Hoover	220
	The Christmas Ship	224
	Belgian Gratitude	228
	Cardinal Mercier's Pastoral Letter	235
	Patriotic Clocks	241
	Alarums and Excursions	245
	Internal Conflicts	251
	The Waesland	255
	A Belgian Co-operative	258
	Breathing Spells	262

CONTENTS

CHAPTER		PAGE
VI.	THE BELGIAN NATIONAL COMMITTEE	269
	A Great Financier	269
	Hard Cash	273
VII.	SAVING A NATION	280
	Their Daily Bread	280
	Joyous Entries	286
	Bread Lines and Soup Kitchens	293
	Health, Clothing, and Housing	296
	Unemployment	304
VIII.	DIPLOMATIC CONQUESTS	308
	Hauling Down the Flag	308
	Great Britain Takes a Hand	311
	Feeding the North of France	315
IX.	AMERICA AND BELGIUM	318
	The Golden Legend	318
	La Belle Belgique	322

APPENDIX

I.	Three Famous Socialists	327
II.	Press and Post	331
III.	Public Charity and Exchange	333
IV.	Incredibly Small Expenses	334
V.	Gifts of Service	335
VI.	The First Supplies	335
VII.	Early Food Shipments	336
VIII.	Flemish	337
IX.	The Poor	338
X.	Belgian Committees	339
XI.	The Millers' Belgian Relief Movement	341
XII.	The Priest	341
XIII.	Ante-Bellum Belgium	342
XIV.	The Artistic Temperament	342
XV.	First Aid	343

CONTENTS

CHAPTER		PAGE
XVI.	Bar-le-Duc	344
XVII.	Interlocking Organizations	345
XVIII.	Food Requirements	345
XIX.	Coffee	347
XX.	A Co-operative Society	347
XXI.	The National Relief Committee	348
XXII.	The Contribution of War	349
XXIII.	Finance	349
XXIV.	Wheat and Flour	351
XXV.	Distribution	352
XXVI.	Soup Recipes	353
XXVII.	Selling Gift Goods	354
XXVIII.	"American Shops"	356
XXIX.	The Clothing Workshop	357
XXX.	Temporary Houses	359
XXXI.	Unemployment Relief	361
XXXII.	Bricks and Laces	362
XXXIII.	The Crop Commission	365
XXXIV.	Belgian Harvests	366
XXXV.	The North of France	367
XXXVI.	French Financial Organization	368
XXXVII.	Funding the Relief Work	370
XXXVIII.	Governmental Subsidies	372
XXXIX.	Belgian Gratitude	372

ILLUSTRATIONS

WAR BREAD	*Frontispiece*
	PAGE
YOUNG GERMANY	52
THE AUTHOR'S PASSPORT	74
"BEATING THE CAMERA"	94
BELGIAN REFUGE DIRECTORY	130
THE BREAD LINE	166
BRAND WHITLOCK	188
HERBERT C. HOOVER	194
LOUIS FRANCK	206
MAP OF THE PROVINCE OF ANTWERP	222
CHRISTMAS, 1914	228
CARDINAL MERCIER	238
EDOUARD BUNGE	262
JULY FOURTH, 1915	278
TEMPORARY HOUSES	302
AN "AMERICAN SHOP"	312
FLOUR SACKS	324
ANTWERP'S CLOTHING WORKSHOP	358

WAR BREAD

CHAPTER I

A VOYAGE IN WARTIME

OFF TO THE WARS

THE Holland-America liner " Nieuw Amsterdam " lay fuming at her Hoboken pier. It was midnight, August 24-25, the first month of the war. The air was heavy, like hot oil; pier lights scorched the dark with their electrical glare; and the ship's funnel spat smoke into the starless vault overhead.

Gangways vomited stewards and hastily swallowed them again, for we were sailing in less than an hour. My trunks were lined with cartons of condensed soups, egg powder, and *Erbsenwurst,* for reports on European food conditions were already alarming; the money-belt about my waist was uncomfortably heavy with British and American gold-pieces, for the newspapers said there was no reliable exchange abroad; my pockets were full of important letters, passports, and a bulky life insurance policy. The times were inauspicious for travel. Yet the ship appeared to be full. Everywhere were strange faces. Heavy featured, gruff voiced men, nineteen to forty years old, with thick silver watch-chains looped across their waistcoats and little sausage-roll satchels in their hands, streamed into the ship and shouted good-bys to the crowds of friends who lined the pier.

"Who are they, steward?" I asked.

"German reservists, sir."

"But I thought the ship would be empty."

"Nearly a thousand of them, sir."

In the steerage twenty or thirty men strolled aimlessly up deck and down, droning, with impartial enthusiam and tunelessness, "The Watch on the Rhine," "Hail, Kaiser, to Thee," and a song from the latest musical comedy on Broadway. The night grew more and more electric, and half an hour before sailing time the tension suddenly snapped like cord. A steerage passenger with hair clipped convict-close and face fiery red, shirtless and hatless, reeled slowly down deck, singing. Others followed him unsteadily, and at the end of the song they leaned together, arms linked, and he led them in three "hochs" for the Kaiser. Passengers from the first and second cabins cheered. The mob of friends ashore in the glare of the pier lights waved handkerchiefs and shouted applause.

There was a sudden stir beside me. On the promenade deck a huge reservist, his cheeks slashed with the rapier scars of his German student corps days, bellowed a ripping "hurrrrrrrrrrrrah!" and instantly, as if a military command had been given and an army had obeyed, the masses of men fell into triple lines across the decks, facing the pier, and began to sing "The Watch on the Rhine." They roared and rumbled and trampled the music out, so that it beat in a steady series of explosions against the high walls of the pier. If Krupp guns could sing they would sing like that. There was more menace in the music than in any I had heard before. It expressed no wild, universal human longing, such as one feels in the chant in the "Marseillaise"; it seemed part of the vast, age-long, irresistible march of the Teutonic races.

They sang *Deutschland über alles.* Volleys of voices beat my ears with a shock like battle. The singers, I learned afterward, had come from Alaska, Canada, the United States, Mexico, Brazil, the Saskatchewan, but they sang as if they had been drilled to sing together since childhood. Then came "Hail, Kaiser, to Thee"; then the Austrian National Hymn; then the old Swabian folk-song, *Muss i denn, muss i denn zum Städtele hinaus,* the farewell which German soldiers have sung for centuries to their sweethearts when they go to the wars.

And there were sweethearts at hand; the pier was lined with them, waving their handkerchiefs and cheering at every pause in the singing. There were mothers and wives and brothers and sisters and friends, all there on the pier, three or four yards away, packed against the rail and plainly visible in the white electric glare. But while the men sang there were no tears, and when the singing stopped there were no tears, and when at one o'clock the ship began slowly to move out into the black river and the cheering rose to salvoes of enthusiasm, until the Captain had to blow his whistle to drown the partisan noise, still there were no tears. The grief of parting hid itself under a stern and pitiless joy at being able to share in Germany's war. The men were off to win personal glory, but far more than that they were to win national glory; glory for Germany, for German might, German efficiency, German organization, German intelligence, German capacity for taking pains—for "Germany first," *Deutschland über alles.*

The passengers on the "Nieuw Amsterdam" did not trouble to think that America was a neutral country; that the ship on which they sailed was a neutral ship. They did not trouble to think what a scandalized New York City press and public would say of them next morning. They were off to the wars at last. They cared for one thing—for *Deutschland über alles,* over neutral ships and neutral nations, neutral thoughts and neutral silence, too; for they were going home to the wars.

Mutiny

"It can't be; it can't be, I tell you!"

A group of reservists pounded the ship's bulletin-board with their fists and yelled in fear and hate. Others clawed at them, struggling and swaying to and fro in an effort to read something newly written on a square sheet of white paper, posted under the heading "Marconigrams." The day's war news, picked up by wireless and posted at noontime, was already old. A sketchy war map pinned to the bulletin-board by Dr. Hendrik Willem van Loon showed the victorious German armies sweeping like a sickle through France toward Paris. Louvain was burning. Belgium was overrun. Lille had fallen. Cossacks were in East Prussia.

But a more sensational message had arrived. Men came running from up and down the saloon stairs and fought those ahead of them to read it.

"What had happened?" they demanded breathlessly.
"What is it?"
"Bad news?"
"The English?"
"Is it the damned English?"
"Are we going to be captured? Are we going to be captured?"

We had been seven days at sea. The "Nieuw Amsterdam" was more like a military transport than a neutral liner. Of her thousand passengers only seventy-five were women; two hundred Dutch reservists were in the steerage—they were wanted at home to keep Holland out of the war—and more than seven hundred and fifty German and Austrian citizens of military age were scattered throughout the ship. There was a Prussian staff officer in the steerage; a nephew of Count von Bernstorff, German Ambassador to Washington, was in the second cabin; there were privates in the first cabin, and one and all they tramped the sanded decks from morning till night like infantry on the march. They cultivated bristling mustaches, and the ship's barber grew rich clipping their hair.

And always they talked of the war. They knew to the slightest detail the organization of their armies, the number of corps, and the broad strategy of the war. War to them was a science, not a thing of horror. War was to recreate Europe. War was an incident in national life; a step on a long road, deliberately planned for, deliberately entered upon, the end of it long foreseen. Let the nations fight: Germany would conquer. In the end Germany must dominate Europe, and confer upon it German order, German system, German efficiency.

Things like Belgian neutrality were unimportant when the evolution of the German Empire was at stake.

But after the first wild burst of enthusiasm, the reservists grew anxious. Fear, laboriously held in check, lurked always beneath the surface of their thoughts. Every smudge of smoke on the horizon suggested a pursuing British cruiser. The thought of England became a nightmare. Every league nearer the English coast made England bulk larger in their imaginations, and they

MUTINY

talked less and less of Germany and more and more of England. The steerage passengers lay all day like sleepy, watchful cats, stretched out on slack gray canvases covering the life-boats, and studied the pitiless open sea. First cabin passengers promenaded the hurricane deck and swept the waters with glasses or demanded news at the door of the Marconi room. Rumors flew from mouth to mouth, and fear and hatred throve.

Thick fog came with the seventh day at sea, and the spirits of the reservists rose again. "It will probably hold until we reach Rotterdam," they said. "But the British won't dare to touch us, even if they stop us. This is a neutral ship. The Germans will be in Calais by the time we reach the English Channel. We'll put a pistol to the Captain's head and make him take us inside the three-mile limit and land us right with the German army!"

But Captain Baron of the "Nieuw Amsterdam" now turned the tables on his passengers. On the bulletin-board was a short and ominous message from the captain of our sister ship, the "Rotterdam," *en route* to New York:

Noon position 50.9 N., 15.30 W. Foggy in Channel. Since good weather. Was held up by British cruiser between Downs and Lizard. "Potsdam" was ordered by English warship to proceed to Falmouth. No news about passengers when I left Rotterdam, but probably Germans and Austrian reservists taken off. Pleasant trip.

(Signed) STENGER.

The group about the bulletin-board roared threats and suggestions. "We must fight! We must do something! Go to the Captain and make him take us back! Make him take us back to New York. Make him go north around Ireland. Make him take us to Hamburg. Shoot him if he won't do it!"

I raced up to the Captain's office, just below the bridge, and waited for the next move. Fog deluged the ship, screening her from all eyes, and the waves roared beneath. Sky and sea and air were a dirty, dangerous gray. But the fog horn was dumb and the wireless gave no sign. We were silently running toward the British patrols. Somewhere hidden in the fogbanks before us the liner "Rotterdam" was hurrying toward New York and safety. Would the Germans compel our Captain to put them aboard her? Would they make him turn back with the "Nieuw Amsterdam"? I knew they were desperate. The men clustered about the bulletin-board were half frantic with fear. Their next move would be interesting.

There was not long to wait. Six officers of the reserves suddenly appeared in line at the door, bowed, removed their caps, and in perfect silence filed over the threshold and ranged themselves about the Captain.

"*Herr Kapitän,*" the senior German began, clutching his North German Yacht Club cap in his nervous fingers, "we have seen the marconigram from the captain of the

'Rotterdam.' We request that you turn the ship about and sail her back to New York."

The Captain's chilblain cheeks glowed crimson and his walrus mustaches stiffened as he answered in halting German, carefully picking his words. "Gentlemen," he began, "this is a neutral ship. I go on, or I lose my ship and my commission."

"Then, Captain, you must set us on board the 'Rotterdam' to be returned to America."

"But," objected Captain Baron, "the 'Rotterdam' is crowded already. Every ship for America now is full with Americans anxious to get home; *nik wahr?* There are eight hundred of you. How could I transfer so many?"

The spokesman flushed. He decided to be brutally frank, to think only of his own safety. "We do not ask you to transfer all," he said sullenly.

"Who then?"

"I speak for myself and my friends." He indicated the committee with a wave of his cap.

The Captain retorted hotly, "I will not do for you what I would not do for the others!"

"All the first-class passengers, then!"

"I will not do for the first-class what I cannot do for the second-class and steerage." Then he added, persuasively, "Think, gentlemen; there would be riot down there if I transferred only you."

The committee muttered. "Transfer all, then. Captain, you must——"

"Transfer in this heavy sea?" The Captain stared. "My boats would be knocked to pieces. If one boat is smashed, if one life is lost, I am responsible; *nik wahr?*"

The committee grew openly angry. One after the other they snapped out orders, and the Captain answered more and more stiffly.

"You must take us to Spain!"

"To Spain?" The Captain shrugged his shoulders. "I have only enough coal to reach Rotterdam. My papers say I go to Rotterdam. I go there—not to Spain."

"To the Azores!"

"But, gentlemen, the Azores are two thousand miles away."

"Around England to the north!"

"But coal?"

"By God, Captain, you must do something for us! It was understood when we bought our tickets of your company——"

"Gentlemen, gentlemen, nothing is understood at sea. Anything can happen at sea; *nik wahr?* On the back of your ticket it says you agree this company shall not be held responsible for loss or damage arising from acts of God, accidents at sea, or any acts of princes or rulers of peoples."

"But, Captain——"

"I cannot do anything."

"But——"

"I say I cannot do anything."

Perspiration started on the brows of the committeemen. They stared at each other and at the Captain helplessly. Each man was thinking only of himself. Freedom or prison until the end of the war hung in the balance, and the Captain held the scales. They itched to settle the matter by a fight, instead of argument, but the old Captain was stubbornly firm. "If there is outbreak I put the troublemakers in irons; *nik wahr?*"

The committee decided to surrender at discretion, and its spokesman addressed the Captain again. "*Herr Kapitän*, will you allow us to send a marconigram to the captain of the 'Rotterdam'?"

"Certainly, gentlemen."

"We will ask him to take us off."

"Of course, of course. But I know what the captain of the 'Rotterdam' says. He says, 'I have already three thousand passengers. I cannot take one more.' But you may send the message."

The committee climbed slowly down the ladder, brushing aside nine-year old Hans, a little lonely German boy who would never march or fight because of a lame hip, but who played constantly with toy soldiers. The crowd of passengers rumbled with excitement. They rushed on the committeemen and overwhelmed them with questions. "What did the Captain say?" "Will he set us on the 'Rotterdam'?" "Are we going back to America?" "What are we going to do?" "Shall we get through?" "Are we going to Hamburg?"

"To the smoking-room!" ordered the senior member loudly. "To the smoking-room! to the smoking-room!" echoed the crowd, and rushed down the decks and through the narrow doorways, hunting for places of vantage among the tables, chairs, and heavily upholstered seats.

The chairman walked to the center of the room, ceremoniously removed his cap and placed it beside a plate of sandwiches, cleared his throat, and waited for absolute silence before he began.

"Gentlemen," he said, ignoring the presence of the ladies, "the Captain permits us to send a marconi to the captain of the 'Rotterdam' to ask that he take us back to New York. We can do nothing else. How many favor?"

Twenty or thirty hands flew up. There was consternation on every face, but no attempt at debate. The chairman clutched his yachting cap, placed it on his head, and strode out to draft the wireless message.

Half an hour later Captain Baron gave the answer. The "Rotterdam" could do nothing. She was less than ten miles away from us, blanketed in mist, but every stateroom was filled to bursting with Americans frantic to get home, and Captain Stenger could give no aid to the passengers on the "Nieuw Amsterdam." There was nothing to do but to sail straight on into the jaws of the British Lion—jaws which stretched from Cape Town to Bergen—and chalked up on the bulletin-board beside Captain Stenger's first marconigram appeared this warning:

Passengers will please pay their Wine Bills to the Head Steward before leaving the Ship.

CAPTURED AT SEA

A dull echo of thunder awoke me. It was five o'clock. The haze of early morning swam dizzily past the clouded port-holes, so one could see nothing outside. An excited Teutonic voice began calling in the passageway; then another and another. A child cried out. Suddenly the engines stopped, and the ship slid forward noiselessly except for the lapping of waves.

I tumbled out of my berth and ran upstairs, in pajamas, dancing pumps, and overcoat. Others ahead of me had made equally impromptu toilets and met each new arrival with grim laughter and jests.

We were stopped, but were we captured? The thunderclap that woke me had been the sound of a shot fired across our bows.

Standing on the slippery deck and clinging to the dripping rail, we saw a passenger ship of about the tonnage of the "Nieuw Amsterdam," with big red funnels and black hull, slowly bearing down toward us. A gun or two peered from her forecastle; two large signal flags—

a white cross on a blue field and a blue-and-white checkerboard—the code which means "stop immediately"—flew at her peak. A gull, the first we had seen for a week, swung lazily in the level morning light between the two ships, and a shark undulated alongside.

But what was the nationality of the stranger? I looked twice for her flag and could hardly believe my eyes. It was the tricolor of France!

"She's not British: she's French!" I gasped to a German beside me.

"*Donnerwetter!*" he groaned, "France; not England after all. It will be worse for us than if the English had captured us. This is the second of September—Sedan Day—the anniversary of the battle where we captured their Emperor. A bad day for us! a very bad day!"

The newcomer slid broadside to us. We could see seven or eight guns pointing wickedly from between her decks or from the bridge; a moment more and we could read her name: she was "La Savoie," a passenger ship of the French Line, plying ordinarily between Havre and New York.

On the boat-deck one of the Dutch marconi operators was leaning over the rail behind a life-raft. His white, angular profile was turned seaward, but he heard my step and wheeled. To my astonishment his face was radiant. "Good," he hissed exultantly; "*Vive la France! Vive la France; n'est-ce pas?* These damned

Germans are going to get what's coming to them. Why, they've treated me like a dog, sir. They've bullied and hectored and abused me, because I wouldn't tell them the news. They'll cool their heels in prison while this war lasts, I hope. Hurrah! *Vive la France!*"

A little white boat appeared at the side of the stranger and was lowered rapidly to the water. Five minutes later it was alongside the "Nieuw Amsterdam," and a dainty French lieutenant, neat as a doll, in blue coat, gold braid, and ceremonial sword, scampered up the ship's ladder. Behind him climbed two tars who looked like house-painters tricked out in white overalls and blue sailor caps, and armed with pistols and cutlasses.

At first it was difficult to take the capture seriously. The little lieutenant's sword got in his way, and he fell flat on the fog-soaked deck to an accompaniment of gruff chuckles from the German passengers. But he was on his feet in an instant, and he took time on his way to meet the Captain to remove his blue-and-gold cap and bow gracefully to a pretty lady who was watching. Our ship had been a man's world until that moment—the reservists ignored women—but the first Frenchman who met us restored womanhood to its gilded pedestal with a single bow.

The conference in the Captain's office was brief. Our papers were seized, the wireless apparatus was dismantled, the marconi room sealed, and the ship and all on her were declared prisoners of war. Captain Baron was asked to leave his office and the bridge, and the dainty little lieutenant assumed command.

The cutter next brought a detail of marines, armed with rifles, fixed bayonets, and pistols thrust into wide black belts. The armament was impressive, and it was disquieting to think of the havoc one fool might cause; but the faces and bearing of the marines were most amiable.

It was not until evening, however, that we made a startling and reassuring discovery regarding our warders. My friend, Dr. van Loon, who was in constant demand as interpreter, and who changed from English and Dutch to German and French without shifting verbal gears, was in quizzical conversation with the master at arms in charge of the detail of marines—a fat, sedate little Frenchman, wearing a huge medal for service in Dahomey.

"Who are you?" he asked the Frenchman. "Who are you, I mean, when you aren't capturing Dutch steamers on the high seas?"

"I am steward of 'La Savoie,' monsieur."

"You are what?"

"Head steward of 'La Savoie,' monsieur. I have charge of the dining-room."

"Ye gods! And what about these fellows you have charge of here—these fellows with guns and bayonets?"

"They are stewards, also, monsieur."

"*Gott strafe* stewards! And do you do this sort of thing often?"

"Pardon, monsieur?"

"Do you often capture ships and put prize crews on board of them?"

"Monsieur, I will tell you the truth; you are our first capture! But it is pleasant capturing ships; pleasanter than being always a steward; *n'est-ce pas?*" And he beamed amiably.

Morning passed, and still we lay where we had first been arrested. "La Savoie" grimly circled round and round us, trying to train all her seventeen guns on us at once, but still we did not move. Wild rumors of our fate spread like fire about the ship, but the little doll-like lieutenant sat in the Captain's office and waited patiently.

"Why are we waiting?" he was asked.

"Orders from Paris, messieurs."

"Then where shall you take us?"

"I do not know." He shrugged his shoulders eloquently. "Maybe Cherbourg, maybe Brest."

"And how long will it take us to get to Cherbourg?"

"I do not know." Another shrug. "Maybe three hours, maybe five hours, maybe twelve hours."

"For the Lord's sake! And then what are you going to do?"

"We take you off."

One of the German officers spoke up insolently. "Monsieur," he drawled, "Cherbourg is not far from Paris, is it? We shall get there in time to join the German armies marching in."

The lieutenant smiled placidly. "We take you off," he repeated. "Orders from Paris."

Days afterward we learned that during those heavy hours when we lay at sea under the guns of "La Savoie" Paris had ceased to be the capital of France. The encircling Germans were close. Archives, records, and the Government itself were removed to Bordeaux, and the armies and the shell of Paris awaited the invaders.

After noon we were ordered to proceed to Brest, so, with "La Savoie" leading the way and covering us with her wicked stern guns, we steamed slowly southward over the summer sea. It was night when we anchored off the harbor entrance. Through soft evening haze two lighthouses winked drowsily at us, and a pale moon looked down in sympathy. It had been a hard day. So small a thing as the pounding of a salt-cellar on a table in the dining-room at luncheon brought us to our feet as if we were shot. Lame little Hans, clumping along the deck, alone seemed untroubled by the general misery. In the afternoon I strolled into the smoking-room to find that haven of masculine comfort occupied by one German, and he playing solitaire.

But the Dutch stewards and some of the crew seemed actually to enjoy the situation. In a week the German passengers had made themselves almost universally unpopular. They abused the stewards, quarreled with the Captain and Purser, and wrangled among themselves. They insisted on maintaining small, mutually hostile groups, apparently based on military or nationalistic lines. Hungarians, Austrians, Prussians, and Bavarians flocked by themselves, but all united to despise our Dutch hosts. In retaliation, the stewards were quick to strike up acquaintance with their French guards, and at night, as I passed the drying-room on Deck "C," I overheard the tailor and his helper gaily whistling the "Marseillaise."

FLOATING MINES

At nine o'clock some of us were standing on the boat-deck of the "Nieuw Amsterdam" when suddenly a searchlight blazed out of the darkness and fingered rapidly along our decks and superstructure. What made the light most interesting was the fact that it was borne over the water at extraordinary speed and in our direction. It came like an express train in a vast and splendid curve, probing us every instant with its calcium glare, till ropes and spars and davits lay bare to its gaze. The light was very close now, and we could see a vague snaky hull and two small black stacks.

"Torpedo-boat!" muttered a reservist.

The little craft tore along behind, then around us; all the time examining us with her searchlight. Suddenly the light snapped off, and we were left in Egyptian darkness, straining our eyes after the vanished ship.

A few minutes more, and little bunched lights, like clusters of fireflies, appeared in three directions at once drawing toward us. They slid across the calm summer sea like water-skaters across a pond, and there was something so ethereal, so ghostly about them that it seemed impossible to imagine that they were instruments of destruction. They ranged about us, two or three thousand yards away. A hoarse voice began a megaphoned conversation. Another voice coughed back a brief answer. A glaring searchlight flashed on and examined us again—nook and cranny, wireless apparatus and waterline. Then the bunched lights began to flash off and on in rhythmic order, changing colors as they flashed: red—red—yellow—red—yellow—yellow. The torpedo-boats were signaling.

One of them drew closer to us, and a megaphoned voice retched out a query and was answered from our bridge. The firefly lights flashed new signals; then the boats ranged about us—one dead ahead, one astern, one on either side—and the "Nieuw Amsterdam" steamed forward.

"Damned little French rowboats!" grunted a reservist near me. "You should see our High Seas fleet," and he leaned across the rail and began to explain to me the superiority of the German craft.

I left him abruptly and went to find the Captain, for

an uncomfortable thought had just occurred to me and I longed for confirmation of my fears. "We're going over mine fields," I said to myself. "If one of the mines has happened to get loose from its anchorage, *pfzzt*—up we go! The night is black as ink, and there are just four torpedo-boats to rescue more than a thousand passengers and the crew!"

"No. It is the other way round," said Captain Baron.

"How do you mean?"

"The boot is on the other foot. It is not the French mine to be afraid of, but the German mine. There are no mines here at the entrance of the harbor of Brest, but the French have found floating mines in the Bay of Biscay, and they say German passengers on neutral vessels have sown them.

"You have not a mine with you?" He looked at me smilingly. "That is good. The torpedo-boats turn their searchlights on the ship for fear the Germans sow mines here."

A tall, angular Prussian officer with whom I had struck up an acquaintanceship joined me on the hurricane deck to watch the ship's manœuvring. His right cheek bore the purple welts of rapier scars and he stood erect as a pine tree, peering into the darkness ahead.

"It will soon be over," I said.

"*Ja*," he answered. After a pause, some shaft of feeling seemed to pierce his temperamental armor-plate, and he began to tell me of his experiences as an officer in the German army. "Uhlan officer ten and one-half year," he went on in English. "Now I am prisoner, without the fight. It will be hard. It will be hard for all, *nicht?* but most hard for me, I think. Harder than for those others. You see, I am officer; I am in the regular army ten and one-half year; *nicht?* The others, they are only reserves. It do not matter for them."

His face lightened suddenly with a new thought, and he turned to me with animation. "But in prison I am better off as them. I am officer, *nicht?* And in the prison the German officer gets same pay as French officer in the battle. French officer in German prison, he gets same pay. So I do not have to work. Maybe I report once a day; write my name down on a paper. The others must work. Not so bad for me, *nicht?*

"And not long, either. We take Paris, *nicht?* The war is over in six weeks. Then we take London. Then we sign the peace. A short war, *nicht?*"

"Perhaps," I said.

"If it is long, then I am better here as in England. Brest is not so far from Paris. I know all France. I escape from the prison, *nicht?* I get so to the German army, and am officer of Uhlans. *Ach,* that is fine, fine; *nicht?*"

Half an hour later our flotilla had passed the black

cliffs on either side of the channel and was in the harbor. Like pinpricks of yellow light in a misty screen, the distant city of Brest appeared. Passengers stood in awed silence on the decks of the "Nieuw Amsterdam." It was a cruel contrast with our departure from New York, and we were full of fears and hopes and wonder.

Two young reservists leaned side by side against the rail. They had their arms about each other, and once I saw the younger rest his head for a moment on the shoulder of the other. It was the only bit of tenderness I noticed during the time I was with the reservists.

We slid slowly on over the calm water. One by one our torpedo-boat escorts flashed their signal lights for a moment, and then made off into the darkness. Ahead of us loomed the black bulk of "La Savoie" at anchor. We moved slowly toward her; then around to one side. The propeller ceased churning. There came a yell from the bridge, "*L'ancre!*", the splash of a heavy weight and the wrenching grind of chains as they slid over the side. Then silence fell, and we lay at rest in the moonlight near the black silhouette of our captor, under the guns of Brest and prison.

INTERNED

After the cool freedom of the voyage the confinement and midsummer heat of the harbor were almost unendurable. There was nothing to do but walk and talk. We were reduced to a democracy of misery. All morning long a snaky blue-black torpedo-boat circled about us, and flotillas of destroyers and submarines glided past on their way to the open sea. Guns peered down from fortifications fringing the hills above the harbor, the seven picturesque Norman towers of Brest suggested nothing but prison walls and donjon keeps, and on the decks of the "Nieuw Amsterdam" stood groups of dour-faced marines and *gendarmes,* for the ex-stewards of "La Savoie" had been replaced by stout Breton guardsmen. We were prisoners, and we were made to feel it.

Immediately after noon we were notified to prepare to leave the ship at once. Only Dutch citizens and the women, of whatever nationality, were to remain on board.

All restraints melted away. A Bedlam of emotions seized the passengers. No one in the ship was sane. Frantic women walked the decks weeping, and the lips of many men were bleeding, half-bitten through in the effort to keep back curses and tears. Our ship and all her cargo were said to be confiscated; Holland was rumored to be on the verge of war with France; the women were reported to be prisoners of war like the men and were to be interned in a Breton fishing village until the end of the war. Under orders from the French officers in charge of the ship Dutch stewards herded the male passengers on deck and left them, surrounded with hand-luggage. Some wrote farewell letters, resting the paper on their knees or on the backs of valises. The few whose wives were on board were half-crazed with horror at thought of the inevitable separation, and, what made it hardest to bear, the women were penned in the dining-room where they could not see the disembarkation.

The steerage passengers went first, climbing down the ship's ladder to a military tugboat crammed with French *gendarmes* and sailors. One by one the men were searched, and their pocket knives, matches, razors, and other small possessions taken from them and dumped into wicker baskets. Their hand-luggage was passed hand over hand to a barge, and then the men were marched into another *bateau*, where they sat crowded together on benches or in the bottom of the boat. Awkward immigrant bags, an English horn, a 'cello, and a phonograph lay in the sprawling heaps of *impedimenta*. The men kept up bravely, and when the tug panted off down the Bay, towing the two barges, the captives cheered and waved their hats to those still on the ship.

A wailing shriek from the dining-room suddenly startled us. One of the steerage women, mother of six small children, had fainted at separation from her husband. She, like most of the women, believed the men were to be taken to the nearest landing-place and shot down by the French. She had come expecting to have her husband's pay while he was in the army, or to have his pension if he fell. There was nothing for her in

America; there was less than nothing for her and her children in Holland, where they would be landed penniless and friendless if the ship were allowed to proceed. And her plight was the plight of a score of others. But the men on deck could do nothing. They were drowned in their own misery.

Among the second-cabin passengers was a German Lutheran minister about sixty years old, who staggered down the ladder painfully dragging a big hand-bag behind him. *Gendarmes* stepped forward to search him like the rest, but the Captain stopped them with a word, and then eloquently waved the old man to a seat on a coil of rope; not in the barge, but in the tug with the French officers.

Our time came. We marched slowly down the stair; down under the sweetly smiling face of Queen Wilhelmina, powerless to protect those who travel under her flag; down past the frantic women in the dining-room, crowded to the doors, sobbing and calling good-bys; down past the stewards, even in those tragic moments anxious only for their tips; down to the French officers who were to decide our fate. Each of us had grown colossally selfish. The only problem which mattered was, "What are they going to do with ME?"

Five of us were American citizens. We had little in common but our citizenship, yet that bond suddenly became stronger than anything else in the world. We kept close together as we marched down the stair. We were determined to fight the matter out as a group. We were free-born Americans, we told ourselves. We were not to be ordered off any ship. We would go when we were ready, and not an instant before. We would fight, if necessary. Those Frenchmen would have to take us off at the bayonet's point, if they took us at all! . . . It was all very childish, no doubt.

The foremost officer looked quickly at our papers, bowed courteously, and waved us back. "You are not to go, gentlemen," he said.

We ran back upstairs in a frenzy of selfish joy. It was like a reprieve from a sentence of death; as unexpected and as precious. We were a handful of lonely passengers now. Already the barges were moving away, and the prisoners were calling good-bys and waving. The women were released from the dining-room and rejoined us on the deck. Half an hour later the barges were little sooty specks moving far out across the blue waters of the Bay, and on the topmost deck were a dozen women and nine-year old Hans watching them out of sight.

A Night on Devil's Island

The French declared our cargo contraband, so that one million dollars' worth of silver bullion, consigned to the Dutch Government, large quantities of flour and tinned meat, and perhaps other supplies, had to be removed before the ship could proceed. All day we watched the green-jacketed Dutch crew helping French marines to transfer flour from the hold of the "Nieuw Amsterdam" to the deck of a barge appropriately named "Le Corbeau"—the Crow. The blazing September sun smote us like fists from the surface of a painted sea and sky; the green Breton hills and the Norman towers of Brest were an agony of invitation to the eye, but we could not set foot on shore; we could not see a newspaper; we could not communicate with the American Ambassador in Paris, and there was no American Consul to whom we could appeal in Brest. The women were forbidden to write to the German prisoners. Yet suddenly, from no one knew where, came news.

"They were taken to Devil's Island. One was shot on the way. A French marine said so!" Rumor, like a hot wind, ran through the groups on the ship.

As the day waned, a second barge drew alongside the "Nieuw Amsterdam." We watched its approach indifferently, when suddenly there came a woman's wail, horrible as keening for the dead. "My husband is there!" she screamed. "My husband is in that barge! He is there! He has come back! He has come back! Oh, why has he come back? What are the French going to do with him?" Her hysteria swept all the passengers. Women crowded the ship's rail, sobbing and calling, and men standing in the barge beneath answered and waved their handkerchiefs.

We waited breathlessly. Seven hundred and fifty-one

Germans and Austrians had been taken from the ship. How many were to be returned? Or were any to be returned? We could only wait. Then five old men and a boy of seventeen staggered to the deck, and we fell upon them with questions. "Where are the others?" we demanded. Only the boy had strength to answer, "They are at Devil's Island—all but the officers and Red Cross doctors. Those are down in the barge on their way to the penitentiary in the city of Brest. Thirty-two officers; five doctors."

A clamor of farewells arose from the barge, for the tugboat was puffing away. The mad wailing began again, and the horrible tragedy of separation was played a second time to the end.

One of the old men who was returned to the ship was a veteran member of the Hungarian Parliament and had been in America just before the war broke out, representing the International Peace movement. It was bitter irony that such a man should be prisoner of war. He was more than sixty years old, big, spiny, and uncouth, with a skin like a sun-dried cactus. He returned to us unshaven, dirty, so exhausted that he could not stand without support, and with his wide eyes fixed and terrible. We helped him to a steamer-chair, and he told in short, apoplectic gasps of what had happened to the prisoners.

"They took us to le Fret," he began; "a fishing village. It is in the Bay. We were unloaded two by two. French fisherwomen came and cursed us. They shook their fists. But there was no violence—not yet. Then a man was shot. He was a German Pole. A steerage passenger. He carried a little satchel with all his money in it. The French officer shouted to him to drop the satchel with the rest of the luggage. The Pole held on. Maybe he did not understand French. Fisherwomen crowded up very close and yelled ' Shoot him! Shoot him!' Still he held on. The officer tried to jerk the satchel from him, but he held on. Then the officer cried out very loud, and they shot him four times.

"After the shooting I saw his body lying in the roadway, but he still held his little satchel.

"Then we were marched four miles, very fast. The younger men could do it, but the old men——! One was a Lutheran minister, sixty-one years old, very heavy, and he soon had to stop. The soldiers drove him on. Then two of our young men caught him by the arms and dragged him with them. But the old man seemed to be dying, so the young men left him in the road.

"It was dark when we had done our four miles. In front of us was a black fortress named Crozon and a causeway over the sea. We had to run into the fort. We were told off into squads of sixty-six and put into bomb-proof steel and concrete caves in the bottom of the fortress. Then they locked us in.

"There was no light. The vault was air-tight except

A NIGHT ON DEVIL'S ISLAND

for two small windows. It was ninety feet long, eighteen feet wide, and seventeen and one-half feet high. The windows were two feet by three and one-half feet high, heavily barred with six railroad irons. It was horrible!

"There was straw on the floor. Nothing else. The air at first was stale. It soon became moist and foul. A man died. Another man was dying when we left the fortress today. Some of the men fought to reach the windows, until we organized ourselves into squads of tens and marched up in turn to the windows to gulp a clean breath. We marched all night long. It was pitch dark in the vault and very dirty. The night was hot. The stenches grew more and more frightful. . . . There are things I cannot tell you. You must imagine. We were there twenty-one hours, and the others are there yet.

"They call it '*L'île du Diable*'—Devil's Island."

Days dragged by on leaden feet. Captain Baron made formal protest against the seizure of the "Nieuw Amsterdam," but still we were held. He twice visited Brest under guard to interview the Dutch Consul there, but the city was a chaos of suffering. Belgian refugees begged in all the streets; women were in mourning; fifteen hundred wounded Frenchmen arrived there in a single day, and were hastily crowded into the small municipal hospitals. People lived in hourly expectation of the fall of Paris and the retreat of the French armies to the south and west. An atmosphere of tragic depression had seized on every one, so that it was impossible to learn anything definite regarding the final disposition of the ship.

The reservists and other German and Austrian citizens were interned on September third; the flour was removed on the fourth; three hundred and ninety massive bars of silver, valued at more than a million dollars, were taken on the fifth; the *maizena* was seized on the sixth, along with six hundred tins of meat; and still no decision had been taken so far as the ship was concerned.

Then came the magic "orders from Paris." Five German Red Cross doctors were returned to the ship, and we sailed at six o'clock in the evening of September sixth.

On the morning of the eighth we were in Rotterdam. Our mails were five days late, and we were the poorer by a million dollars' worth of silver, and a cargo of flour, meat, and *maizena*. Out of about eight hundred Germans and Austrians, there remained only twenty-six to report to their consuls in Holland. Some of these were of military age. One of them was a German Doctor of Philosophy, who stowed himself in a lifeboat and lived there for five days on ship's biscuit and water; another hid himself in a small hollow in the ship's walls, and although he had lived four and one-half days without food or water seemed none the worse for his experience; others had traveled with Scandinavian or Swiss or

A NIGHT ON DEVIL'S ISLAND

American passports, several of them being *bonâ fide* Americans citizens who wanted to volunteer in Germany, and so escaped the French.

Seven hundred and forty were left as prisoners of war in Brest.

CHAPTER II

BERLIN THE TERRIBLE

OSNABRUCK TO BERLIN

"Why did you Germans destroy Louvain?"

"Louvain?" said the man from Mannheim. "Remember Heidelberg! War is war."

"Heidelberg?" I recalled vaguely that over a hundred years ago the German university town was burned by the French. "What has Heidelberg to do with it? This is the twentieth century."

"The twentieth century has grown from the nineteenth, and the nineteenth from the eighteenth, and the eighteenth from the seventeenth, and the seventeenth from the sixteenth. You must think in centuries to understand Germany."

"*Sub specie æternitatis!*" I sneered, quoting Spinoza's famous phrase. "Under the form of eternity; eh?"

We were riding to Berlin on a military train which had come directly from the battlefields in France. A heavy smell of ether drenched all that one breathed, and waxen-faced soldiers, unshaven and dirty, crammed the little compartments. There was no distinction among first-, second-, and third-class passengers.

A splendid young Uhlan wearing a wisp of mustache leaned negligently against a compartment-door, his spur scratching the panel. The front of his green-gray uniform was a clotted mass of what seemed to be brick dust: it was dried blood. Infantrymen with bandaged heads, bandaged arms, bandaged legs or bandaged shoulders, blocked the narrow aisles and lay on the floor between the seats. A soldier with his jaw shot through breathed noisily. Occasionally some one groaned through clenched teeth as he shifted his position.

These men were only slightly wounded. . . .

The man from Mannheim had never heard of Spinoza, but he knew his Kant and Karl Marx and the new Freud psychology. "You must think in centuries to understand Germany," he repeated doggedly.

At every station, women from the Red Cross came to meet the soldiers with hot bouillon, hot coffee, stretchers, and ambulances; and at almost every station we picked up new recruits, mostly officers, just being called to the colors. They came in brand-new uniforms with shining swords at their sides, invariably accompanied by friends who cheered them and called, "Bravo! bravo! congratulations!" as the train pulled out of the station.

In Hanover two women, who seemed to be mother and wife of a young hussar just starting for the front, were at the station to see him off. He was all smiles, but the women were in agony. They fought to keep their self-possession. The mother's fingers clawed holes in the handkerchief she held in her hand to wave as her boy left her, and the wife's lips trembled as she tried to say the happy nothings which would be everything in the world to her soldier in the field. They smiled to the very last minute, and when the train started and the young officer leaned far out of the window, laughing back at them and waving his handkerchief, they shouted after him, "Congratulations! congratulations! God bless you! Congratulations!" . . .

The man from Mannheim sighed heavily. "Generation after generation they have done that in Germany: century after century. Do you understand?"

There was an air of heroic happiness about our train. Every time another train passed we were cheered and waved at; car-windows flew open; men, women, and even children leaned out, calling, waving, and smiling—always smiling. Factories and canals were idle, but the land was alive. Everywhere peasant women, in bright red, green, or yellow costumes, worked in the rich harvests. Children, even six-year-old youngsters, picked up potatoes. Baby-carriages were common conveyances.

Two troop-trains went by us, west-bound for France, and their loud "*hurrrrrrahs*" were electric with feeling. Little boys, dressed in diminutive uniforms, perfect even to spiked helmets and miniature swords, hung from the windows of houses to shake German flags in salute, and little girls in the turnip and potato fields called shrilly as we went by. It was a continuous ovation. To come home wounded was to come in triumph, and ether and bandages and painful mutilations were forgotten in the joy of such a welcome.

So we reached Berlin. The broad platforms of the Friedrichstrasse Bahnhof were crowded with eager men and women awaiting the arrival of our train. It was a confusion of laughter, happy tears, the tight grip of hands, smiles, furtive touching of the weeks' growth of beard on military chins, men kissing men, and shouts of "*Gepäckträger! Gepäckträger!*" The porters—forty-five, fifty, sixty years old, all of them—hobbled about collecting the luggage. Red Cross workers crowded up to take charge of the wounded. Soldiers, in every variety of uniform, stood waiting for other trains; some of them in neat, clean, brand-new outfits with yellow boots that squeaked as they walked, and with sprigs of green in their gun-barrels; others, just back from the battles in East Prussia, in muddy, war-worn uniforms which they had fought in and slept in and traveled in without change, knapsacks on their shoulders, rifles at their hips. It was a crowd shifting like quicksilver, and every face smiling. Even the sixteen-year-old *Spreewald Mädchen* in charge of the news-stand laid down her knitting to watch.

Among the first to leap down from the train was a tall Prussian Uhlan on furlough. He had been fighting under von Hindenburg in the East and von Kluck in the West, he told us. " Such luck!" as he expressed it. He bounded to the platform like an athlete, although I knew he was wounded; stood stiff for a moment, clicked his heels, saluted with an abrupt mechanical snap of the forearm which is the very perfection of impersonal, unemotional recognition; then flung his arms out like a little boy about the shoulders of a gray-bearded giant in general's uniform, and kissed him like a girl.

That nineteen-year-old boy wore over his heart the Iron Cross of 1914. The man he kissed wore the Iron Cross of 1870-'71. . . .

" His father, his grandfather, his great-grandfather and great great-grandfather fought the French. We Germans remember in centuries," the man from Mannheim said.

Prussia Enthroned

Consciousness of history seemed the most vivid feature of wartime Germany. Men talked of the religious wars of three centuries ago as if they had been fought in our lifetime. They talked of Napoleon as of a contemporary, and of the sorrows of the medieval and modern Germanic states with the fervor and poignant suffering of a citizen of those bygone days. Jean Paul Richter

PRUSSIA ENTHRONED

or Theodor Körner have not painted the humiliations of old Germany with more skill and feeling than the German-on-the-street in 1914. It was like a loyal son telling of the sufferings and hardships of a devoted mother.

One pleasant afternoon I called on Baron von Nimptsch, president of the Berlin branch of the New York Life Insurance Company, in his offices at the corner of Leipzigerstrasse and Wilhelmstrasse.

"You cannot understand our militarism?" he asked. "Listen! Century after century the Fatherland of the Germans was fought over, burned over, plundered and pillaged over, from the time of Cæsar until Prussia emerged to lead the Germanic Federation. Germany's trade history is a long history. It is no nineteenth century discovery. The Hanseatic merchants of Hamburg, Bremen, and Lübeck were famous when the English still were pirates. During the Thirty Years' War, from 1618 to 1648, Germany's population fell from nineteen millions to four millions. Before that war we Germans had a culture higher than France or England. Every vestige of it was lost. That is the explanation of our militarism.

"A century ago came Napoleon. The city of Königsberg only recently paid off the last of the assessments levied on her in Napoleon's day. That is the explanation of our militarism.

"The thought of a helpless Germany is intolerable to Germans. To survive at all, we have to be strong. To survive at all, we have to give up what you Americans call your 'personal liberty.' We must obey. We must organize. We must be ready to fight for our lives and the life of our country. And that is German militarism."

A few nights later I was guest at a weekly meeting of one of the innumerable artistic circles of Berlin—one of the little groups of painters, sculptors, and their friends who meet on Friday evenings about long tables in Charlottenburg for beer and conversation. Some of the men and women about me bore famous names; all had amiable, healthy, florid faces; all were cosmopolitans by education and training. The men were over military age.

"Prosit!" said my host.

Twelve of us lifted our mugs and drank solemnly.

My nearest neighbor glanced at me and frowned. "Germans observe measure in everything," he said reprovingly; "even in drinking beer. The first drink should empty the mug down to the hasp of the handle; the second to the boss of the mug; the third to the bottom. You have only sipped your beer."

I liked the idea of classic measure in beer drinking, and we discussed it solemnly. "Measure is everything. Restraint. The 'golden mean.' Order. Discipline. That is the German way," they said, when a clenched fist struck the table beside me a tremendous thump. My beer splashed from the mug, and the crackers flew. The fist descended again and again, and an agonized voice repeated "*Nein! Nein! Gott!* It cannot be! It cannot be!"

"What is it? What has happened?" I asked.

"One of our friends, a sculptor, a member of this Circle. We have just heard that he has been killed. He volunteered three weeks ago."

The group buzzed with unhappy conjecture. "It is horrible! Horrible! *Ein bildlicher Mensch,* a German genius, shot down by the Cossack, the Jap, the Indian, the Nigger. This is England's work. Oh, it is horrible! Horrible!"

I realized with unpleasant astonishment that German discipline and restraint hid oceans of vast, wild feeling, uncritical and elemental; that the intellectual and physical order of the Empire was built upon these.

"See!" The man at my right drew a pencil from his pocket and nervously sketched on the tablecloth a little map. "It is very small, our civilization," he explained. "Here is Germany, and Scandinavia, Holland, England, America. That is all. France and Italy have another culture. Theirs is Latin; it is decaying. All the rest of the world is *barbarisch.* The Russians, the Japanese, Africa, Spain, South America—all that is *barbarisch.* There is only this little island of our civilization, and we are fighting to the death to save it."

"But France?" I remonstrated. "The whole world loves France."

"France?—*la grande nation* is always hysterical. Think only of the Caillaux trial. On July twenty-sixth the French newspapers talked of nothing but that dirty case; one week later we were at war. In France everything is done with uproar and outcry—*immer mit Geschrei*. One morning in Paris I was awakened by horrid noises in the street. Men screamed and fought. They ran in and out of the hotel. They bawled from the windows. They cursed and wrestled on the sidewalks, and howled—*immer mit Geschrei*. It was all because an Englishman had won the Gordon Bennett cup!"

"And Italy?" A strapping, sunburned artist at the far end of the table took up the story. He had come that day from Rome. "Italy is a kindergarten full of naughty children. They sob and squall and squabble like four-year olds.

"A few nights ago in a Roman restaurant an Italian soldier jumped to his feet in the midst of the dinner and cried, '*Viva l'Italia! Viva la Serbia! Viva la Francia! Viva l'Ingleterra!*—our friends! Down with the *Tedeschi!* Down with the barbarous Germans!'

"I arose," the artist continued. "I took a table nearer the speaker, and when the excitement had died down I stood up close to him and called on all the other Germans in the room to stand. A dozen big, muscular fellows got up. They were splendid!

"'What do you think now, Signor Soldier?' I cried to the disturber.

"'Ah, pardon, pardon, Signor! I did not mean it! I did not know!'

"So the little fool apologized," the narrator ended contemptuously.

They had spoken of Frenchmen and Italians as a Southern colonel might speak of negroes. It was not simply the historical antagonism between Romantic and Teutonic peoples, it was the physical feeling of repulsion which a Southerner feels in discussing racial amalgamation.

In fertile ground like this the war spirit grew unchecked. The theaters played to crowded houses, and the theme was always war. "*Die Waffen her!*" "*Deutschland über alles!*" "*Kriegsbilden*," "*Mein Leben dem Vaterland*," "*Ein' feste Burg ist unser Gott*," Schiller's "*Wallenstein's Tod*," and "*Wilhelm Tell*," were advertised on all the pillar posts, and I heard at the Deutsches Opernhaus the first performance of Engelbert Humperdinck's opera "*Die Marktenderin*," with the old Prussian Marshal Blücher as hero.

The famous theatrical manager, Max Reinhardt, wished to produce Shakespeare, but considering the intense bitterness of feeling against England and things English he laid the matter before the German public for arbitrament. The *Berliner Tageblatt* of Sunday, September twenty-seventh, was favored with the following letters:

"Shakespeare belongs to the whole world."
CHANCELLOR VON BETHMANN-HOLLWEG.

"First, we are fighting the living and not the dead. Second, the majority of men's masterpieces belong to the whole world of culture and not exclusively to their fatherland. Third, Shakespeare especially has for more than a century been so far incorporated in our German flesh and blood that we may consider him our own. Proof: any production of Max Reinhardt's."
Bürgermeister Geheimrat GEORG REICKE.

HOW THE POOR FARED

But Germany's racial and historical dogmas tired me by their reiteration. All men thought alike, all men spoke alike. The intellectual mobilization was too perfect. I longed for revolt and self-criticism, so I telephoned to the Reichstag to Dr. Karl Liebknecht, the famous Socialist leader, to whom I had letters, in order to make an engagement with him to talk over the Socialist situation.

The gentle-voiced telephone operator interrupted me. "*Sie müssen aber Deutsch sprechen, Herr. Es ist verboten English zu sprechen.*"

"I beg pardon, *Fräulein*," I answered lamely; "but I don't speak German very well——"

Her answer was in perfect English. "Perhaps I can translate for you, sir," she said coldly. . . .

Twenty minutes later a police-detective visited my room to examine my passports and papers. He was profuse in his apologies for disturbing me, and bowed himself out with deep regret for the trouble he had caused me.

The incident rankled. "Why is it?" I demanded of Herr Nicholas Arps, as we walked down the Dorotheenstrasse on our way to visit soup kitchens. "Why do you Germans submit to so much police interference?"

His delicate face, with the deeply graven lines about the dark eyes and mouth, looked at the moment like a saint's carved from wood in the confession-stall of a cathedral. Like thousands of sensitive men in all lands, the war was visibly breaking him to pieces. He suffered night and day from horrible dreams. He wanted to go as a volunteer, but his weak heart made that impossible. Besides, he was over the age-limit. But he shouldered a rifle daily and stood from one o'clock until five, guarding a railroad bridge in Charlottenburg.

"We must have police. We must obey. We trust our Government because it is wiser than we and because it does better for us than we can do for ourselves. That is what you will see today in the soup kitchens. Your country is so different from ours that you do not yet understand the virtue of obedience. We must have police; we must have soldiers.

"But where is a policeman now?" he added. "We

must ask our way to the *Kinder-Volksküchen.* Do you see a policeman?"

There was no blue-coat in sight, and I could not remember having seen one since I had left the hotel. We were in the midst of the old Ghetto of Berlin—a place so clean that it shone, but the poorest part of the city. In New York, it would have swarmed with police. . . . The Jews were preparing for their New Year, and all about us was activity and a happy stir.

"See the prices for food and clothing," said Herr Arps.

"They are lower than in Holland or America," I said, and I told him laughingly of my trunkful of *Erbsenwurst,* condensed soups, and egg powder, which I had brought from America for fear I should starve in Germany. I could have bought them more cheaply in Berlin than in New York. . . . "But we must find the way to the *Kinder-Volksküchen."*

We questioned several passersby. None could tell us where the children of the poor could receive free meals thrice a day. The need, apparently, was not great. Block after block we walked where formerly stood the most hateful rookeries in Germany. There are no slums in Berlin. Everywhere were clean, wide streets, tenements with open courtyards so sunlight and air could reach all the windows, and window-boxes of asters and geraniums to brighten the view. We wandered past the unfinished theater which the German Socialists are

HOW THE POOR FARED   47

building—the *Neue Freie Volksbühne*—a marvelous monument by, for, and of the working-people; made without a penny of help from the upper classes.

"There are no more Socialists now," said Herr Arps. "There are only Germans."

"And I am half inclined to think there are no more policemen," I retorted. "That one who visited me this morning was the last of his race."

"There has been a marked decrease in crime since the war began."

"So?"

"But it is strange that we cannot find a policeman."

An awkward squad was drilling behind a high board fence, and a sharp, high-pitched voice shouted orders. Over a little butcher-shop was an advertisement of fresh horse cutlets. The pillar posts at street corners advertised theatrical offerings and what seemed an endless series of educational advantages: trade schools, night schools, art schools, manual training schools, technical schools, kindergartens—all as if it were peace time. But everywhere one felt the presence of the paternal Prussian state. The awkward squad consisted of the raw material from which the Imperial armies are made; the butcher-shop was regulated by the State; the theatrical offerings were censored by the State; the schools were subsidized and coerced by the State. The Kaiser's photograph, and cheap post-cards of Kaiser, Kaiserin,

Crown Prince, Bismarck, Hindenburg, Häsler, and Zeppelin were in almost every window. Confectionery shops were arsenals of sweets, where candies shaped like cannon balls, shot, cartridges, bullets, and packed in boxes decorated with the national black-white-and-red, or made in odd shapes like Uhlans' helmets or forty-two centimeter shells, could be bought at astonishingly low prices.

It was nearly half an hour before we caught sight of the familiar blue uniform of a guardian of law and order. He knew exactly where we should go; in fact, he took us to the door. On the way we remarked on the lack of police protection. " Yes," he said, " the people are good. We do not need so many policemen. Germans are comrades and brothers."

The *Kinder-Volksküche* was about an open courtyard, behind a diminutive lawn decked with formal flowerbeds. Its dining-room was tiny but immaculate. Only eight children were being served as we talked. The women in charge explained that there was provision for many more, but there was no need. " It is as in peace time," they said.

In a nearby beer garden, beside a huge brewery, we found a Red Cross soup kitchen for adults. One hundred and fifty men, women, and children stood in line at the door, where a volunteer worker passed them inside. The children and some of the women carried pitchers in which to take the provisions home. Most of the adults ate inside. They were surprisingly neat and clean; their pressing poverty obviously was new. Yet I learned that sixty thousand were then being fed in Berlin, and that in peace time the number is about thirty thousand.

Upstairs we went with the line of the destitute. Each of the women and most of the men bore with them little books in which stamps were affixed for every day the man of the house had been at work. The day when the stamps left off was usually the day when charity began, for the poor have no opportunity to lay up reserves in Germany or anywhere else. They accepted the proffered help cheerfully and as their just due, without obsequiousness.

The director of the soup kitchen was Herr Held, a Reichstag deputy; big-boned, healthily florid, and as proud of the kitchen as a father of his household. His helpers were women volunteers. In Germany the rôle played by women of the leisure classes did not seem important. Knitting for the soldiers, nursing, and amateur relief work alone seemed to be allowed them. Herr Held and his assistants ate with the soup line, and Herr Arps and I joined them at a little table with a heaping platter of liver hash, boiled potatoes, a thick slice of bread, and a glass of water.

"But you have no police here," I remarked.

Herr Held beamed at me as he dipped into his hash. "Not since the beginning of the war," he said. "See, all is clean and quiet and orderly. We have forty-five hundred people every day, but never a disturbance. That is because of the war. Rich and poor, we are one; all Germany is one; there are no more Socialists; there are no more revolutionists. Germans all are sisters and brothers."

War Worship

Berlin, the flat-faced, heavy, portentous *parvenu* among cities, was completely possessed by the devil of war. The mark of the sword was on everything. Among the quiet, serious crowds which thronged the downtown streets during afternoons and evenings, and which overflowed into a few uptown avenues, every fifth man was a soldier. And the civilians never tired of the sight. They paid each uniform the flattering attention of staring as if it were the first they had ever seen. There was worship in their eyes. All sorts and conditions of men strode by in uniform: Prussian generals, in gold and gray and blue; a haggard military doctor, just come from the hospitals and still smelling of ether; dirty, tired infantrymen, just back from the firing-line in East Prussia, limping along in the gutter; a *Jäger* in Alpine green uniform, with a green feather in his peaked cap; aristocratic hussars in uniforms of blazing red, marching along erect as automatic dolls; an officer of the famous Death's Head Hussars, a white skull grinning down from his black shako, and the cords across his breast pulsing as he walked; companies of drab, middle-aged *Landsturm* marching down the street; a crack regiment of the Guard doing the "goosestep" at the corner of *Unter den Linden,* and smacking the pavement until the streets echoed like a forest under volley fire; a squad of Red Cross workers marching in civil dress, each wearing his little white-and-red arm-band and each carrying a tiny satchel; cavalrymen riding by like centaurs on coal-black horses; a new regiment off for the railway station, with band blaring and colors snapping in the wind; an adjutant in a gray military automobile with a horn that boomed like a cannon; wax-faced convalescents, by ones, twos, half-dozens, dozens, walking the streets to get the air, limping painfully or guarding a bandaged arm or shoulder or head from the jostlings of the crowd. Then, like a travesty of all these, twenty small boys, in improvised uniforms, with spiked caps, wooden swords, and an ingenious wooden cannon mounted on a gun-carriage which would lower and raise and pivot about like a real field-gun, marching down the Friedrichstrasse with patriotic flags and a drum.

If two soldiers talked together in the street, they immediately attracted a circle of respectful listeners. If a single soldier walked along in the gutter where the sidewalks were overcrowded he was made immediately the cynosure of all eyes. Street-cleaners and 'bus-drivers made way for the soldier; pedestrians nudged each other to give him room; in the restaurants he was given the best place. And all these attentions seemed to be unconscious; certainly they were ungrudging. They were given as if the German soldier were obviously a superior order of being.

I was walking down Dorotheenstrasse one morning when I saw the street crowds gathered on the curbs and looking upward. There was a soft purring sound in the air—a new theme introducing itself into the staccato music of the traffic—but the sea-blue sky was empty.

Then I saw the German army of the air. A tremendous amber-colored nose pushed its way across the heavens, thousands of feet above our narrow canyon of street. The nose became a face—eyeless, mouthless, expressionless—but still a face. The face became a head, and the head a great golden body, like the woodcuts of Leviathan in old family Bibles; then the Zeppelin sailed into full view.

A Bavarian soldier standing beside me turned his head away and caught my eye. His face was radiant with happiness. He grabbed me impulsively by the shoulder. "God!" he said, and I know the oath was a prayer; "It's beautiful! It's beautiful! And you can bet your life it will blow hell out of anything the English have!"

One night I was walking near the Dom—the monstrous cathedral which stands opposite the Kaiser's palace—when I noticed a large crowd gathered about one of the exits. At least five thousand men and women

A war game in Berlin.

Attacking the trenches.
YOUNG GERMANY

were thronged on the marble steps, overflowing on to the sidewalks and streets, and all standing in absolute silence, waiting. Their faces were turned toward the church porch, where the big yellow eyes of a waiting automobile stared out at them from beneath a marble archway.

There was a stir in the dusk of the porch. An automobile horn, deep-toned as the bass in a cathedral organ, boomed out, and the car began to move down upon us. The crowd slowly made way. Men bared their heads, still silent. A large woman, veiled to the eyes, sat in the tonneau, bowing stiffly to right and left as the car crawled down the drive.

"*Die Kaiserin*—the Empress," whispered a woman in front of me, never taking her eyes off the figure in the car. A moment later, and the crowd was dispersing as quietly as it had assembled.

There had been no display of enthusiasm; not so much as a cheer. It might have been a religious procession which had passed. The Empress had been like Augusta to the temple, praying for the success of the German arms.

German "Preparedness"

To such a people its army was an instrument, keying up the machinery of civilization, giving direction and purpose to myriads of whirring wheels. The army was an essential part of a conscious universe of order, a universe in which civilized society has constant drastic work to do, the work we call "civilization."

Against such a background, war was a world grown plastic; but wars were only recurring incidents in history. The killing, the maiming, the robbery and rape were only a small part of warfare. Relatively few had even the chance to become beasts. Relatively few actually served on the fighting-line. Wars are actually fought by minorities; wars are made by whole peoples.

The mobilization and drilling of noncombatants was just as important to the German mind as the drilling of soldiers. The whole strength of the people must be thrown into the balance. The Germans launched armies as one launches ships, full of profound faith that they would return to port bearing all that the nation desired. Even their jingoism seemed moral. They shared none of the common Anglo-Saxon feelings that war is a dirty business, soon to be finished, hands washed, and apologized for. They felt none of the mixture of pride and shame which made my English friends say, " We'll muddle through it somehow, I suppose." The year 1914 was called by the Germans " The Iron Year," and the war they called the " Folk War." Every German knew the object of the war. It was to fulfil the destinies of the Empire.

Significant of this was the constant recurrence of the

phrase *Die Zukunft*—the Future. Magazines and newspapers teemed with it, and always in the German future, as in the present, war had a prominent place. War was "the father of all and the king of all." When Germans spoke of a "lasting peace" they added, "a peace for forty years." Now it is already more than forty years since 1870-'71, but with the typical German habit of thinking in centuries the seers were already anticipating 1954, when the old sad round would begin again and the nation would draw a step nearer to its sky-topping goal.

But Germans wondered at their own unanimity. Quietly, irresistibly, all life, all thought was warped to the one end of making war. The *Odeon Werke,* a small phonograph factory which I visited, was turning out one hundred shrapnel shells a day; the canning factories had accumulated stocks to supply the armies for four years, yet they were working at maximum capacity. I talked with Herr W. Türke, manager of the immense Eckert Plow Factory, makers of agricultural implements, three-fourths of the product of which is commonly sold abroad. "We make nothing but munitions now," he explained. "Our machinery was specially designed so that it could be transferred at once to munition work. There is no such thing as that anywhere where private enterprise persists. Government officials are absolutely in charge of my factory, and they are turning out grenades, shrapnel shells, bombs, pressed-steel trucks, and ammunition transports. You see, we Germans organize victory."

Another day I spent with Herr Konsul Marx at 44 Charlottenstrasse, learning how the Germans withdrew their financial deposits in foreign countries before the outbreak of the war and thus were not "caught napping."

"Germany foresaw everything," he concluded.

Industry, commerce, finance, as much as ammunition and armies, were looked upon as the property of the Empire. And much the same attitude was observable toward the Kaiser. Germans looked on him as an asset, personally and politically. I remember one half-humorous conversation in which I upheld the republican ideal and condemned the imperial.

"We must have the best men in the administration of affairs," agreed the German. "You Americans get them in a republic, we in an imperial form of government. But remember that if Germany became a republic tomorrow we would go to the polls and elect as president Mr. William Hohenzollern. Don't laugh! He is our greatest man. He understands us, and we understand him thoroughly. There is an immense advantage to a people in watching their ruler from the cradle to the throne. You can never know your American presidents as we know our German Emperor."

It is this same historical sense of the Germans which led them to the theory of the defensive-offense—the military theory that one must strike the enemy before he is prepared in order to defend oneself against him. And it was the acceptance of this theory by Socialists and monarchists, laborers and capitalists alike which enabled the German Empire to launch upon a sleeping world the war it had prepared.

But the silence of the Socialists seemed a profound mystery. The German *Sozialdemokratie* had been fighting Prussian militarism for years. Hardly an election passed without increases in the strength of the Social-Democratic party, in spite of appallingly unjust laws directly intended to keep a large part of the laboring class disfranchised and in spite of a Socialist Code which hampered the spread of the movement by bullying its press and breaking up its public meetings. When the war broke out the German Socialists had one hundred and twelve deputies in the Reichstag, all of them, like their Socialist brethren the world over, pledged to peace.

On August first Socialists were called to the colors, like everybody else; and they responded without a dissenting voice. On August fourth the Reichstag Socialist *bloc* voted for the war budget, and went so far as to cheer at the toast, "Long live His Majesty, the Kaiser; the people, and the Fatherland!" Eight days after the mobilization the Imperial Union for Fighting the Social-Democrats—a powerful organization, having locals in all parts of Germany, and organized by a general in the Imperial army for the one purpose of annihilating the Socialist movement—this powerful Union disbanded, declaring that there were no more Socialists to fight; that all now were Germans and brothers; and that it was giving its books, its money, and its office furniture to the Red Cross.

Vorwärts, the daily newspaper published by the Social-Democrats, which had always been anathema to conservative Germans, and which had never been allowed on news-stands in public places such as railway stations, subways, and hotels, now appeared on these news-stands cheek by jowl with the *Berliner Lokal Anzeiger*—the inspired organ of the German Government.

On my way to see Dr. Karl Liebknecht at the Reichstag I stopped at the Central Hotel to see if I could buy *Vorwärts.*

"We haven't it today, sir," said the clerk.

"But you have it on other days?"

"Oh, yes, sir."

"Well, why haven't you the paper today? Have you sold all your copies?"

"No," the clerk explained; "the Government forbids it."

"Forbids you to sell it?"

"Oh, no, sir. The Government has forbidden *Vorwärts* to appear at all!" And he handed me a folded leaflet on which was printed in large letters:

THREE FAMOUS SOCIALISTS

To the Subscribers of "Vorwärts":
The Commander-in-Chief in the Mark sent us the following notice Sunday evening at 9 o'clock:

"The appearance of *Vorwärts* is hereby forbidden until further notice."

(Signed) VON KESSEL,
Major-General.

Berlin, S.W. 68, Lindenstr. 3.
28 September, 1914.

Editor and Manager of *Vorwärts*.

THREE FAMOUS SOCIALISTS

The first floor of the Reichstag was full of refugees from East Prussia and volunteer officers administering relief. It was quiet and reverential as a funeral. There was something strangely dead about the Reichstag. As I went up to the office of Deputy Dr. Karl Liebknecht I passed a series of little cells with doors marked "Polish Party" and "Social-Democratic Party"—catacombs of ambitions and hopes.

But there was nothing deathlike about Dr. Karl Liebknecht. Son of Wilhelm Liebknecht, the famous revolutionist of 1848, his own record has been as lively. In 1907 he was sentenced to serve eighteen months in prison for high treason because of his book *Militarism and Anti-militarism*. In 1908 he became a member of the Prussian Diet; in 1912 he was elected to the Reichstag, where he rapidly assumed a position of leadership among the Socialist Deputies; in 1913 his charges in the

Reichstag led to scandalous revelations which touched even the Imperial Court and the house of Krupp.

I remember him chiefly as a dark round face, semicircled by the sort of black ringlets which come from a hair mattress; not a keen face at first glance, not the face of a man of action apparently; a sort of professorial, cloistered, comfortable face. One felt like talking over the college courses one might take in the next semester rather than discussing the affairs of the Empire.

Then Dr. Liebknecht began to speak, leaning forward over the little table in his private office. His voice was very musical and very gentle. He spoke German in a way to soften all its angles, but what he said contradicted the delicate tone in which he said it.

"It is a war of lies." He looked me straight in the eye. "Every nation concerned lies. The German newspapers lie as a matter of course. When the war began the Socialists were fully aware that it was due to the capitalistic incentive of Austria-Hungary. We held dozens of protest meetings here in Berlin. *Vorwärts* published stout editorials. We had demonstrations against the war. Then came the censorship. We could do, we could say, nothing."

"But why?" I asked. "Americans expected you to do a great deal."

"You do not understand the power of the censorship," he said quietly. "You Americans cannot imagine the awful power of the military. In one day, in one hour, we were cut off. Every man became like a separate cell in the body politic. Every man was isolated with his own thoughts or else he was drowned in the flooding ideas of the war. From the moment the censorship shut down there was no more exchange of ideas. Every thinking man in Germany became a mental prisoner."

"But what is the war for, Herr Doktor?"

"It is a war of conquest. Whatever its causes may have been, we know that the Imperial Government intends it to be a war of conquest. There are rich mines in France and Belgium. They will never be given back. The Government will do with them and with us just as it pleases.

"It has done as it pleases with all the German people. I am a member of the Reichstag. The Chancellor of the Empire sent an ultimatum to Belgium on August second, 1914. That ultimatum was never reported to the Reichstag until August fifth. The war budget was presented on August fourth and passed on August fifth, with the concurrence of all the Socialists except fifteen. That is abominable duplicity on the part of the Government. Those fifteen Social-Democrats who voted against the war credits were the only real revolutionists. They were not for reconciliation with capitalism, but for fists.

"But they were helpless. The lying press was inflaming the people against our enemies—against the Russians and the French and the Belgians and the English. The

German papers were flooded with stories of atrocities committed upon German soldiers which to my certain knowledge were afterward disproved but never publicly denied. The people were told that the Russians were barbarians, the French fools, the Belgians superstitious weaklings, and the English cowardly sneaks.

"The causes of the war were obscure. The Socialists really thought that Germany could not be responsible for such a catastrophe. Czarism was ostensibly the issue on which the war began, and it was on that issue that the Social-Democratic *bloc* voted the war credits on August fifth. Nobody exactly understood the situation. The Socialists had lost their press at one stroke, for the censorship was absolute, and so they were like sheep without a shepherd."

"How do you feel about Belgium?" I questioned.

Dr. Liebknecht's voice continued in the same even, professorial tone. "I was in Stuttgart at the time that von der Goltz was appointed Governor-General of Belgium. I tried to get up a protest meeting against annexation. The military government would not permit so much as a public poster advertising the meeting. Indeed, the Government forbade meetings of any sort for any cause.

"But you can see that the newspapers are preparing the nation for the final annexation of Belgium. 'We have bought this province with our blood,' they argue, without thinking of the Belgian blood. 'We have paid for it with our lives. The Belgians,' they say, 'are little higher than brutes. They are completely dominated by their clergy, they are ignorant and superstitious and backward, they do not deserve to possess their own country.' All such nonsense as that passes current for wisdom in Germany today."

"But what have the Socialists really done about it?"

"Very little," he said. "*Vorwärts* has been closed twice and has had to agree in writing that it will not mention the class-war. Here is another example of what has taken place. My wife is Russian, and the war had barely started when my house was searched, my private papers were seized and carted off, and the sanctity of my whole establishment was violated on the pretext that my wife might be a spy. And in spite of the fact that I am a member of the Reichstag, not one word of this affair ever got into a Berlin newspaper."

"But, Herr Doktor," I said doubtfully, "you Socialists seem to us Americans to have lost a great opportunity. Frankly, we cannot understand your attitude as a party. We think you have been—to put it very frankly —cowardly."

"You think we have been cowards," he repeated gravely, never taking his eyes from my face. "Well, perhaps we have been. Remember, the German Social-Democrats own property worth more than twenty million marks. They own printing-presses and halls and theaters and the like. You know, property makes men cautious. Perhaps our possessions have made us conservative. Perhaps the German Socialists do not dare to risk all."

Herr Karl Kautsky, the veteran commentator on Marx, I found on the top floor of a Charlottenburg apartment-house, in a little den crammed with books and pleasantly odorous of old bindings and printer's ink. His face was cameo white, and its expression scarcely changed throughout our talk. Only the dark eyes seemed really alive. His white hair and white beard looked rather like silken adornments for the cameo face; they seemed to have no relation to the personality of the old man.

I was irritated with Herr Kautsky, and my attitude was frankly unsympathetic. I was irritated with his cautiousness and his bookishness and his air of letting the world go about its business. That may have been because Herr Bernstein was with him—a keen, obviously Jewish "intellectual," black as Mephisto, who seemed anxious that Herr Kautsky should tell nothing, and whose every statement seemed to come through double lines of internal censors before it reached his lips. A copy of the New York radical mazagine *The Masses* lay on Herr Kautsky's table, and I took its presence as a good omen. I was mistaken.

"Did you Socialists make no effort to stop the war?" I asked.

"The party did not," said Herr Kautsky. "We saw

THREE FAMOUS SOCIALISTS

long ago, we German Social-Democrats, that we should be powerless in the event of war. The French Socialists thought that they could stop war. They talked of general strikes and immense movements for peace. We German Socialists knew better. We had our meetings of protest. There were great Socialistic demonstrations on *Unter den Linden* just before Germany declared war on Russia. We had stirring protests in *Vorwärts.* We did our best to prevent the war, but we were powerless the instant martial law was proclaimed. Now we can do nothing. *Vorwärts* has been suspended. We have no press, we have no forum. We are heart and soul against a war of conquest, but we cannot even protest against the annexation of Belgium."

"But why did you do nothing in the Reichstag?" I asked.

"What could we do?" said Herr Bernstein, speaking slowly and gravely in English. "The Kaiser does not ask permission of the Reichstag to make war. He asks only for money to carry on war. When the time comes to make peace, he will make peace without consulting the Reichstag, and the terms of peace will be those he arranges."

"And so you are not going to do anything until after peace is made?" I asked, again turning to Herr Kautsky.

"We can do nothing," he repeated. "We are leaders without followers. There are two million German Socialists in the army. That means half of our members are gone. No Socialist in Germany knows what that half of our party is thinking, no Socialist can be sure what those two millions think of this war. We cannot talk to them, we cannot even send them letters by the army mails. They are cut off, isolated, every man of them. Perhaps they may talk together by twos or threes, but each man is thinking alone. What do they think? That is the great question for German Socialists to answer."

I grew more and more irritated. The atmosphere of caution and inaction seemed to me unworthy a man calling himself a Socialist and an internationalist. I blurted out a rank criticism or two. Herr Kautsky went on, prompted occasionally by the watchful Herr Bernstein.

"You are an outsider," he said. "The picture is not so black as you may think. For years we have been living under the Socialist Code—laws framed by the German Government to prevent our meeting or reading or even thinking. We have learned how to convey information to each other secretly. Intelligent Socialists are not being misled by the silence of *Vorwärts*. Some are confused, no doubt, but not all, and *Vorwärts* will do all it can. We have learned how to read between the lines."[1]

[1] See Appendix I, page 327.

The Attack

On October second I was invited by the Foreign Office at 76 Wilhelmstrasse to interview the Imperial Vice-Chancellor, Vice-President of the Royal Prussian Ministry of State, and Secretary of State for the Interior, *Excellenz* Clemens Gottlieb Ernst Delbrück. The invitation was formal as a summons to court. The ancestry and offices of the minister were recounted; the place, time, and nature of the interview were defined; and special emphasis was laid upon the fact that His Excellency had never before discussed affairs of Empire with an interviewer.

Military automobiles in gray war-paint were flying about the city like hawks; black-white-and-red flags fluttered from all the public buildings; five Belgian cannon huddled at the base of the bronze Frederick Second on *Unter den Linden;* French machine-guns squatted in an irregular line before the palace of the Crown Prince; and a dozen battered and dented Russian field-pieces lay in the gutter before the Kaiser's *Schloss* as symbols of German victory. On the window glass in the offices of the *Lokal Anzeiger* were pasted bits of white paper telling of new successes: von Hindenburg's advance into Russia and capture of Suwalki, the fighting before Verdun in France, and the fall of the outer forts of Antwerp.

The plain-clothes watchman on guard at the Foreign Office led me into a tiny cubbyhole, where I waited while a cold autumn wind blew in from the beech wood where Bismarck loved to walk. A lithograph map of Germany, a plain uneasy chair, a table, a window—that was the reception room. For the seal of the Iron Chancellor was set on the Wilhelmstrasse. The Foreign Office was as severe and barren, as secret and as stout, as any medieval donjon keep. Men with iron masks might live there and never a word of them reach the outside world. The very air in the offices seemed colder and more mysterious than the usual atmosphere of officialdom.

After a quarter of an hour the door to my cell opened and I became one of a group of seven or eight press representatives, American, South American, Swiss, and Scandinavian—the few neutrals left in the world!— making my bow to a chubby, unctuous diplomat, Baron von Mumm Schwartzenstein, former German Ambassador to Tokio. The Baron had the look and air of a successful British banker, but he carried the weight of the world on his rounded shoulders, for he was officially in charge of all the foreign newspaper representatives and of what they told and did not tell their journals.

His office was as gloomy as an undertaker's rooms. A few stray, level sunbeams crawled under the low-drawn curtains, and sparrows chirped outside. The office was decked with much discolored marble at door and hearth, and one caught a glimpse of what seemed to be the popular Prussian painting,—a muscular and very

THE ATTACK

blonde Brünnhilde trampling and spearing the breast of a very dark Latin lady.

We were soon led to another reception hall, where we met the Vice-Chancellor, and were quickly seated at a green baize-covered table. Before each of us was a paper pad and a pencil, and a typewritten abstract of what His Excellency proposed to say. The gentleman before us was a fine-looking Prussian about fifty years old, with sparse hair, open blue eyes, a frank face, and a friendly manner. He seemed like the Dutch uncle of fiction.

As we listened to the formal, scientific statement—a statement like a college lecture or a seminar conducted by a thoughtful German professor at the head of a long table—I caught glimpses of the whole drama of modern Germany. It frightened and weighed upon me like a bad dream.

Behind us lay a chaotic congeries of States and the gaunt, tenacious emergence of Prussia; the slow spread of industrialism into Germany; the riotous days of 1848, when Wilhelm First fled Berlin for the *Pfauen Insel*—his Elba; not his Saint Helena. The German Empire slowly forged in the Prussian furnace, shaped by the Prussian sword; the wars of 1864, 1866, 1870-'71, and the screaming burst of energy, industrial, political, and military, since the Franco-Prussian War. It was a picture of a medieval political organization dowered with the enormous wealth and power of twentieth century industrialism; a *Zollverein* developed into high tariff walls, so that the Fatherland might be industrially self-contained; skeins of strategic railways, Armadas of subsidized shipping, schools and press subsidized, censored, coerced; and more and more mountains of ammunition for a war which was sure to come.

Then the dawn of "the day"; the military mobilization, and with it the marvelous industrial mobilization. How the crisis in the currency was overcome at a stroke; how there was no moratorium; how credit was rehabilitated by the creation of cycles of new banks; how local and provincial employment agencies were consolidated into one Imperial Employment Office; how whole villages of German fishermen were transplanted from the North Sea to the Baltic; how the miners from the Silesian coal fields were transported to the Masurian Lakes after Hindenburg's victory, to bury the hundreds of thousands of Russians sucked under in the swamps, where acres of swollen, festering hands were stretched to heaven from the stinking earth; how minimum prices for grain and flour checked speculation in food; how iron and steel, textiles, arms, leather, and conserve industries were centralized and controlled by the State; how the German people subscribed their four and one-half milliards to the first War Loan as if it were pennies instead of marks—and far beyond the frontiers, eastward and westward, avalanches of guttural-voiced men in gray-green uniforms, falling upon France and Russia and unprotected Belgium.

CHAPTER III

THE FALL OF ANTWERP

Berlin Versus Antwerp

A Page from a Diary

Monday, October 5: left Berlin for Belgium.
Tuesday, October 6: reached Antwerp; arrested as a spy; released.
Wednesday, October 7: at midnight bombardment of Antwerp commenced.
Thursday, October 8: at 3.00 p. m., a 12.09 c.m. shrapnel shell burst in house where I was staying, completely wrecking two floors; nobody killed.
Friday, October 9: Belgians and British expeditionary forces evacuated Antwerp. At noon bombardment ceased, after thirty-six continuous hours. At 2.00 p. m., German army entered.
Saturday, October 10: left Antwerp on foot and walked through German lines to Dutch frontier.
Sunday, October 11: at 3.00 a. m., cabled story to New York from Rotterdam.

Four days after the interview with *Excellenz* Delbrück I was in Antwerp, the beleaguered capital of Belgium.

At Esschen, a little Flemish town just across the frontier from Holland, everything was in confusion. The crowded railway station was vile with every imaginable human stench. Night and day, for almost a month, refugees had lodged in straw littered about the floor. Poverty-stricken Belgians sat hunched up in the corners, or sprawled full-length in the malodorous pile. Babies screamed incessantly. A few women wept. The eyes of all were red. In the dirty, narrow street behind the station stood fifty awkward Flemish carts piled high with bedding and furniture hastily flung together in the panic of departure. Every one was fleeing toward Holland.

"When is the next train for Antwerp?"

"There is no train for Antwerp, monsieur." The sad blue eyes of the station agent hardened as he stared at me.

"Then I must drive to Cappellen."

"Impossible, monsieur."

The agent whispered to some one behind him. A man in a faded and very dirty blue uniform, with a round blue cap, came out and whispered to another in the station. A curious group of people crowded behind me to listen. I could hear them stirring and whispering suspiciously.

"What is your business, monsieur?"

"I am on official business. I must see the American Consul General in Antwerp."

"You have papers?"

"Of course."

The group crowded close. The man in the blue uniform was at my elbow, breathing hard as if he had been running. It was a ticklish moment. I showed the latter half of my passport, bearing the round red American seal; but one part of the pass I did not show—the part which read, "*Gesehen! Gut zum Eintritt in das Reichsgebiet. Haag, den 17. Septbr., 1914. Gesehen. Berlin, 28. September, 1914. Auswärtiges Amt des Deutschen Reichs Pass-Bureau,*" stamped with the eagle-crested seals of Germany.

The harassed ticket-agent and the bystanders were convinced. They murmured approvingly, "American! Mynheer is American!" There would be a train for Antwerp, perhaps at three o'clock, perhaps at four, perhaps at five. Who knows? Monsieur could wait where he would.

This was war I thought: sordid, unhappy, disorderly; the fearful flotsam of the floods poured out from Berlin. It was much more real than the mechanical perfection which I had seen in Germany. In Esschen there was a hideous droop to the shoulders of every one, as if they carried unbearable burdens. Only half a dozen children, playing noisily at soldiers with broomsticks and pans in the cluttered street behind the station, seemed untouched by the general misery.

The train came; late, of course. There were perhaps a dozen passengers, all men. The little train lurched painfully through timid towns, past neatly cultivated fields and forests where acres and acres of trees had been cut down by the Belgian soldiers and piled in tangled heaps, while the naked stumps, left standing knee-high, were sharpened wickedly to impede cavalry charges, past belts of barbed-wire entanglements stretching as far as one could see, past earthworks hidden in fringes of woods, past beautiful old *châteaux* and the country-houses of millionaire Antwerp merchants, stark and empty now, past high old-fashioned bastions of forts dating from Vauban's and Napoleon's day.

Twice my passport was examined by Belgian sentries, and twice I succeeded in concealing the German *visé*.

So at dusk we jolted into the dark Central Station of Antwerp.

An American Spy

A few oil lanterns gave the only light in the station. People hurried by in the darkness like ghosts; they conversed in undertones.

At the wicket I was stopped and my passport demanded. This time I could not conceal the German *visé*, and the Belgian official peered at me in astonishment.

"Why has monsieur come?" I explained that monsieur is an American *rédacteur*—an editor. The official was sorry, but he could not admit monsieur to the city. But if monsieur were determined to enter? . . . A group formed quickly about us, and their remarks were not reassuring. I explained myself clumsily.

THE AUTHOR'S PASSPORT

"Yes," said the official, "but the seal of the Belgian Minister at The Hague has been placed on monsieur's passport before that of the German Minister. The seal is four weeks old. Meanwhile monsieur has been in Berlin!"

"True," I acknowledged, "but I am an American, and besides I have friends in Antwerp who can vouch for me."

"Monsieur has friends? Monsieur must come into the station and wait for the commandant."

My two hours' detention in the marble waiting-room of the Central Station was strange as hysteria. I was thoroughly frightened. My imagination played strange tricks. It tried and convicted me without mercy. It sported with me as cruelly as a cat does with a mouse, and before the bar of my conscience I pled guilty to espionage in its worst form,—the pitiless artistic desire to witness catastrophes where one can be of no assistance.

Ghostly soldiers, black-robed priests, and Red Cross nurses flickered past me in the gloom. There was a table spread in a far corner with great round loaves scattered upon it, and oil lamps shedding a little glow of light which made it seem like a parody of da Vinci's "Last Supper."

At half past seven the Belgian colonel in charge of the railway station came to quiz me. He stood before me as stiff as a statue, and as cold.

"Your papers, monsieur!" he ordered crisply. "Why have you come to Antwerp?"

"I am an American *rédacteur.*"

"Yes?"

"I am here to study war conditions."

"Yes?"

"You will see from my papers that I have been in Berlin. It was for the same purpose: to study war conditions."

"Yes?"

"I have friends in Antwerp."

"But when were you in Berlin?"

"I left there yesterday morning."

"Yesterday! ! !" He looked at me in amazement. "Yesterday?" he repeated. "The *visé* is dated September twenty-eighth, but you were in Berlin yesterday?"

"Yes, *mon Colonel.*"

"I must send you to military headquarters!" He beckoned to a soldier. "Take mynheer—" he began in Flemish.

I followed the soldier through the black corridors of the station and out into the night. There was not a light in the streets, for fear of Zeppelins. Twice during the month of August the great air-craft had hung above the city and dropped bombs, and fear of them still ran high. The cold October sky arched over us like a cave. There were crowds about us. I could hear them walking in the street and on the pavement. Occasionally I caught a scrap of muffled conversation in Flemish. Once there was a suppressed sob. Some one opened the door of a *café,* and there was a sudden burst of light, immediately extinguished as the man slipped inside. I heard a glass clink and a girl laugh, but I could see nothing.

A military automobile hurriedly rounded the corner, and its blazing white searchlight illuminated for a moment herds of scurrying figures on the avenue.

Sentries challenged us in the dark. My guard talked with them in whispers. We passed on. . . .

Headquarters consisted of several small, ramshackle buildings, full of little offices. No one seemed to know where I should report. I went into a little bare room, half full of lounging soldiers who stared at me curiously, then into a second, and at last to a third. There a fine young major, his eyes pathetically anxious, examined me. My guard watched in silence.

"You have been in Berlin?"

"Certainly. I left there yesterday to come to Antwerp."

"Why?"

"To learn the truth about war conditions."

"Your papers!"

I showed my papers; all that I had with me.

The major evidently had had to do with other Americans, for his next question was, "Do you wish to see the battlefields?"

"No, I do not," I said.

The major spoke in Flemish to a second officer. Then he turned to my guard and addressed him in French. I have never heard more comfortable words.

"It is plain," he said slowly, "that monsieur is an American. But monsieur must go to the American Consul General early tomorrow morning and get a paper certifying that he is entitled to a pass admitting him to Antwerp. Monsieur may go now." And the major wished us a very good night.

My soldier escort presented arms, and we marched out into the dark. I bade him and the sentries *adieu,* but they would not have it so. "The night is very dark," they said. "Monsieur might lose his way." So they saw me safely to my hotel.

England Aids Belgium

I woke at four in the morning. Down the gray canyon of street below my window a long procession of Belgian artillery pounded and rattled over the cobble-stones. For half an hour it rumbled and jolted past—a line of dejected-looking horses and silent men. Then, when it had gone out of ear-shot, I heard far away the *boom——boom——boom boom——boom boom boom* of the big guns in the forts.

Automobiles full of officers, English as well as Belgian, were flying about the streets when I left the hotel after breakfast. Mr. Winston Churchill had paid a hurried call to Antwerp on the preceding Friday, when affairs looked darkest, and an expeditionary force had come from England to the relief of the Belgians. The force consisted of a marine brigade and two naval brigades, with some heavy naval guns manned by a detachment of the Royal Navy. It numbered all told eight thousand men. But the reinforcement seemed singularly haphazard. The First Lord of the British Admiralty dashed into Antwerp late in the evening with half a dozen armored motor-cars, arriving unheralded and unexpected to take charge of the situation. In the Hôtel de Londres I met a blithe young man named Julian Arthur Jones, son of the English playwright, Henry Arthur Jones, who told me in whispered confidence that Churchill had brought sixteen thousand first-rate British soldiers!

But conditions looked grave. The narrow Flemish streets still blazed with Belgian, French, and British flags, and most of the shops were open, but there was an alarming proclamation on all the pillar-posts, signed by the Belgian General Deguise.

ANTWERP, October 6, 10 P. M.—The situation of Antwerp is serious. Lieutenant-General Deguise, commanding the fortress, has addressed this evening to the burgomasters of the towns in the fortified zone the following letter:

"I have the honor to bring to the attention of the population the fact that the bombardment of the agglomeration of Antwerp and its environs is imminent.

"It is self-evident that the menace or the execution of

a bombardment will have no influence on the length of the resistance, which will be carried to the last extremity.

"Persons wishing to avoid the effects of the said bombardment are requested to withdraw without delay in the direction of the north or the north-east."

The forts of Lierre fell on Tuesday, October sixth, and King Albert, the Queen, and the Government moved to the town of Saint Nicolas on their way to the coast. The morning newspapers were calm, but by no means reassuring. People were leaving the city. They hurried anxiously to and fro, dragging with them hastily packed bundles of clothing, hand satchels, baby carriages, trunks, valises, umbrellas, and innumerable boxes. Street-cars were crammed with refugees and their goods, and outside the railway stations hundreds and thousands of people crowded together clamoring to be let inside. The rich left their houses to caretakers and departed in automobiles and carriages. The poor went on foot without giving a thought to what had to remain behind. There was almost no order; no direction. Wednesday's exodus was already a rout.

Banks were mobbed by people clamoring for their money. The gold reserves of the National Bank were sent for safe-keeping to England. Shops and warehouses closed as fast as they could. Hotels and *cafés* shut their doors and barricaded the windows. Citizens piled sand-bags against the cellar-ventilators of their houses as a protection against shells. People in general, even those who intended to remain in Antwerp come what might, seemed unnerved.

In the American Consul General's anteroom on the top floor at number 24 rue des Frères Cellites, I found an excited assistant imploring everybody who called for advice to get out of Antwerp as quickly as possible.

"What are *you* going to do?" I asked.

"I have to stay," he answered. "But if I were in your shoes, I would leave the city at once. It is going to be bombarded." His voice shook.

"I came here to get your *visé* on my papers, so I can stay," I said.

"Get out of the city at once!"

"But I intend to stay. Surely there will be plenty of people who stay."

He stared at me as if I were a lunatic; then he disappeared into the inner offices.

I looked up one of the Consular clerks, and she made out a little paper for me and stamped it with a big blue seal.

"Are you going to stay through the bombardment?" I asked her.

"Oh, yes," she said. "All the Consulate people have to stay. You'll find us here in the cellar if they shell the town."

"I'm glad to know that," I answered. "I shall look you up. It will be pleasant to join the American Colony.

... *Auf Wiederseh'n,*" I added. "Oh, I beg pardon. That's German!"

War Correspondents

At the Belgian military headquarters things were in a chaotic state. Weeping women and excited men stormed the place to ask advice. It took me more than half an hour to find my Belgian major, and when I found him he had no time to make out the formal pass for me. Sentries, orderlies, and officers were worn out. The whole atmosphere of the place was one of despair. I knew that if I were arrested in Antwerp without a pass, I might be shot as a spy, but there was too much misery and anxiety at headquarters for me to intrude further.

I saw two men arrested on the street outside the military offices. Fifteen minutes later I was told they had been shot against a wall.

I was walking down street in front of the deserted royal palace and the rococo mansions on the Place de Meir, when a German *Taube* flew directly overhead. It was like a beautiful bird sweeping across the sky, but the sight of it terrified the crowds beyond measure. In less than a minute the streets were absolutely deserted. Shops and banks and hallways of private residences were suddenly crammed with people, their faces blanched, eyes staring with horror, their mouths open. Antwerp had been terrorized by the Zeppelins, so that every one was afraid. The *Taube* flew serenely away, and the streets gradually filled again, but people walked closer to the buildings and hurried when they passed exposed places.

Shops were rapidly closing. By afternoon, less than half of them were open, and by five o'clock in the evening most of the hotels had shut their doors. From the southeast came the incessant *boom——boom boom ——boom* of the big guns. Bombardment was imminent. Hugh Gibson, secretary of the American Legation in Brussels, had gone through the lines carrying to the German General, Hans von Beseler, a chart of Antwerp on which were shown the principal architectural treasures, so that the German guns might spare them if possible. Belgian soldiers by twos, threes, and halfdozens, weary and discouraged, slouched along the pavements. Many probably were deserters. An English major said that it was practically impossible to hold the Belgians to the trenches. They had had their bellyful of battle, and no wonder! With almost no help from their allies, they had borne the brunt of incessant attacks from an invincible enemy. Rumors of a great French advance flew about the city, and some even believed that the sound of the cannon portended a Belgian action in the rear of the Germans. But such tales could no longer buoy up the spirits of the troops. It was up to the British expeditionary forces to hold the lines, so the English major said. And as evening fell, whole companies of Belgian infantry and cavalry passed, all going westward. Troops were being drawn off from the forts; the officers called it "making a change of base."

Red Cross ambulances clanged by bringing wounded to the hospitals, but those who could walk from the battlefields straggled into the city as best they could.

In the Hôtel Saint Antoine on the Place Verte I found a group of American and British war correspondents and photographers. Horace Green of the New York *Evening Post* was there; gentle-voiced, observant, and calm as a Harvard *Crimson* scribe writing up a collegiate lecture. Julian Arthur Jones dropped in, eager as a cub reporter on his first assignment, and explaining to all of us what was going on. And there was a mysterious looking British intelligence officer named Montfort and a number of reserve officers, lounging about the lobby; for the Saint Antoine was British headquarters.

"Are you going to stick it out?" asked Julian Jones.

"Yes," I said. "Are you?"

"My paper orders me to stay. Look at this pile of telegrams; fifteen if there is one, and all came today, too. Bally trick, I say, to order a man to stay in this hole while the Germans capture it. I suppose I'll date my next despatch to the *Chronicle* from the Kingdom of Heaven; eh what?" . . .

A thin-faced Westerner in immaculate riding-breeches

and puttees came into the lobby and slouched down wearily into a chair.

"Have you had anything to eat?" I asked him by way of introduction.

"No," he answered listlessly.

"Well, this hotel is closing. Come along and let's see what we can find. My name is Hunt."

"I'm Donald C. Thompson," he said, "photographer for the New York *World*. Guess I'm better known in America now than President Wilson is. I've been taking *the* pictures of this little war!"

I showed interest. "Are you going to stay and take pictures when the Germans come in?"

"You bet your sweet life!" exploded Thompson, recovering his animation.

"I'm staying too. But is there really going to be a bombardment?"

"Yes," he said, "you bet your hat there is! Come and stay at my house, won't you? I've got a fine little shack with all you want to eat and a good bed. It belongs to some Belgian friends of mine, but they've gone to Holland."

I accepted gratefully. To exchange hotel quarters for a home was bliss indeed. A hotel always seemed to me a poor place to die in. So that night Donald Thompson and I went to number 74 rue du Péage, a pleasant dwelling house near the avenue du Sud, which was to be our fortress during the bombardment of Antwerp. A press photographer for the Chicago *Tribune* named Edwin F. Weigle and the Dutch Vice-Consul, Mynheer de Meester, shared the house with Thompson. A large American flag hung over the front door, and Thompson's full name and New York address were scrawled with indelible pencil on the white panels.

We climbed the darkened stair and lit a match. It was an attractive house, but the rooms were cluttered with shoes, clothing, boxes, and *bric-à-brac* abandoned in the hurry of departure. The beds were unmade. The dishes were unwashed. In an oven of the big Belgian stove in the kitchen we found a soldier's uniform and cap hastily crammed out of sight. Jams, pickles, cured meats, soups, wine, mineral water, a bin of apples, fresh bread, and plenty of butter were in the cellar. We were not to starve! And best of all, the basement was a couple of feet below the ground level, so there would not be too much danger from flying fragments of shells.

A pile of books lay beside my bed, and I glanced at them before putting out the lamp. They were *L'Epouse du Soleil, Cadet la Perle, Quo Vadis,* Sudermann's *La Femme en Gris,* and Ella Wheeler Wilcox's " Poems of Passion "! With these incongruous spirits to guard me, I fell asleep with a sense of comfort and security.

The Bombardment of Antwerp

I was awakened by a tremendous roar and a shock which seemed to lift the house from its foundations. Immediately there came a distant *boom!* a shrill snarling whistle, then another explosion which pounded the air like storm.

Boom – wheeeeeeeeeeeeeeeeieieieiekkkkkkkkkBANG-GGGG! Boom – wheeeeeeeeeeEEEEEEEIEIEIEIE-KKKKKKKKBANGGGGGGGG! Every pane of glass in the house blew out in the chaos which followed the bursting of that fourth bomb. It had hit directly across the street, less than thirty-five feet from where I was hurrying into my clothes. I could hear screams and sobs; then the sound of people rushing by the house, and the crash of glass which littered the sidewalks, splintering to bits as the people ran. But above every other sound clamored the continuous mad-dog snarling of the German shells. *Boom – wheeeeeeeeeeieieieiekk-kkBANG – boom – wheeeeeeeeeeeeeeeeeeieieiekkkkkk-BANG – wheeeeeeeeeeekkboomBANG – wheeeeeeeeeee-ieieieboomieieikkkkkBANG – boom – wheeEEEEEEEE IEIEIEIEIEIEKKKKK – BANGGGGGGGGGGGG! !* My watch read 12.05, Belgian time. . . .

From the cellar came a frightened, unintelligible voice.

"Everybody all right?" I yelled, strapping on my belt of gold-pieces and flinging on my clothes.

"All right!" answered Thompson shrilly from the next room. "Y-yes," called Weigle from upstairs. And we bolted for the cellar.

There, fully dressed even to his overcoat, was the Vice-Consul. His teeth were chattering. He stood ankle-deep in coke in a small fuel closet under the stairs, which we Americans had entirely overlooked in our inspection. A single candle-flame lighted the place. "Sh-sh-shut the door," he begged. "Where is the g-g-g-gas meter? We must turn off the g-g-g-gas meter. It isn't safe. We must turn off the g-g-g-gas meter. Where is the g-g-g-gas meter?" The poor fellow's state was pitiful.

To my astonishment, the cannonade gave me an intense feeling of exaltation. It was like the exhilaration of fever. I was convinced that we should all be killed, so I wrote on the walls of our cyclone-cellar the names and addresses of Thompson, de Meester, Weigle, and myself. My senses were keenly alive to danger, but there was a strange joy in the thought that life was to be obliterated in a mad chaos of flame and steel and thunder. Death seemed suddenly the great adventure; the supreme experience. And there was something splendid, like music, in the incessant insane snarl of the shells and the blasts of the explosions.

Thompson and I ran upstairs and brought down mattresses and blankets, then we all lay down side by side in the coke, with the flimsy door shut to keep out stray shells. The shell fire at first had excited; now it seemed

THE BOMBARDMENT OF ANTWERP 89

to soothe me, and I went quietly to sleep. Occasionally I was awakened by the Vice-Consul and Weigle arguing whether or not we were in the direct line of fire, and whether or not the last shell had burst nearer our house than the first. Outside, fugitives fled sobbing along the streets; but I slept, indifferent to them.

Such sleep is like drowning. It has the double effect of a stimulant and a narcotic. Pictures of my past life rushed out of the dark in streams and flooded my sleep with bright and somber visions. I saw them, but I slept. . . .

At four o'clock in the morning Thompson and I left the others and went out into the avenue du Sud. Refugees, most of them women, were hurrying by in every direction, half-dressed, only half sane, and horribly afraid. Many, no doubt, were crouching in the cellars, but most of the people ran. Old and young, in little coveys of fours, fives, half-dozens, dozens, ran along the sidewalks, slipping and crashing over the broken glass, making a terrifying and unearthly racket as they ran. Whenever a shell snarled unusually near, the groups fell cowering on hands and knees against the nearest houses. Women covered their heads with their shawls and waited breathless and motionless for the smash and roar of the explosion. I saw a shell burst in the avenue within a few yards of some of these fugitives. A woman dropped her baby and ran on without it. Two old men, dragging a heavy bundle of household goods between them, abandoned it in the street and fled screaming. A priest ran plump into me, completely unnerved. The shell had struck just at the corner of the rue du Péage and avenue du Sud and had torn a hole through curb and cobblestones and earth three feet deep and seven feet in diameter.

In the house just across the street from ours, a shell had gone into the front door sill and had blown out the entire hallway. On our side of the street, four doors away, a shell had burst in the third story, completely wrecking the top of the building. Only a little farther down the street another house had been hit. From the south of the city rose columns of black smoke, where the suburb of Hoboken was burning, but so far as I could see there were still no fires in the principal part of Antwerp.

I stood in the middle of the street and watched the gray sky in the hope of seeing a shell. The idea was absurd, yet I felt an odd sense of being cheated of part of the spectacle. The air seemed full of steel. I counted three explosions a minute: I wanted to see something. One could hear the shells so easily, it seemed ridiculous not to see them. . . .

Belgian soldiers began to pass, hurrying westward. Their eyes were glassy. Often they were breathless and staggered as they walked. One of them pushed into our open door and asked me a question in Flemish. I caught the word "vest," and told Thompson the man was cold and was asking for a waistcoat to wear under his uniform. Thompson brought the garment, but the soldier shook his head. "*Kleederen*"—clothing, he said, and he showed us by signs that he wanted a whole suit. The rout had begun. Soldiers were deserting by wholesale and attempting to escape from the city in civilian dress.

We left our front door open until nine o'clock. In the panic of flight some of the fugitives seemed to take comfort in stopping, if only for a moment, in the flimsy shelter of our hallway, then darting out on their aimless course. Once or twice I tried to talk with them in French, but they were beyond words. They seemed to be of all classes of the population: well-to-do burghers, dock-dwellers, servants, and peasants.

What a Shrapnel Shell Did

Daylight brought comfort, but the panic continued. The exodus seemed endless. Little carts, wheelbarrows, baby carriages, Flemish milk-wagons drawn by dogs, two or three old cabs, and an occasional farm wagon piled high with goods, went by us. Old men and women, invalids, cripples, and young children were carried past in that ghastly rout. I saw a man with hideously deformed feet and legs madly propelling himself along on home-made crutches. A wrinkled old woman came by leading a cow. Dogs were howling everywhere. There was the incessant rattle and crash of broken glass on the sidewalks and in the streets as the fugitives stumbled past. But one sound dominated everything. It was to left of us, to right of us, behind us, before us, and overhead. It was the smack and boom of the big guns, and the everlasting crazy uproar of the bursting shells.

The air was bitter with powder smoke. Later I smelled kerosene. The Germans were shelling us with shrapnel and incendiary bombs. Fires began to shoot up in the heart of our section. There were heavier explosions. A fifth house in our block was struck, and the entire front was riddled with lead—great jagged holes showing in woodwork and bricks and plaster. The house looked like a colander.

We did not know it then, but the bombardment was systematic as a game of checkers. The city was blocked off on checker-board charts; each battery was given its share of work to do, its time for rest and refreshment, and square by square the Germans shelled.

Hours dragged by. With methodical regularity the German steel was pumped into the doomed city, except for brief pauses once every hour, when the artillery corps stopped to cool the guns. It was almost amusing to think of the calm young Prussian lieutenants of artillery—the same sort as those I had seen in Berlin two days before—now five miles or more away from us, quietly and unemotionally directing that cyclone of shells. . . .

Fire slackened at noon and we had visitors. Our front door bell jangled violently, and in came Horace

WHAT A SHRAPNEL SHELL DID 93

Green, cool and collected as always, but keenly sensitive to the horrors of the situation. He confirmed the worst fears of Weigle and the Vice-Consul by telling us that our house was in the direct line of fire, and that no shells had as yet fallen in the center of the city. While he was talking, the door bell jangled again. Thompson answered this time, and I heard his piping voice raised in hearty greeting. "Hello, Jimmie," he yelled, "how are you? Come right in. Glad to see you."

"It's Jimmie Hare—James H. Hare—photographer for *Leslie's Weekly*," explained Green.

I had never met Hare, but I knew of him as the veteran photographer of a dozen wars; seventy-two years old, they said, and spry and bold as a boy. So I left Green and ran upstairs. Thompson had vanished completely. There was no sign of Hare. I went to the door and threw it open. A German shell whizzed close overhead: the bombardment had commenced again. The Germans had taken only half an hour off for lunch!

But where was Hare?

A little gray man, about five feet tall, wearing a boy's cap and a brown Norfolk jacket, was hopping about on the other side of the street in a litter of broken window glass, bricks, and plaster dislodged by the shells. He had a small black box in his hand, and he was sighting it at the house. The box was a camera. The little man was Hare.

"Hello! hello!" he yelled in the tone of an enraptured camera fiend. "Hold that! Fine! Hold that pose! Duck your head behind the door! Great!" He pointed the camera. *Wheeeeeeeeeeeeeeeieieieikkkkkkk-BOOM!* . . . A German shell burst only a quarter of a block away. Hare dodged, but kept the camera pointed. "Hold that pose!" he yelled again. "Look scared!" I obeyed without an effort. "Fine! Great!" he said again. *Snap!*—the picture was taken, and we ran for the cellar together. . . .

We learned from our visitors that the American Consul General, Vice-Consul, and the entire Consulate staff had fled from the city to Ghent. What were we going to do? We were going to stay in Antwerp, and we intended to remain in our house until we were burned out or shelled out.

We had not long to wait. Our visitors had scarcely left us, and we were amusing ourselves in our little cyclone cellar, when our billet arrived. I had just completed a drawing of Weigle and the Vice-Consul lying on the coke. There was the familiar dull, distant *boom*, and the snarling *wheeeeeeieieieiekkk,* but the blast that followed was exactly over our heads, and it sounded like all the thunders in the universe rolled into one. The shell had exploded directly over us. It seemed to bring down half the house about our ears.

Thompson and I raced upstairs with a bucket of water in either hand, ready to put out any fire which might have started. We could not see a thing. The

"Beating the Camera."
The author's head just shows in the half-open door.

plaster dust was thicker than smoke, and the stairwell was choked with *débris,* but luckily for us, part of the wall had been blown out, and the air soon cleared sufficiently for us to take stock of our situation.

Two floors and a part of a third were completely wrecked; five rooms and a hall in all. The shell had gone through three thick brick walls. In the ruin was a broken couch, a smashed wardrobe, shivered mirrors, chairs, beds, and bed linen, a collection of stamps, a rosary, a crucifix, and quantities of small, intimate possessions of no intrinsic worth, but great personal value. The walls were scarred and splintered. There was an acrid smell of powder smoke in the air, gray plaster dust covered everything, but no fire was visible.

Our door bell rang sharply, and we ran downstairs to find our kind Belgian neighbors standing at the door with buckets of water in their hands, all ready to help us. There was plenty of cowardice in Antwerp during the bombardment, but I think gratefully of the unselfish bravery of those Belgians in the rue du Péage who were so ready to help the strangers.

A Bath and a Forced March

We hurried a second time to the top of the house and looked about us. Half a dozen serious fires were blazing up in our immediate neighborhood. One of them seemed to be in our block. The air was calm, but the fires might spread. Dusk would soon be on us. If we intended to move at all, we ought to take advantage of what daylight still remained.

We decided to move.

I was dirty and tired, and felt a sudden longing for a bath. It was the last chance of soap and water, perhaps, for many days; so while the others packed their motion-picture cameras and other belongings for the *trek* northward, I sputtered and lathered and scrubbed and rough-toweled to my heart's content. I can remember few more luxurious sensations in my life than that steam-hot bath under fire of German shells. . . .

The streets were almost deserted when we began our long walk north. Smoke obscured the sky. To some it must have seemed like the Day of Judgment. Ruin was everywhere. An unbelievable number of houses in our neighborhood had been struck, and wherever shrapnel hit, half the house had been demolished. Streets and sidewalks were plowed and pitted. In one of the squares stood a statue with its arm blown off by a ball. Many houses and shops were burning, but no one was paying any attention. The water supply had been cut off a week before by the Germans; the fire department was demoralized, and a few houses did not matter when one's whole world was falling.

We came out at last on the water front by the river Scheldt. Away to the southwest the immense Hoboken oil tanks were blazing, and tremendous columns of jet-black smoke were pouring up into the gray sky. Across the river, from the Tête de Flandre, a Belgian fort fired intermittently, and from the southeast still came the boom and shriek of German shells.

Refugees were jammed along the quays, all trying to get across the pontoon bridge to East Flanders. We moved slowly along with the crowd, not quite certain what to do. Fate decided for us. While we stood watching the fugitives, the pontoon bridge closed for the night, and thousands of unfortunates who had stood in line for hours, hoping to cross, were driven back into the city again. As a matter of fact, a retreat was in progress, and the military needed the bridge.

First they transferred the wounded. Six thousand five hundred in all were taken from the Antwerp hospitals to places of safety across the river. Three hundred and fifty, the worst wounded, were left to the Germans. Down the street from the Town Hall came rocking and bouncing twenty or thirty old double-decked Piccadilly motor-buses. Even their familiar advertisements were still pasted on them, and their London destinations. They had come with the British expeditionary forces, and they were returning filled with wounded.

Hospitals were rapidly emptied. Calm-faced nurses in white overalls with Red Cross brassards on their arms, black-robed Belgian priests, soldiers, and civilians helped in the transfer, and nothing was more heroic in all Antwerp than the work of the devoted Red Cross doctors and nurses who quietly removed the wounded from hospitals to ambulance under fire. There was panic in some of the wards. Mutilated men dragged themselves from their beds and pulled on what garments they could; they screamed and implored the nurses not to let them fall into the hands of the Germans. Some begged revolvers so they might shoot themselves. And in the crisis both the English and Belgian nurses were angels of mercy indeed.

Troops followed the wounded across the Scheldt. When night fell, Belgians and British were marching over the bridge by squads and companies and regiments. Tugboats puffing excitedly to and fro aided in the transfer. The narrow bridge of boats was crowded all night long, and the quay below the Steen—the picturesque old Spanish fortress on the river's brink—was heaped high with knapsacks, uniforms, shoes, blankets, and other *impedimenta* of war.

At the Queen's Hotel, overlooking the Quai van Dyck and the pontoon bridge, we put up for the night. Here we found Green,[1] Hare, Arthur Ruhl [1] of *Collier's Weekly,* and the British intelligence officer. There was a little grate fire in the hotel sitting-room, under a shallow glass skylight, where we gathered and talked. Those hours were strangely revealing. The nerves of the men

[1] Both Green and Ruhl are authors of excellent books on Antwerp: *The Log of a Non-Combatant,* by Horace Green, Houghton Mifflin Co., Boston, 1915, and *Antwerp to Gallipoli,* by Arthur Ruhl, Charles Scribner's Sons, New York, 1916.

were so badly shaken they could scarcely stand. Hare had been arrested by a Belgian officer and narrowly escaped shooting as a spy; Green had had an unusually close shave from a shell; Ruhl had been in the trenches and was worn out. Things ordinarily hidden under the surface of life came up that night like bubbles from a stagnant pool, and perfect strangers confided to each other their hearts' secrets.

That night I slept in room number one in the Queen's—not five hundred yards from the pier and the pontoon bridge—and my sleep was troubled all night long by the weary tramp of beaten men, marching to the boats and the possible security of East Flanders. The night was very cold and dark, except for the ghastly light of the burning buildings. Antwerp had fallen. This was the aftermath. . . .

That night Sub-Lieutenant Rupert Brooke crossed the bridge of boats. Insolent and beautiful and young, he marched with his men, mercifully ignorant that seven months later he was to die of disease, not battle, in the Ægean. I have wondered since if he was then composing the sonnet he called " Peace ".[1]

"Now, God be thanked Who has matched us with His
         hour,
     And caught our youth, and wakened us from sleeping,

[1] This sonnet is one of five which originally appeared in *New Numbers* and may be found in *The Collected Poems of Rupert Brooke*, published by the John Lane Company, New York, 1915.

With hand made sure, clear eye, and sharpened power,
  To turn, as swimmers into cleanness leaping,
Glad from a world grown old and cold and weary,
  Leave the sick hearts that honor could not move,
And half-men, and their dirty songs and dreary,
  And all the little emptiness of love!

"Oh! we, who have known shame, we have found release
    there,
  Where there's no ill, no grief, but sleep has mending,
    Naught broken save this body, lost but breath;
Nothing to shake the laughing heart's long peace there
  But only agony, and that has ending;
    And the worst friend and enemy is but Death."

BLOWING UP THE BRIDGE

At six o'clock Friday morning the pontoon bridge was blown up. It was a magnificent and terrifying spectacle. Fugitives had been pouring across in the half-light of early morning. Later they came flying back toward the city as fast as they could run. The river front was lined with helpless hordes of people and piled high with things thrown away by the retreating Belgian and British troops. Some of the correspondents were trying frantically to engage a boat so they could get out. The Dutch Vice-Consul and Weigle had disappeared utterly. It was *sauve qui peut.*

Then from the middle of the bridge came the explosion. A sheet of flame leaped from the water; there was a deafening roar, and a rain of fragments. The river was littered with wreckage. The crowd screamed and

BLOWING UP THE BRIDGE

ran—anywhere, nowhere—dropped their bundles—lost their friends and relatives—fell down and clambered up again,—all the time screaming in brute fear.

There was another burst of flame, another roar, another rain of wood and steel. The bridge still hung across the stream, but it lay like a snake with its back broken. A Belgian gunboat crawled near and began to hammer the floating barges with solid shot. The roar of the discharges was practically continuous. The firing was less than fifty yards from us, and the leap of the flame from the gun seemed almost to reach the pontoons where the shells were striking. Two or three of the barges listed slowly. Several sank. The remainder floated, a tangle of wreckage, moored in the rapid tidal current of the Scheldt.

Down the Canal au Sucre came soldiers flying from the battlefields. Fifty Belgians appeared, then two English Tommies. Their despair when they saw that the bridge was gone was pitiful. I could not stay to see if they got across in some other way.

For Thompson and I retrieved our kits from the Queen's and started off for the American Consulate. We were absolutely alone now. Our friends had left the city, and only we two were left to see the Germans come in. The bombardment had ceased temporarily, although we still could hear the booming of guns in the southern forts. The Belgian black-yellow-and-red flew high on the cathedral tower, untouched as yet.

A few Belgians were about the streets. One of them suddenly threw up his hands, spun half round, and fell. He was dead of apoplexy before we could reach him.

At the Marché aux Lits, a fire, larger than usual, arrested us, and Thompson unpacked his moving-picture camera and calmly cranked away until the falling walls of the shops compelled us to move on.

The street-corner shrines of the Virgin, which one always associates with Antwerp, were empty of their images; only the tinsel canopies remained along the Place de Meir. The Red Cross hospital was idle; the palace was deserted. Great holes showed in the street and sidewalks and there was everywhere the dreary wreckage of shops.

At the Consulate we found only the Belgian caretaker and his wife. The American Consul General, the Vice-Consul and the entire staff had left Antwerp by automobile the day before. We were not exactly proud of our countrymen, but in a panic no one is master of his actions and no one can judge another.

Soon the cannonading recommenced, and panicky refugees came to the Consulate door for protection. That Friday morning bombardment was the severest of all, and did, as we discovered later, the greatest damage. Yet right in the midst of it there was a sound of carriage wheels in the street below the Consulate windows, the bell rang, and up came the coolest person in Antwerp.

BLOWING UP THE BRIDGE 103

"I'm Mrs. Ide," our visitor said. "I'm from Chicago, and I live here *en pension*. I'm not afraid of the Germans, but *he* is."

"Who is *he?*" I questioned.

"*He* is the man who keeps the boarding house. *He's* out there." Mrs. Ide motioned to the carriage. "He's the driver. He wants to be under the protection of the American Consul."

We explained our anomalous status, but added that we thought we could do as Consul General and Vice-Consul respectively, and that in any event we intended to defend Antwerp from the German invaders.

"My!" said Mrs. Ide when we had ended this rigmarole. "It sounds fine to hear good 'United States' again when we have to listen to so much German." And she pointed skyward, where the shells were screaming.

She had hardly gone when a Belgian refugee ran in and begged protection of the Consulate. His sister was American Minister Brand Whitlock's cook, he explained, and the poor fellow had reasoned it out that American protection certainly was due the brother of such a functionary.

All through that unhappy morning people came, and we gave them what comfort we could. It was little enough at best, yet they were pathetically grateful, and I think it did all of us good to stand for an hour or two in the shelter of the American flag.

ENTER: THE GERMANS

At noon the bombardment ceased. It had been practically continuous for thirty-six hours. One hundred and eighty-one houses had been destroyed by incendiary shells, thirty-one houses had been partially burned, nine houses totally destroyed by explosions, and five hundred and fifty-six badly damaged. How many people were killed or wounded I have never learned; shrapnel fire is notoriously uncertain in its results, but there were about twenty dead and wounded picked up in the streets and there must have been bodies in the ruins of houses and shops.

Friday morning the military authorities authorized the city officials completely and without reserve to negotiate to stop the bombardment. General Deguise and his staff had gone westward with the army. Antwerp's old burgomaster, Jan de Vos, the Spanish Consul, Senator Alfred Rykmans, and Deputy Louis Franck presented themselves in an automobile before the German outposts. They were blindfolded and taken through the lines to the town of Contich. Mr. Franck in his tall hat and frock coat was spokesman.

It was a common story in Antwerp afterward that the German General, Hans von Beseler, could not believe his eyes when the deputation appeared before him, for there was not a man in uniform among them! "I will not receive them," he stormed. "I will not treat with civilians. I have conquered one of the great fortresses of the world," he burst out, turning on Mr. Franck, "and a civilian comes to render it up! You come to render it up!—a man in a top hat!" . . .

But the citizens of Antwerp did not yet know that their beautiful city had capitulated. I left Thompson at the Consulate and made a rapid inspection of the center of town. In the Place Verte four big shells had plowed into the earth, and the cathedral of Notre Dame had at last been struck. Most of Belgian cathedrals are not like Dutch Protestant churches—whitewashed sepulchres, with barnacles of shops about their bleaching hulls, so the destruction in its neighborhood had not menaced the cathedral itself. But now in the south transept, thirty feet from the ground, yawned a hole four feet in diameter. I endeavored to find the custodian, but they told me that he had fled. Later I found a priest and a bystander named Peeters, and together we searched for the keys. The priest babbled mournfully to me of the sacrilege of the Germans: the mad ruthlessness with which they make war, the brutality with which they treat priests and nuns, and their impious vandalism.

At last we were inside. The beautiful old cathedral of Notre Dame had stood inviolate and sacred since its completion in 1450. It held the carved masterpieces of a host of sculptors, and the famous "Descent from the Cross" of Rubens, but fortunately all the paintings had been removed and hidden away before the bombardment began, for there, on the flag-stones, directly in front of the high altar, I picked up half a howitzer shell—one of the latest and most terrible weapons known to men. Fragments of the stone of which the cathedral is built had been blown one hundred feet away from the spot where the shell entered. Five sections of the great stained-glass window in the south transept had been shattered, another had been completely demolished, and an altar rail was gouged with shot. "What sacrilege! What scandal!" the poor priest reiterated in an undertone. Our shoes gritted on bits of priceless stained glass as we walked.

Three shells had struck near the Town Hall and had pitted the south side of the building, but the Germans had spared the principal architectural treasures of the city. The museums were untouched.

New fires were springing up. New fugitives were hurrying past, all going northward. But most of the population still in Antwerp waited with the calm of despair for the occupation by the Germans. No more soldiers were to be seen, the Civic Guards had been disbanded and had disappeared, and a policeman at the Town Hall told me the city had surrendered and that the Germans were about to enter.

I walked up toward the avenue des Arts. The streets were deserted and the city silent, except for the snapping of flames in the burning houses. Suddenly I heard

THE ARMY OF OCCUPATION 107

a new sound—low, insistent, measured—the sound of men marching. I turned a corner and looked. . . . There, coming down the avenue in absolute silence, were the Germans.

THE ARMY OF OCCUPATION

The troops were advancing cautiously, like men who fear a trap. There was no music, there were no flags. First came some of the bicycle corps, then masses of infantrymen and a few cavalrymen, then came floods of soldiers. Column after column they rolled past, all in the gray-green service uniform which is the most remarkable disguise ever invented by mortal man. Line after line they tramped by, anonymous as swarming bees, indistinguishable from the mass at fifty yards, stamping the cobble-stones in perfect time, with the remarkable, tireless, springy march-step of the German recruit. There were sprays of field flowers in some of the guns, and sprigs of green in the soldiers' coats.

The men glanced suspiciously at the shuttered windows, as if they suspected that snipers lurked behind in the darkened rooms. One madman's work just then would have precipitated a massacre and the destruction of the city. . . .

Von Hindenburg was still on the offensive in Russia, and tremendous battles were in progress in France, yet the captors of Antwerp were as fresh as if they had been newly mobilized, and they were literally the flower of the Kaiser's armies. I did not see a man older than twenty-eight, except two officers who flew by in a motor-car.

Then came what seemed to be endless trains of artillery, rumbling along behind the infantry. Field guns and Austrian howitzers went past, each drawn by six splendid horses, and nervous military automobiles appeared, skirting the columns. Belgian civilians began to come out, their curiosity having got the better of their discretion. Several timidly gave directions to members of the bicycle corps or officers in automobiles who stopped to inquire the way.

Through the rue des Tanneurs to the Place de Meir came another infantry column; but like the first, it entered in silence, without music and without show of any sort.

The infantrymen stacked arms in the streets and rested. At the end of every alley and side street I could see frightened people peering out at their masters. Occasionally some one hurried furtively along close to the buildings. Women wept and wrung their hands. A few, perhaps more frightened even than the rest, appeared in side streets with cups of coffee which they offered to the Germans. A *café* in the Place de la Commune opened, and long files of soldiers quietly formed and bought beer from the trembling proprietor.

I walked up to a group of twenty German soldiers resting in a little park, and introduced myself.

THE ARMY OF OCCUPATION

"Are you English?" a young lieutenant asked mildly.
"Oh, no," I said. "I am an American."
"*Ach,* so! . . . Where are the English?"
"You must not ask me," I laughed. "Americans are neutral."

Trains of artillery kept pouring in. Down along the water front beside the old Spanish Steen, a dozen big guns were unlimbered and began shelling the west shore of the Scheldt. The pontoon bridge was a hopeless wreck, and the Belgians had scuttled all available river craft and jammed the machinery of the canal locks, so pursuit by the Germans was impossible. They contented themselves with shelling the rearguards of the retreating army. *Boom, boom——boom, boom, boom* went the German guns; but the weary population of Antwerp was past caring.

And I found myself careless too. Now that the thrill of the bombardment had subsided, I felt an apathetic calm. The sufferings of Belgium ceased to interest me. . . . I looked up Thompson, and together we walked leisurely back to our little house in the rue du Péage as if we had left it only for a stroll. On our way we saw new ruins caused by the shells, and a number of new conflagrations. We picked up bits of a shell which had penetrated one of the round towers of the National Bank building, and stared at the holes in the Palais de Justice. Little house dogs, deserted by their masters, were scratching and whining disconsolately at locked doors, but we walked by, indifferent to them. Our house we found still intact, although the third and fourth floors where the shrapnel shell had struck were little more than kindling. The American flag still hung protectingly over the front door.

We went inside. A starving cat yowled from the backyard, and we found dry bread and sour milk, and fed it. Beside a rosebush in the yard was a sunken spot, like a grave. Probably our Belgian hosts had buried household treasures there.

But our curiosity was dead. West of us the Germans were pounding away with their field guns. Occasionally we heard dull reports which sounded like the Belgian forts or the British armored trains replying. It may have been the Belgian troops blowing up their forts. At intervals came the sharp crackle of infantry firing in platoons close at hand. But we did not care. We had grown callous and careless from the strain of two days.

First Aid to Antwerp

Saturday morning, October tenth, the rest of the German troops about Antwerp poured into the city. They entered, like their predecessors, in perfect order and in silence. We two lonely Americans stood in the office of the deserted American Consulate overlooking the rue Leys and watched the line of troops roll by. They, like the others, were young and fit. We did not see *Land-*

sturm among them. They passed like an army going into action: gun after gun, regiment after regiment, Red Cross wagons, commissariat wagons, more guns, more regiments, and still more regiments. It seemed to be arranged especially for our benefit, and Thompson unlimbered his moving-picture camera and took photographs of the entire proceeding.

Belgian *agents de police* were still at their posts, reinforced now by German sentries. It was interesting to see how quickly the latter assumed the task of cleaning up the city. By seven o'clock Saturday morning, squads of citizens, men and women, were sweeping the sidewalks and streets under guard of German soldiers, and as I threaded my way slowly along among the soldiers massed in the narrow downtown streets, I found them passing from hand to hand buckets of water to put out the street fires. At the Marché aux Œufs, Belgian firemen were working on the ladders, German soldiers were passing buckets below, and in one place the soldiers were energetically engaged in working an old-fashioned six-man fire pump.

On the Vieux Marché au Blé, soldiers crowded into a little food shop. "Ah, ha," I said to myself; "here's where I catch them looting." I wedged myself into the shop in the wake of a stocky private. The tiny space was jammed with Germans, and the nervous proprietor was hacking away with incredible speed and skill at a huge cheese. Sausages, cheese, cake chocolate, and bread were what the soldiers were buying. The stock went like wildfire, but not a soldier left the shop without paying for his share. They paid in Belgian money. Some of them had to stand about for eight or ten minutes after they had received their purchases before they had an opportunity to pay, but they paid. They were more like a crowd of picnickers buying out a rural grocery than soldiers of a conquering army occupying the capital of a kingdom.

A dozen Bavarians stood in the rue Aqueduc listening to the vituperations of an old Flemish woman. She was berating them like schoolboys, absolutely fearless, but they seemed to be taking it in excellent humor. I think they understood about one word in six, for the Flemish language is just enough like the German to be hopelessly confusing at first. Suddenly one of the soldiers looked up at the cathedral spire, where the Belgian flag had hung ever since the tragic day that Germany sent her ultimatum to Belgium. There, crawling slowly toward the top, was the black-white-and-red flag of the invaders. It reached the peak and began to flutter in the light breeze. The soldiers yelled delightedly. "We must sing! We must sing!" shouted some one; and the long compact lines began to chant, *Deutschland, Deutschland über alles.*

German marines were hard at work on the wreckage of the pontoon bridge when I came out on the water front. A line of German cannon stood below the Spanish Steen, and across the Scheldt smoke rose lazily from ruins of buildings set on fire by the shells. In the mountain of *débris* discarded by Belgian and British in their retreat, German soldiers were searching for serviceable trophies. I saw a soldier worm out of the pile a brand-new fencing mask and foils. He stared at them as if he had no idea what they were for; and indeed they looked amusing enough in the heap of uniforms, rifles, bayonets, cartridge boxes, cartridge clips, camp knives and forks, swords, and scabbards which lay scattered in disorder for more than one hundred and fifty feet along the edge of the quay. Another German fished out of the mass a beautiful Belgian presentation sword. He threw it aside in disgust. The searchers were taking only serviceable things—leather straps, holsters, knives, and the like.

The old Steen loomed dark above them as they searched. The stony eyes of the tenth century seemed to look very calmly on this last taking of Antwerp. The Steen had seen many conquerors: William the Silent, Alva, Farnese, Marlborough, Napoleon, Marshal Gérard —why worry over one more? . . . I walked up the steep approach. A solitary Belgian guard stood at the portal, his face haggard and his hands twitching. He touched his cap to me very gravely. "Yes, monsieur can go up; but it is sad, very sad." "What is sad?" "Why, what the Germans have done." . . . The antique door had been hacked through with an ax, the wrought iron lock had been broken, and the quaint old halls invaded in order that men might tear down the Belgian flag which had floated there so many years. All over Antwerp, Belgian, British, and French flags still stood, untouched by the conquerors, but from the cathedral, the Town Hall, and the summit of the Steen, Germany's black-white-and-red now hung triumphant in the quiet air.

On the Road to Holland

I had seen enough. Thompson elected to stay in Antwerp with his beloved cameras, so I set off on foot for the Dutch frontier.

The streets in the northern part of Antwerp were deserted, except for a few weeping women and children. I saw men lurking in the alleys, but I did not stop to talk with them. Twice I saw American flags floating over shipping still in the river, but for the most part town and river were deserted.

At the first bridge stood a detail of German soldiers. "Is to pass *verboten?*" I asked. "No," they answered, and I went on.

The northern basins were crowded with barges, but the locks had been jammed and rendered useless. What small boats there were had been stove in, so that they could not be used to set troops across the river, but the larger shipping was uninjured. Along the wharves were piled thousands of tons of coal and grain; probably the most valuable booty in Antwerp. But the wharves, like the streets, were deserted.

People still were fleeing from Antwerp. A few bolder ones drifted back, evidently reassured since the firing had ceased, but most were headed north. Many young men went by me on bicycles, pedaling as if for dear life. I stopped two of them and asked why they were leaving. They told me incoherently that if they stayed in Antwerp they would be sent away by the Germans to fight against the Russians. . . . An old, old woman in stiffly starched peasant cap and black gown, was borne along in a wheelbarrow, bumping through the ruts in the narrow road. Her wooden shoes jolted against the barrow rim, and her head nodded to right and left as if she were a queen acknowledging the greetings of her subjects. Her face had lost all human expression. It was like lead, or like ashes. . . .

Suddenly I found myself in the very midst of fortifications. They were to right of me, to left of me, and in front of me,—immense, silent, grassy banks, scarred here and there with trenches and embrasures and gray concrete gun-bases. My heart flew to my throat, for those half-invisible, silent works seemed far more menacing than any number of visible enemies. The Germans might be there, or the Belgians. In any event, I had no business spying about the defenses.

Then, for my need, an old peasant appeared. He seemed like a gnome which had popped from the ground, for I could have sworn the place was empty a moment before. He was dressed in rags, and there was an odd stubble of beard about his leathery face, but he looked intelligent. He hobbled near and peered up at me in silence.

"Do you speak French?" I asked uncertainly.

"Oh, yes, monsieur."

"And will you show me the road to Holland?"

"Gladly, monsieur."

The old fellow was a natural philosopher. He would have delighted Voltaire or Rousseau. He had thought deep thoughts, uncontaminated by the influence of the schools, and as we walked he poured out his wisdom in a feeble wheezy monologue.

"The war? Ah, monsieur, the war, it is a curse. But then, much in life is a curse, and we must bear it tranquilly. To live, that is the important thing. Men fight each other, cheat each other, steal each other's land, lust for one another's wives—yes, monsieur, it is true—but we must live. We must bear all tranquilly. It is war. It is life, *n'est-ce pas?*"

We walked together for a quarter of an hour through the lines of fortresses and saw not a living soul. Those great fortifications of Antwerp, the impregnable ring which General Brialmont had drawn about the metropolis of Belgium, lay deserted and useless while an old man and a boy walked through them and moralized of war. . . .

I was alone beside the Scheldt again, sheltered by the dykes from hostile eyes, but the impulse to see was irresistible. I ran to the top of the ridge and looked back. There was the dark silhouette of Antwerp, the lace-like cathedral spire, the high buildings and factories, and the low mass of houses. But up from the pile still rose black columns of smoke to trouble the dark day. Antwerp still was burning.

Eastward were the green embankments of the forts, westward the broad dark river, and the reedy levels of East Flanders. But northward! . . . Suddenly I felt as if I had fled from a nightmare, as if nothing in Antwerp had been real, from my arrival and arrest as a spy, through the terrible thirty-six hours of the bombardment and the coming of the Germans. Before me were long, level meadows, cultivated fields, patches of wood, and little winding lanes with avenues of slender trees, alder hedges, ditches, and lines of pollard willows. It was a landscape to make a painter shout for joy. Hundreds of cattle loafed beside the ditches or lazily browsed in the grass. Colts and young calves frisked about, utterly indifferent to war. A flock of small birds flew by me, singing. Far away a windmill turned, and thin church spires marked quiet villages, sheltered in groves of oaks and elms. Here there was no wreck; no devastation. Here life was real. Antwerp had been a dream.

Vluchtelingen

But an endless line of unhappy fugitives moved northward through the quiet lanes. The flight, begun on Wednesday, continued unabated on Saturday. Sometimes the narrow paved roadway was blocked with carts, bicycles, and people. High-pooped Flemish farm wagons piled with goods, abbreviated prairie schooners, queer copies of the Deadwood coach, hand carts, dog carts, ox carts—anything which ran on wheels or legs made part of that tragic procession.[1]

A man hailed me from the door of a roadhouse. I shouted back that I could not stop, but he insisted so earnestly that I turned and went to him. He was a very old man, bent with rheumatism and shrunken like a ghost. He stood crazily clutching the jamb of the door as he talked. To my amazement, he spoke English in a voice that thrilled like a trumpet. He had seen and recognized the little American flag in my coat.

"For God's sake, sir, can't you help us?" he cried. "You're an American, aren't you, sir? Isn't America

---

[1] Yet these fugitives, these "vluchtelingen," as they are called in Flemish, were only part of an age-long flight. Flanders means "land of the fugitives." A Fleming—it used to be pronounced "flē-ming"—etymologically is a man who has fled from the old German forests.

going to help us? Can't you do something for Belgium? Don't you see that something must be done? Surely your country will help us! Oh, this is a black day for Belgium!"

If only I had known how America was to help! If only I could have spoken with the tongue of prophecy and told him of the work to be done by the Commission for Relief in Belgium! But I did not know; I did not know, and I could not answer him a word.

There were three men whom I passed, pushing a hand cart. Half a minute afterward there was a shout behind me, and I looked about to see one of the three running toward me. He held a bottle of light beer in his hand, which he insisted that I drink. The cart contained only a few household treasures and half a dozen bottles—all that the man had left in the world—but he felt that he must share with the stranger. I drank, with tears in my eyes, to him and to Belgium.

In all the little towns along the way, refugees rested in utter exhaustion or camped out under frail shelters in lanes, dooryards, and streets. I never before realized how many old people there are in the world. Half of these refugees seemed over sixty years old and practically helpless. War kills the old like flies. Life owed them a warm chimney corner, a friend or two, a pipe and a bottle; instead of these, it had hurled them out into the center of one of the most terrible cataclysms of history and had chased them in panic from their homes and native land. What such as these suffered during the reign of terror in Antwerp and afterward can never be imagined or described.

Every ditch along the roadside was littered with things thrown away by the fleeing soldiers. There was no escape over the river for the garrisons of the northern fortresses, such as Saint Philippe, Oudendyk, and Stabroeck, so they had joined the civilian fugitives and had cast aside in their flight, uniforms, side-arms, wine bottles, and every other sort of military *impedimenta*. Caps and uniforms lay trampled in the mud; empty bottles bobbed grotesquely in the canals; the culverts were stuffed with refuse; and all the farmers in the neighborhood were salvaging military supplies.

Little peasant boys, their trousers rolled high, waded thigh-deep in ooze and ditch water, fishing out clips of cartridges and arms, and quarreling over their finds. . . .

Late in the afternoon rain came, but the procession did not slacken speed. Cyclists went by with heads down and pedals spinning. Weary horses and wearier men plodded steadily along in the face of the drizzle. Absolute terror still was upon them. No one thought of stopping for rest, for the Germans were somewhere behind.

They were in front of us, too. The rain stopped and some of the fugitives seemed to have grown calmer, when down the narrow, tree-bordered highway came a huge military automobile. Half a mile ahead I saw people run out of the road, jump the ditches, flatten themselves against the hedges, and clamber over gates into the turnip fields. An old man tumbled into a ditch and lay motionless, half immersed in muddy water. Panic was on again.

The car came thundering along, a great white flag flapping from its wind-shield, and when it got nearer I saw that two German officers and a civilian sat in the tonneau. The civilian was one of the Belgian notables told off to surrender the forts to the Germans, and the car had just come from Fort Stabroeck. The eyes of all in the automobile were fixed on the straight road ahead. I do not think they noticed the panic their passing caused. They flew by without giving us a glance, speeding back toward Antwerp.

AT THE FRONTIER

Hours passed. Austruweel, Wilmarsdonck, Oorderen, Beerendrecht, and Sandvliet lay behind us. The frontier could not be far away.

In the road ahead some one raised a happy shout, and the long line of men and carts surged forward more hopefully. Half a mile away appeared soldiers and a number of wagons lying at the side of the road. As we got nearer, I saw a little wooden sentry-box beneath the avenue of trees; still nearer, and a flag—not Belgian, not German, but the red-white-and-blue of Holland—the colors so comfortably like our own. This was the arbitrary, intangible line where war stopped and peace began. A few steps more and we were standing in the midst of a group of friendly Dutch soldiers, all wearing in their caps the *pompon* of the neutral House of Orange.

Most of the fugitives crossed the line and plodded on mechanically as if they were blind and dumb. Some sank exhausted to the ground and lay with faces buried in the grass. A few prayed. Scarcely any smiled. Panic still was upon them,—panic which they would feel for days, and dream of for years. It was the kind of elemental terror which falls on a people once in centuries.

Piles of muskets lay in the grass, where the fugitive soldiers had been disarmed as they crossed the border. The Belgians from the northern forts had come bringing arms, ammunition wagons, automobiles, and even field artillery and regimental flags, and fast as they had come, the Dutch had disarmed them and led them away to be interned until the end of the war.

Hundreds of soldiers had entered Holland by this road. While I watched, two more, both infantrymen, came in from the south. They were in uniform, torn and battle-soiled, but they had already thrown away their rifles, and they passed the frontier with eyes glazed and mouths agape. A sentry led them to the side of the road and left them there to rest. An hour afterwards they came marching up the highway under guard of four soldiers.

One of them asked to speak with me, and the guards willingly acquiesced.

"We are prisoners, monsieur, until the end of the war," the Belgian explained. "Do you think our families should go to London and wait for us there?"

"Are your families here?" I asked in astonishment.

"Oh, yes, monsieur."

"You brought them with you?"

"Oh, yes, monsieur. There is my wife: there is my child." He pointed to a grief-stricken little woman, sitting motionless on the ground; a three-year-old boy sprawling beside her. "I could not leave them to the Germans," the man continued. "My comrade and I went back to our homes and brought our families away with us. Now we must go to the military prison camp and leave them. Will England care for them if they go to London?"

Would England care? England must care! "Oh, yes, indeed, England will care for them," I promised with my whole heart and soul. "Have no fear. Rest tranquil. England will care for them. And when the war is over, perhaps you and they will come to my country—to America."

"To America!" His face brightened wonderfully. "Monsieur is American? *Au revoir*, then; *au revoir*. I will come to America. Some day I too shall be an American, perhaps. *Au revoir, mon compatriote.*"

And he and his comrade marched off with their Dutch

guards, leaving the grief-stricken little wife and the three-year-old boy sitting motionless in the grass beside the road.

A few hundred yards away was a small railroad station where I found two or three hundred Belgians crushed into a tiny train waiting to start for Bergen op Zoom. Most of them had sat in the train since ten o'clock in the morning. Few had eaten any food. There were many children among them, all strangely quiet, like little frightened animals, while their elders whispered breathless stories of the horrors in Antwerp.

"Oh, monsieur!" A fat housewife, wedged into the narrow space between a seat and the car wall, was telling the story. "Oh, monsieur! It was terrific—the sound of them—the bombshells. They screeched and yowled and spat, like cats that fight themselves. Terrible! I ran! Oh, how fast I ran! I am breathless with thinking of it. Oh, those bombshells! Oh, holy Mary!"

An old man took up the narrative. "Yes, and in les Jardins Botaniques such sadness! There the keeper of the menagerie shot down all the wild beasts—all the animals of the jungle—for fear they would escape and bite the poor people in the streets. Oh, it was sad, so sad! When the bombshells began to fall on the Jardins, the keeper took up his gun. One by one he shot them— *boom! boom!*—the big lions, and the wolves, and the foxes, and the panther, and the spotted leopard—they died, screaming horribly. Then the keeper came last to the cage of the brown bear. You remember the brown bear in the menagerie, madame?—he was so kind, so gentle. A child could pet him. And he had been taught to hold up his paws together, as the priest does in the cathedral of a Sunday, praying.

"When the keeper came with the loaded gun, this bear put up his paws, *so,* praying him not to shoot. And the keeper burst out with a great cry, and went up near to the bear, and embraced him lovingly through the bars of the cage. And then he took up the gun—and—*boom! boom!*—he shot him."

"Oh, but it is sad!"

"Yes, and so sad is the howling of the poor forsaken dogs all the night long in Antwerp;—thousands of dogs abandoned by their masters and left to starve. I cannot sleep for thinking of them, locked in the empty houses, scratching and sniffing at all the doors, and all the time howling with fear and the hunger. Ugh! it is horrible, horrible, messieurs. The poor animals! How they suffer! How they suffer!"

"But the atrocities of these Germans! In war they become cannibals. I have an uncle who is of the military, and he found on the battlefields after Malines——"
The *raconteur* spun a yarn as old and as vile as war itself; a tale that was typical of thousands which have been accepted as Gospel truth since this war began.

It nettled me, and I interrupted him in the most dramatic moment of the story. "You must not tell such tales," I said severely. "They will keep Belgians from going back, and you must go back to save your country." The man shrugged his shoulders significantly. "Ah, monsieur, you do not know. If we go back, as you advise, we shall have to come away again tomorrow. The French are going to capture Antwerp. Already their army is only a few kilometers away. Perhaps they too will shell the city. We do not want to go back to be shelled a second time."

"Yes, messieurs, that is true," a third said. "Besides, there are the Russians. Already they are near Berlin, and they will come down through Germany to help us. The Russians are a mighty people. Maybe they will come soon. We will not go back until they come." . . .

I held my peace. Cows were coming in from the fields about the station, ready to be milked. For the time being they seemed more interesting, more intelligent than the sad-eyed men and women in the train. They were calm and even-tempered and self-respecting beasts. They read no newspapers, paid no taxes, went to no churches, and waged no wars. They ate grass and gave milk. That was life.

We milked them almost into the mouths of the little Belgians in the train, for as fast as the tepid milk squirted into the tin pails we bought it and carried it to the youngsters. But it was painful to see the children drink. They sucked at the foaming liquid without a trace of eagerness or enjoyment. They seemed to have grown centuries old and indifferent to everything about them.

DUTCH HOSPITALITY

Shortly before nightfall we pulled out for Bergen op Zoom. That hour's ride is unforgettable. Fugitives of days before were crowded along the roads and out into the fields like grasshoppers. There was not a foot of space along the highway left vacant by their vehicles. One after another, as far as the eye could see in either direction, carts crawled along through the dusk. High Flemish wains rode like ships above a tossing sea of human heads; ponderous, underslung farm wagons came by, hauled by stout Percheron horses; there were milk carts pulled by dogs; delivery wagons, out-of-date family coaches, American carriages, hay wagons, victorias, omnibuses, and ox-carts, all trundling along in that sluggish stream. Thousands were their own carryalls and beasts of burden; they pushed baby carriages or wheelbarrows, piled high with goods; they carried awkward bundles on their backs, pedlar fashion; they bore baskets on their arms, or little parcels done up in towels slung from their elbows. And there were hundreds plodding along the road who carried nothing at all; who had come away from their homes leaving absolutely everything behind.

Cattle and even flocks of sheep marched with the human herd. Once I saw a little goat run out of the throng, bleating piteously. Cats and birds in cages rode high upon the wagons, and scores of tired dogs padded along behind their tired masters.

As night grew darker, fires popped up under the alder hedges. Camps were pitched, pallets of straw spread, and people cooked their suppers over hot coals. Some improvised rough lodgings for the night under their wagons on the bare ground, or in the open fields under the stars. Every farmyard was an oasis of rest and refreshment, where food was to be had for the asking until the supply was exhausted.

Of course there was not nearly enough food for all who asked. Most of that sad army went dinnerless and supperless, and most of it still marched. Its own inertia, not its will, seemed to carry it on, and a strange sound came from it as it moved—a continuous droning, a low murmur, like heavy breathing, which filled all the night air. That sound seemed to come from the earth and the sky and the trees and the grass, as well as from the marching men. It was a sound more terrible than human wailing. It was as if all nature mourned, and as if this vast movement through the night were the funeral procession of a nation. . . .

The little Dutch villages along the way blazed with lights to welcome the wanderers. Every house was full. People gladly slept on doorsteps and pavements to give up their beds to the Belgians. Every drop of milk and every ounce of bread was at their command. Schools were turned into emergency hospitals and churches into lodging houses for them. Factories became refugee camps, and in every imaginable way the Dutch tried to cope with the awful situation which the war had thrust on their neighbors.

The Belgians contributed a remarkable invention to all that the Dutch were doing. This was a refugee directory. I first saw it at Woensdrecht, and afterwards in half a dozen villages in southern Holland. Conspicuous house walls or fences in every one of these villages were chalked over with the names and addresses of Belgians stopping there. The directories were scrawled up along the principal streets, and there were hundreds of names in each list.

> The Myer Family
>   Dordrechtstraat 12
> Marcelline Smit
>   Roosenstraat 50
> Julie le Maitre
>   Waterstraat 17, City

—so the notices read.

But there were scores and hundreds of families whom no directory could help that night; families whose fathers, or mothers, or children, or grandchildren had become separated from the others in the mad panic of flight and had not yet been found. Some of them would never be found. The newspapers of Holland were to be filled for weeks with advertisements for the lost. On that tragic night, every town in southern Holland had its quota of lost children, and every town had its Belgian Rachels, weeping, and not to be comforted.

Bergen op Zoom, a quaint ugly Dutch town on the main line of railway from Flushing to Rotterdam, roared like a metropolis that night. It was jammed with refugees. They lay about in the streets, on the doorsteps and sidewalks. One could not walk without stepping on them. Every house and church and school was at their disposal, but still there were thousands too many. They were bedded down on the bare boards in church pews, and on the polished floors of the best parlors in town. They slept in and under carts standing in the streets. Women in the pangs of childbirth were placed on cots improvised of school benches and mattresses, and the sick and infirm were made as comfortable as possible on loose straw piled in sheds and barns.

Bakeries were commandeered to supply free bread to all who asked. The milk supply was taken up for the exclusive use of the children. Groceries were gutted. All blankets, bandages, old clothes, and household medicines had already been solicited by the Red Cross for the needy by the time we got there. Carriages and wagons were all in the service; men, women, and even children were at work, and Bergen op Zoom on the night of

BELGIAN REFUGEE DIRECTORY

Courtesy of *Leslie's Weekly*

October tenth, 1914, reached the heights of unselfishness. But so did all Holland. From the northern tip of Friesland and Gelderland to southwest Zeeland, there was not a Dutch community which lacked its share of fugitives. The Government appropriated large sums for the relief of the refugees on the day the flight began. It now ran free trains into all sections of the country, thus distributing the burden as equably as possible. The spirit of the Dutch was splendid. They laid aside in a moment the animosities of years: all the sordid inheritance of hatreds and distrust which makes up half the national feeling of the European nations. They forgot the Revolution of 1830, which resulted in a final separation of the Belgian Provinces from those we call Holland. They forgot that it is a Dutchman's patriotic duty to dislike his Belgian neighbor. And it is to their eternal honor and glory that they opened their country, already suffering terribly from the effects of the war among their neighbors, without question and without hope of reward, to the disinherited hordes that overwhelmed them.

Free trains were running east and west from Bergen op Zoom. While we waited on the crowded station platform, three trains were dispatched for Flushing: one for refugees, two for captive Belgian soldiers. Men, women, children, and luggage, we blocked the platforms, shivering and half famished, from seven o'clock until long after ten. A tiny Belgian baby slept in my arms. I had taken it from its exhausted mother, and she had not even turned her eyes to see what had happened to her baby, or why. Another child slept leaning against my knees. The older people stood numb and dumb. We watched human beings ride away like tired cattle, and when they had gone, others dully took their places. The fugitives to the last man seemed utterly exhausted.

Late at night the station gates swung open once again, and there appeared the head of a long procession of captive Belgian soldiers. Some were in civilian clothes and carried awkward bundles on their backs, like many of the other fugitives; some were bareheaded and coatless, shivering in the cold October night air; a few still bore their army blankets in great white sausage rolls across their shoulders and under their arms; two or three had brown loaves of bread in their hands, and bottles, which the Dutch had given them, in their pockets; but most of them had nothing at all except the uniforms on their backs. There were at least two thousand of them.

They slouched in carelessly, without order or direction, between two files of Dutch guards. Going to prison until the end of the war was not a pleasant prospect, even if it is called "internment." But when the refugees on the platform caught sight of the head of that procession and realized that these were the men of King Albert's army, they sent up a cheer which thrilled those tired soldiers like a bugle-call. It was marvelous to hear such a cheer in the midst of so much suffering. The long, irregular lines stiffened and became soldierly once more; the men's eyes flashed as they returned the shouts with a will; and when two long trains came in to take them away to military prison, the Belgian soldiers went into the cars still cheering and singing.

ATROCITIES

It was almost midnight when I climbed painfully into the Rotterdam Express at Bergen op Zoom. Every nerve ached and trembled. My arms hung paralyzed at my sides; my thin clothing crackled with cold; I had no coat. But nothing seemed to matter, for life and death were like old friends and pain was like a brother; all problems seemed simple, and all emotions clean.

I stumbled into the first open compartment of the first-class carriage, fumbling at my belt of gold-pieces to make sure they were safe. There was an empty seat, and I dropped into it, hardly noticing my only neighbor —a dark-eyed lady of about thirty-five, sitting directly across from me.

I leaned my cheek against the cold window-glass and stared out into the night, "seeing things." It was a mental trick I had learned when tired—to visualize rapidly whole trains of pictures, so that they fly by in the darkness as against a screen.

The crisp voice of the lady in the seat opposite interrupted my picture making. Her eyes studied me with the confident look of the born aristocrat who knows and feels instinctively the privileges of birth. It was not strange that she was traveling alone. In wartime everything is possible. Boats from Folkestone to Flushing went at all hours, for German submarines were active; and on this night of nights, all trains were hopelessly off schedule. Our train, the boat-train, would probably reach Rotterdam after two o'clock in the morning.

"You are English?" she asked.

"No, I am an American. But all my ancestors were from the British Isles."

"I should have thought you English." Her eyes examined me carefully: tousled hair, soft collar, and coatless shoulders.

"You compliment me," I said, "since you see me half-dressed and half-frozen. But *you* are English."

"By birth, yes. By marriage I am Dutch. My husband is head of a department of government in the Hague." She spoke a name well-known in Holland. "I have been two months in England visiting, and am just returning. . . . Tell me," she exclaimed, without altering the well-bred modulation of her voice, "have you seen any of those vile Huns?"

"I have just come from Antwerp."

"So I thought. I should like to burn the whole German nation, as one's gardener burns the worms in an apple-tree! Did you see any atrocities?"

"No."

She appeared to be disappointed. "My family is well-known in England," she said. "I have friends—army officers high in the service, you know. They have told me unspeakable things. In an English hospital I saw two little Belgian children with their hands cut off at the wrists——"

"Don't!" I interrupted.

"You don't want to hear about them?" she asked in evident annoyance.

"Forgive me," I begged. "I've just come from the midst of the war. My nerves are a bit on edge. I've seen so much today."

"Then you *have* seen things," she said positively. "Now I want to hear about them. Tell me exactly what you have seen!"

"Shall I tell you how the Germans came into Antwerp?"

"Please do. Did they commit any atrocities?"

"No," I said. "They came in very quietly. I went up to the first officer I saw and began to talk with him. Do you know the first thing he asked me? It was the same thing you asked. 'Are you English?' And he didn't seem to care one way or the other. He asked me politely, just as you would ask."

"But didn't the Germans shoot any citizens?"

"No," I said.

She stared at me with sudden dislike and suspicion. "Are you pro-German?" she demanded.

"Not in the least," I returned. "I am heart and soul pro-Belgian, and I want the Allies to win the war."

She seemed doubtful. Her dark eyes bored into me, as if to lay bare the falsehoods hiding behind my tired face. "Didn't the Belgians do anything?"

"What do you mean?"

"Did they let those murderers come into Antwerp without fighting to the last man?"

"Oh, they fought, and the English fought, too, splendidly," I went on. "But when the bombardment had lasted thirty-six hours, and the army had gone away, there wasn't anything more to do."

"I should have shot at the Germans from the windows! Why, officers I know tell me they have found women's bodies ravished after they were dead, and there was a girl eighteen years old in one of the London hospitals whose breasts had been hacked off."

"Please don't!" I implored her.

"Why?" she asked angrily. "People should know these things!"

"You don't understand; you can't understand. I have just seen some of the saddest and most terrible things in the world: the sight of a whole nation in a panic, running away from its country. I've seen thousands of old people, and children, and even little babies. I've seen people of every sort: peasants, aristocrats, and merchants. I've talked with them, walked with them, ridden with them, and stood with them in the cold; and

ATROCITIES

yet I've hardly heard those poor people say one hateful word. During all this terrible week they've been as simple as little children—just wanting to live, and eat, and sleep, and be in company with other people. They've almost forgotten how to hate."

Her fine eyes narrowed. "Don't say that. It's horrible even to think it. Forget to hate the Huns?—nothing in the world could persuade me to do that! Oh, I hope and pray every night for the time when our soldiers are in Germany and can pay them tit for tat!"

I must have winced.

"The trouble with you is, you have been too close to it. You are abnormal just now," she concluded.

She did not speak again until we were rolling into the station at Rotterdam at half-past two in the morning. I got her luggage out of the racks, and piloted her safely to a taxi-cab.

"Good-by," she said, giving me her cool finger tips. "I'm glad me met, although you've disappointed me. Give me your address. On Monday I am going to send you newspapers telling of the atrocities."[1]

---

[1] A discussion of Belgian atrocities has no place in this book. The foregoing chapter records a mood; not a judicial decision. But for those who desire trustworthy evidence by an American eye-witness, I suggest Arthur Gleason's *Young Hilda at the Wars* and *Golden Lads*, published by the Century Company, New York, 1915 and 1916.

Relief Work in Holland

Ten days later I was speeding from Rotterdam to the Belgian border with a yachtful of victuals and clothing for the *vluchtelingen*. One of the secretaries of the International Court of Arbitration, Dr. M. P. Rooseboom, a nervous, slender, active gentlemen, quick in his sympathies, and in appearance the antithesis of the stolid stage Dutchman, had solicited food and clothing for the refugees as soon as they came into Holland, and borrowed from one of his friends a fine steam yacht to take the supplies to the towns along the frontier where they were most needed. I went as his guest.

All available space on the yacht was piled with bags of rice, beans, coffee, tubs of lard and butter, cheeses big as cartwheels, packages of underclothing for women and children, and more than eight hundred loaves of bread.

Dr. Rooseboom had been in Liége while the battle still was on. He and several other Red Cross volunteers from Holland were working their way up the Meuse, shells flying, bridges being blown up, the shriek and thunder of bombardment deafening them.

Suddenly, he said, they noticed beside the river a slender steel camp table, its legs half buried in mire, three or four wine bottles on it, and an immense map spread across its top, over which hung a general, propped by his elbows, studying the chart oblivious to the din. His chair and four or five other chairs stand-

RELIEF WORK IN HOLLAND

ing in the mud were of priceless mahogany and had been taken from a nearby *château*.

Dr. Rooseboom was introduced to the general. He was von Emmich, commander of the Tenth Army Corps, the captor of Liége. "Ah," said he, "I know you. You are the son of General Rooseboom, whom I met at the Prussian manœuvers in 1897."

When Dr. Rooseboom told his father of the encounter, the latter looked grave. "I remember it well," he said. "The Germans charged in close formation. 'You will sacrifice thousands upon thousands needlessly if you drive your men like that,' I said to a group of German officers who, like myself, were watching the manœuvers. One of them, a young colonel, replied, 'Don't trouble yourself about that. We have them to lose!' It was von Emmich." ...

Barges, loaded with refugees, lay moored on the broad rivers and in the canals. It was wash-day, and their red, blue, white, and gray flannels flapped from lines hung across the decks like jaunty flags in the keen wind.

At nightfall we reached Hansweert and dined in a small hotel crammed with Belgian refugees and Dutch soldiers. Rain beat the roof in a deluge. Clouds of tobacco smoke and the steam of wet clothes drying before a small stove smothered us, and everybody talked of Antwerp.

After dinner, a Belgian in a great fur coat began the

story of a German defeat at Ostend: the Germans were in full flight, King Albert personally was in command of the Allies, and he had just issued a proclamation from Ostend forbidding his people returning to Belgium until the war was over!

"But the Germans occupied Ostend four days ago," Dr. Rooseboom volunteered, "and the King of Belgium is in France."

The Belgian turned on him furiously. "Nay! Nay! That is not so," he thundered.

"Here is the *Nieuwe Rotterdamsche Courant* telling about it."

The Belgian swept the newspaper aside. "It is not so."

"No matter. But where is this proclamation?" The commander-in-chief of our little relief expedition addressed himself to the roomful.

No one answered.

"Isn't it a shame," he said to me in English. "Louis Franck of Antwerp is in Holland appealing to the refugees to return to Belgium. The King and the Government at Havre have told them to go back. But if they spread stories like this, they'll never go home, and they must go, for Belgium's sake as well as for Holland's." He turned again to the fur-coated Belgian. "Look here, mynheer," he began, "can you tell me where——"

His adversary turned the tables very neatly. "These

Dutchmen are paid by the Germans to tell us tales," he whispered loudly to the man at the next table. . . .

Next morning we were in Ter Neuzen, a beautiful medley of one-story houses, steep red-tiled roofs, small mullioned windows, tiny chimneys, claret-red brick walls, and narrow alleys. Refugees were not allowed to stay long in Ter Neuzen, because it is a fortified place, and the Dutch feared that German spies might come with the *vluchtelingen*. But the fugitives were allowed to rest there and even to spend the night. The bare little barn of a Protestant church had been crowded with them, and pious ladies of the town had given up their neatly embroidered church cushions so the refugees might sleep comfortably in the pews.

The church vestibule was piled with these cushions, soiled and much dilapidated after a week under the heads and heels of refugees. The municipal authorities had just condemned them to be burned. An apple-cheeked old *vrouw* was fishing gingerly about in the pile.

"*Ja*," she explained. "I gave them my cushion, the poor Belgians, but it was a very nice cushion, all embroidered, and now I want it back again."

We left her still searching. . . .

In the warm sanctuary of the Roman Catholic chapel, a score of Belgian women and children were at prayer. Incense from the early mass still clung about the pretty little church, and yet it seemed all full of sighs and tears.

Two small girls, with eyes red from weeping, stood apart, their lips trembling as they sent up their childish petitions. I was told that they had lost both father and mother in the mad flight from Antwerp.

In Sas van Ghent on the Belgian frontier, we found five thousand refugees still quartered on the town. More than two thousand were in ships along the canals, most of them able to pay for their support. There were six hundred paupers. For a week the town authorities had been passing fugitives along to the less crowded ports farther north at a rate of several thousands a day.

But the poor who remained were fortunate. Sas van Ghent lies cheek by jowl with the beautiful Belgian town of Zelzaete, where King Albert and Queen Elizabeth spent two nights in their flight to Ostend and the Yser, and it possesses a huge phosphate factory, owned by Belgian capitalists, and idle since the beginning of the war. The Dutch turned all the newcomers into the vast factory. They filled store-rooms and offices with straw, collected all the blankets in town, set doctors promptly to work, and had the situation well in hand from the start.

In the heart of the works was an immense building, large as a circus, where the Belgians camped by thousands. High overhead was a wilderness of tracks and steel supports and traveling cranes, but the dirt floor was clear of obstruction, and people slept, cooked, washed, and ate on the bare ground. After a day or two, a genius got to work, begged lumber from the authorities, and set about building himself a house of uncut boards and straw. Forty or fifty others followed his example, and the results were excellent. The dwellings, no larger than pig-stys, were exactly the sort of houses our ancestors were building three thousand years ago, and formed as quaint a village as the famous Swiss lakehouses. They gave a delightful sense of privacy and ownership. Blankets or old coats hung over the opening which served as door and window, and straw stuck through the chinks between the boards as it does through the ribs of a scarecrow. Little wooden shoes stood beside the huts, for there were plenty of children among the refugees. Once I saw a real French bisque doll lying in a cradle whittled from a piece of board. One of the more aristocratic huts had a little board fence about it, to keep the baby from running away, and the mother was industriously scrubbing at a pile of clothes in a pail, and hanging them on the fence to dry.

There came a *clop clip* of little wooden shoes across the hard dirt floor, and a five-year-old *vluchtelingetje* (little refugee girl) darted by us. She was playing hide-and-seek with another youngster, dodging awkwardly about among the little human stys. It must have been a great adventure for children to camp out with so many playmates in such strange surroundings, to eat strange food, to play strange games, and at night to hear bloodcurdling tales of what the Germans do to little children!

The phosphate factory was paradise compared with camps in some other towns along the Belgian-Dutch border.

Cities of Refuge

In Hulst, which we next visited, the coming of the Belgians had been tragic. A small town in the neighborhood was looted by the frantic fugitives before Dutch troops could arrive and restore order. Hulst itself for two nights and days was like chaos. Men, women, children, vehicles, and a small army of Belgian soldiers overwhelmed the town.

By far the greater portion of the troops got safely to the Yser. Eye-witnesses have told me how they came along the dykes, tired, dirty, discouraged, but how they turned at a word of command and went back into battle, singing. It will never be forgotten how the doughty Belgians held their share of the line in the November battles. The fact that the army retired in safety from Antwerp is counted a Belgian success, in this war of mobile armies and not of fixed fortresses. Stories were current of General von Beseler's chagrin at this. There were even legends of his suicide in Ghent. But in August, 1915, he reappeared again in military annals as conqueror of the Russian fortress of Brest-Litovsk, for

which he received the blue ribbon of the Prussian order
"*pour le Mérite.*"

The British lost at Antwerp three hundred of their eight thousand men. The Belgian losses have never been reported. But in addition to the killed, wounded, and missing, twenty-one thousand two hundred and fifty Belgian soldiers and one thousand five hundred and sixty British soldiers and marines fled to Holland with the civil population, and were interned. At Hulst, automobiles full of high officers of the Belgian army arrived ahead of their troops. Then came the men, the undersized, swarthy, discouraged-looking soldiers whom I had seen marching across the pontoon bridge at Antwerp, completely demoralized now and flying for their lives. Their retreat had been cut off southwest of Saint Nicolas.

A day and a night they came straggling into Holland. There were wounded in that rout—men with their heads awkwardly bandaged up, or their arms in slings made of the sleeves of their shirts. Many limped. Some were bareheaded. Some had thrown away their overcoats, so they could run the faster, and the fronts of their uniforms were soaked with perspiration. Dismounted cavalrymen, their blood-red trousers flapping as they walked, came with the blue uniformed infantrymen. Many of the uniforms were torn and soiled: the whole back of one overcoat had been cut away by a shell. A color sergeant marched in, still clinging to a dirty, drooping battle-flag. Field artillery and ammunition wagons were part of that strange procession, the drivers humped listlessly above their horses, and the lines dragging. Commissariat wagons, hospital ambulances, Red Cross automobiles, and omnibuses came over into Holland with the army. And perhaps most pathetic of all, a bedraggled regimental band marched in, half the men still carrying their cornets and drums and horns—a hideous travesty of the pomp and circumstance of war.

Thousands brought their rifles, but most were unarmed. In Hulst I saw a pile of Belgian guns sixty feet long and six feet high, corded up like firewood, and a heap of cartridges, at least twenty bushels of them, lying under a rough tarpaulin on the ground. In addition to these spoils, there was a small hill of bayonets, cartridge belts, side-arms, revolver holsters, camp kits, sappers' axes, and shovels, piled helter-skelter in the marketplace.

An immense tent was erected in the square before the Town Hall, and civilian refugees were camped on straw under its thin shelter, in a hideous, beast-like commonwealth. The Gothic cathedral in the center of the town, centuries old and marvelously beautiful, became a camp for soldiers waiting to be interned. The town schools were emergency hospitals. There were thirty-seven premature births in one of these. School benches with a mattress over them served as maternity cots. Every rag of cloth and every drop of medicine suddenly became priceless. The sick lay on pallets spread flat on the floor in the schoolrooms, and Sisters of Charity kept the place as neat as the neatest metropolitan hospital.

The bread supply had been exhausted days before we came. Most of the fugitives lived on boiled beans, cooked in ten great cauldrons in an open courtyard. There were crowds of Belgians jammed about the enclosure, waiting to be allowed their turn inside, and they were ravenous as beasts. No dishes or spoons were to be had. Men, women, and little children brought empty tins, bowls, or fragments of old crockery to hold their share of the precious food, and they ate from little wooden shovels which they had whittled out for themselves. No one knew how many *vluchtelingen* were in Hulst, but on the day before, in a nearby village of one thousand inhabitants, there had been twenty-three thousand Belgians.

It had poured rain all day. I stepped out of the incessant floods into the shelter of the tent on the market-place, and stumbled over a baby carriage. I looked further into the stuffy, malodorous dusk of the tent. There was another baby carriage, and another, and another. . . . Some proud poet should write the Ode to the Baby Carriage!—that democratic chariot of the children of men. It had been everywhere in the tragic procession from Antwerp. It had trundled over roads, it had ridden high on carts, it had traveled strapped to the handlebars of bicycles, and always it had held the most precious possessions of its owners. Sometimes these possessions were family pictures, or silver, or fine linen; but usually, more precious than all these, it held the Belgian babies. Reverently I bare my head to the Baby Carriage: it is the vehicle of civilization.

A Story of King Albert

Human beings in agony are prone to curse Fate and to blame even friends for their pain. The tear-worn faces of the refugees masked bitter fancies. They told many tales of treachery in connection with Antwerp.

And it is hardly to be wondered at. Fast as the Germans advanced through Belgium, a part of the population retreated before them. These migrations flowed in great waves. There was a general exodus from Brussels before the German troops occupied it on August twentieth: the rich going to England, the poor to Antwerp, or over the border into Holland. And as the tides of battle ebbed and flowed through the country between Malines and Ghent, the peasant population joined the urban fugitives, most of them crowding into Antwerp. They felt absolutely safe in the circle of the famous Antwerp forts. Had not military experts declared the fortifications impregnable? Then, in less than a week, three of the outer forts fell, and the Germans were hammering at the gates.

Stories of collusion between Belgian officers and the

Germans found many believers. Accounts of reinforced concrete gun-bases found under tennis courts in Malines, Duffel, and Contich, were common. When I visited Dr. Henry van Dyke, American Minister in the Hague, his first question bore on these stories of treachery. "There are many rumors here in connection with the fall of Antwerp," he explained. "They seem to have some foundation. There undoubtedly were Germans in the Belgian army."

Many Belgians blamed Churchill's ill-fated expedition to Antwerp, declaring that the city could have been saved a useless bombardment and its inhabitants spared the horrors of flight, if the British had not interfered. They had forgotten the devotion of their King and Queen; they had forgotten the self-sacrificing patriotism of the Common Council of Antwerp which unanimously voted on October fourth that it was "the unchangeable wish of the population to see pursued to the very end the defense of the fortress of Antwerp, without any other thought than that of the national defense, and without any regard to the dangers run by persons or private property."

A slant-eyed Belgian girl, with wet hair, and a big shawl drooping about her narrow shoulders, sat in the malodorous tent on the market-place in Hulst, telling a story to a group of refugees. Outside, the rain fell steadily. It sluiced and spotched and oozed from the atmosphere, as if the air were a cold, wet sponge. It crawled down necks and up trouser-legs. It sopped cheeks and beaded eyebrows. It snuggled into the roots of the hair, and churned up mud that clung like cottage-cheese.

The *vluchtelingen* were huddled together in the dismal shelter of the tent. A couple of lanterns gave all the light there was, except the glow of a pipe. An old Belgian sat smoking, in spite of the regulations imposed by the Dutch, and underfoot was enough loose straw to fire a city.

The girl allowed me to join the group, and retold the story for my benefit.

"It is a story of King Albert, m'sieu," she said, by way of preface. "A story of our King and of my brother. You would hear it?"

"Please, mademoiselle. If you please."

"In French, m'sieu," she went on; "yes? Well, then! Our officers were bad, all bad. That is why we lost."

I nodded in sympathy.

"Always they were drinking or idling. My brother, he was of the artillery, stationed near Antwerp. And one afternoon comes the King, alone, marching into the fort on foot. The King stared about him as one does in a dream, for there was not an officer, not one single officer, only private soldiers and one sergeant, there beside the big guns.

"'Where are your officers?' cried the King.

"'Sire, they have gone to an inn—to—to drink champagne,' says my brother.

"'What?' thundered the King. 'They have gone where?'

"'To an inn, Your Majesty,' says my brother again.

"'Leaving the forts in charge of a sergeant?'

"'Yes, Your Majesty.'

"'Send for them at once,' cried the King, and his eyes glittered.

"After a quarter of an hour they came, very shamefaced, riding on their fine horses. From the pocket of one of them there stuck out a champagne bottle!

"The officers saluted the King, much frightened.

"'Get down off your horses,' he ordered.

"They climbed down awkwardly, with legs of wood.

"'You are under arrest,' said the King. He thrust out his hand suddenly and pulled the wine bottle from the pocket of him who had it. 'For this you betray a kingdom—for wine and an hour at the inn,' he said. 'Give me your swords.'

"They gave them up.

"Then the King took the swords and snapped them in two across his knee before the faces of the officers and men. And the King wept."

CHAPTER IV

BELGIUM AS A GERMAN PROVINCE

Antwerp Again

On a cold, clammy afternoon in late November, three young Americans stood in the Pass Bureau at Antwerp, chatting with Lieutenant Sperling, aide to Baron von Hühne, the German Governor of the fortress and province of Antwerp. The bureau was a rambling suite of offices in the old Belgian Ministry of Colonies on the Marché aux Souliers. The floor was bare planks. The furniture was cheap oak, scarred and dented. Outside, under the wide windows, stood rows of military automobiles, their gray hoods marked " General Government, Fortress Antwerp," and sentries scuffed to and fro in the paved courtyard. The street before the bureau was clear of pedestrians, for the Germans did not permit Belgians to walk past headquarters, unless on official business. Next door, in the Hôtel Saint Antoine, where British and Belgian officers had lodged during the siege, and where German officers now lived, a shell had punched a neat round hole near the roof facing the Place Verte, and across the street, in the Marché aux Souliers, stood the gutted hulks of a score of shops, burned during the bombardment. The ruins were partially hidden by a neat wooden fence which served as bulletin-board for the Antwerp Animal Rescue League, the Belgian Red Cross, and the German General Government.

An official proclamation, still posted, although Antwerp had fallen a month and a half before, read:

> The German Army enters your city as a victor. No harm will be done to any citizen, and your property will be spared if you avoid any hostile action. Any insubordination will be punished by court-martial, and may result in the destruction of your beautiful city.

In the offices of the Pass Bureau, a lithograph of Kaiser Wilhelm Second and two cheap picture postcards showing German soldiers off for the front were pasted on the walls, and perched above a bookcase stood a plaster bust of Leopold First, Belgium's first king. Four or five soldiers sat about at little tables laboriously writing out passes in longhand, or interrogating sad-eyed Belgians who filed in one by one from the long, black, silent queue waiting outside in the cold. While we watched, the bureau closed for the night.

"*Geschlossen!*" muttered an under-officer, rising from his chair.

"If you please, monsieur——" began one of the Belgians.

"No! It's shut! Out!" he exclaimed. And a soldier hustled the applicant to the door.

"Please, Herr Lieutenant."

Sperling wheeled and faced an orderly standing stiffly at attention.

"The passes are for——?"

"Lieutenant Herbster, U. S. N., Mr. G. Evans Hubbard, and Mr. Edward Eyre Hunt," he answered in German.

"*Danke sehr.* The gentlemen are from——?"

"Hague, Holland."

"Citizens of——?"

"The United States of America. All the gentlemen are Americans."

"To go from Antwerp to Brussels and return?"

"Antwerp to Brussels."

"For civil or military automobile, Herr Lieutenant?"

"Military automobile, of course. The gentlemen are *'Americans.*"

The Lieutenant turned again to us and continued: "It is fine, eh? Everything for me is paid. I have a suite of three rooms in the Hôtel Saint Antoine, where His Excellency the Governor and the others of the staff live. I have a bedroom, a drawing-room, a bath, worth twenty-seven marks in Berlin. My breakfast, that is two marks; a cigar, one mark; lunch, six marks; benedictine, two marks; another cigar, one mark; coffee, one mark; dinner, seven marks; liqueur, three marks; cigars and coffee, two marks. Then I have my chauffeur and my valet. All free. I pay nothing. Fine, eh? Altogether

I have seventy or eighty marks' worth every day here."

"That sounds like an easy way of getting a living. Don't you pay the Belgians for anything?"

"No," he said. "If one is a German officer, one goes into any restaurant, any hotel in Antwerp, and one signs one's name for the things one eats. Like a club in America, eh? It is by the *menu de requisition*. How do you say that in English?"

"Requisition bill-of-fare."

"Yes. And the city pays all. The restaurant keeper sends the bill to the city. Fine, eh? And we Germans eat and drink very much! Everything is requisitioned."

"Do they pay even for champagne suppers?"

"Please?"

"Does the city pay your wine bills?"

"Certainly."

"Don't the people object?"

The Lieutenant drew himself up proudly. "They are Belgians; we are Germans. They make no objections. . . . Ah, here are your *Scheins*."

A soldier clicked his heels and presented three sheets of green paper, duly filled out in longhand and stamped "*Kommandantur von Antwerpen*."

"Thanks, Lieutenant. Thanks especially for arranging it so we can go to Brussels by auto. The English newspapers say you haven't many automobiles and no benzine. We appreciate your kindness."

He smiled broadly. "So? You can see we have many automobiles in Antwerp, and we have benzol instead of benzine. We have potatoes for alcohol; we have coal; so we have plenty of benzol, eh? . . . A moment," he added. "Perhaps I go to Brussels tomorrow morning. Then I take you. I will show you the ruins. Very interesting. Very nice ruins."

"Oh, thanks awfully."

"Eight o'clock, then, we start. I will show you the ruins."

We three Americans bowed ceremoniously and walked out. On the steps below the sign lettered "*Pass-Zentrale, Antwerpen*" and "*Intendantur*," a sentry drew aside and stood a salute. Herbster, U. S. N., smiled happily at the compliment. "The 'Deutschers' aren't so awful, are they?" he asked. . . . "Now let's go look at what the Zeppelins did to Antwerp!"

THE CONQUERORS

At eight o'clock in the morning, German time, Lieutenant Sperling's gray Mércèdes car stood puffing outside our hotel. We climbed hastily into the tonneau and buried ourselves to the chin under fur rugs and lap robes. It was mercilessly cold and black as ink. A drizzle of icy rain fell, and the streets were dark and dead as a buried city. The Lieutenant flashed a pocket lamp over the car and its occupants. By the flashlight we saw two rifles standing stiff and forbidding beside the military chauffeur, and in the bottom of the car, two packets of official mail destined for the Governor-General in Brussels.

"Right?" asked Lieutenant Sperling, slipping into a balloon silk raincoat and preparing to drive the automobile himself.

"Right," we answered, our teeth chattering.

"You remember the musical-comedy, 'Pink Lady'?" he asked. "I have seen her in New York." And as we slid from before the lighted hotel into the dark, dead tunnel-like streets of Antwerp, he began lustily to sing:

"To you, beeyoutifool ladie, I raise my eyes;
My heart, beeyoutifool ladie, to your heart sighs." . . .

A red lantern, waving in crazy arcs, stopped us at the city gates. "*Halt! halt! wohin?*" bellowed rough voices from the gloom. "General Government!" the chauffeur answered. "Good!" came the response, and we dashed on down the road. This happened seven times in an hour's ride, except that the lantern gave place to a red flag as morning advanced.

Darkness and a misty rain still hid everything. We could scarcely see each other's faces. There was no sunrise on that cold November morning. It seemed instead as if the rain slowly became luminous as light fought its way from the east. The landscape lay blurred and drenched—a vista of burned villages and muddy roads. It was a country seen through tears.

Lieutenant Sperling's pleasant chatter roused us at intervals. "You see that?" he asked, pointing with pride to a hillock near the road. I fancied I saw the pin of an old windmill and a clutter of ruins. "A Zeppelin did that," he went on. "It was a practice shot."

We raced along beside heaps of bricks and ashes which had once been picturesque Flemish villages. The whitewashed walls were shrapnel-pitted, so that the bricks showed through red, like blood. In frozen, muddy fields along our route, bent old peasants worked on turnip mounds. Cabbages lay heels up in hillocks which looked as if they must have served some military purpose. There were trenches in almost every line of brush or trees along the Antwerp-Brussels highway: careless, grubby trenches built by the Belgians, mathematical, business-like, criss-cross trenches built by the invaders. There were quick burrows which a man could throw up in a quarter of an hour with his kit shovel, pits with sharpened stakes in them to break up cavalry charges, and brambly barbed-wire entanglements which looked as if they had been woven by a crazy spider, and which were frosted and dripping like a spider web on a winter's morning.

The rain changed to a drizzle, and we could see much better, but our depression grew. I was fated to travel that Antwerp-Brussels highway for a year, but always with the same feeling of sadness which I felt on first seeing it. Innumerable trees were scarred by shells. Huge holes, half full of mud and ice, were gouged in roads and fields. Farm-house after farm-house had been burned or else destroyed by shell-fire. And once we noticed a broken cradle beside what had been a doorway in the murdered village of Waelhem.

"Good shooting," remarked Lieutenant Sperling. "Our artillery, I think it is the best in the world, eh?"

At the bitterly contested crossing of the river Nèthe, where the Belgians fought to hold the enemy from the advance on Antwerp, where they flooded the country, blew up all the bridges, and charged again and again in the face of overwhelming artillery fire, there stood a little earthen mound and a big black cross. The inscription was in German script, lettered white on black. I caught only a part of it while the sentries examined our passes. "Thirty-eight brave soldiers who died for the Fatherland," it read. I do not know if the dead were Belgians or Germans. The conquerors write the same words over fallen foes as over friends.

Beside the bridge stood a Belgian with a collection box, begging contributions for the poor of Waelhem.

The embankments and gun-cupolas of Fort Waelhem, first of the Antwerp forts to fall, were plowed up as if by a gigantic steam-shovel. "Forty-two centimeter shells," explained the Lieutenant. The fort was a gravel bank. And all along the road were graves. Men had been buried as they fell; sometimes singly, sometimes in groups. Each grave was marked with a new lath cross. Some of the crosses bore bunches of artificial flowers or wreaths, or simple crowns of tissue paper, dripping with wet. Some of them held a German *Pickelhaube,* or else a shapeless, flat service-cap.

But the village of Waelhem was most pitiful. It was a living grave. Of its two thousand inhabitants, twelve hundred had already returned. Not a house in the village had been spared, yet the refugees came back to their hearthsides, and were living in huts constructed against the empty brick walls, with curtains of bed-clothing to keep out the beating rain.

And romantic, unworldly Malines was a city of gray ghosts. The gray rain fell incessantly, but we could see the south side of the famous cathedral of Saint Rombaut, a mass of repulsive wreckage, in which the big stained-glass windows hung shattered and inert, and the gigantic tower—the "eighth wonder of the world," according to Vauban—punctured with shrapnel, where the dead bells of the *carillon* still hung. German soldiers lounged before the dilapidated old Cloth Hall. Our automobile passed through a Red Sea of *débris* piled higher than the tonneau on either side of the market-place. Walls were sheered away like theater-sets, showing flowered wall-papers and battered furniture, and floors cascading crazily down to the street. Three hundred and fifteen houses had been totally destroyed and fifteen hundred damaged, for Malines was bombarded four times.

Near Eppeghem a white swan paddled serenely in an ornamental pond. On the borders of the pond were crosses marking graves, and willows burned and slashed by shells.

A few farm-houses, made habitable again, bore the magic words "chocolate" and "milk" chalked up on doors, so the returning refugees might buy.

It was with vast relief that we reached Brussels, where there had been no fighting and no destruction, where beauty was unmarred by the ruin of war, even if bedraggled and ashamed.

A stiff line of German Boy Scouts stood before the beautiful hôtels on the Parc, where Governor-General von der Goltz had his offices. They looked pathetically tired and lonely so far from home, but kept eyes front and shoulders back like maturer servants of the Kaiser. Lieutenant Sperling smiled as we drew up before them, but he returned their salute gravely. "*Jung Deutschland!* Young Germany," he whispered to us. . . .

"And now for the Hotel Astoria, on the rue Royale, eh?" he said. "You will be the only foreigners in the hotel. It is for Germans. Requisitioned." As we drew up at the curb, he was still singing lustily:

"To you, beeyoutifool ladie, I raise my eyes;
My heart, beeyoutifool ladie, to your heart sighs;

Come, come, beeyoutifool ladie, to Paradise.
Dream, dream, dream, and forget
Care, pain, useless regret,
Love, love, beeyoutifool ladie, in my heart sings."

HUMOROUS HERR BAEDEKER

Several times after that we had occasion to use our military passes and to ride in German automobiles. The officers always seemed glad to have us, and they seemed to us amazingly boyish and care-free. What they wanted, they took. They even requisitioned women's underwear from lockers in the Brussels Golf Club, and of course wine was always fair spoils, whether paid for by the *Intendantur* or not. Almost every one of them had an automobile at his disposal, and they appeared everywhere, riding freely about the country in spite of the fabled shortage of gasolene and tires. The peasants, whether on foot or in their little dog- and donkey-carts, were desperately afraid of the "joy-riders." The screech of a Klaxon, or the shrill, frivolous yodel of an automobile fife, such as many of the German motorists affected, would clear the narrow Flemish roads quick as light. But that was not always enough to satisfy the officers. They howled picturesque German curses at the ignorant peasant drivers, apparently for the fun of the thing, and then whizzed off down the road, giving horn with all the delight of a coaching party in a Dickens novel.

Among themselves they were a good-natured, sentimental lot of warriors, in spick and span uniforms and well greased boots. Most of them were typical, square-headed, smooth-shaven, slash-cheeked giants, who seemed to be playing at a game called war. Many times they carried with them in the automobile, gifts for the sentries along the route: cakes of chocolate, cigars, or copies of the *Kölnische Zeitung, Berliner Tageblatt, Kreuz Zeitung, Die Woche,* and *Frankfurter Zeitung.* Sometimes the sentries stopped us; more often they did not; but on one occasion when a conscientious sentry did his full duty and compelled every one in the car, officers included, to show passes, a major told me the classic story of Kaiser Wilhelm Second at the Prussian manœuvers, attempting to dash past a sentry. The sentry promptly presented his rifle and compelled the imperial automobile to halt.

"Do you know me?" demanded the Kaiser angrily, removing his automobile goggles and glaring at the soldier.

"*Ja, Majestät,*" answered the sentry, "but I have orders to stop everybody."

"Umph!" snorted the Kaiser. Then his stern face melted into a smile. "You are right, my son," he said, and he saluted the soldier and ordered the car to go back by the way it had come. . . .

I have seen the sentries give money or other little gifts to Flemish children. Frequently the men on sentry duty were old *Landsturm* soldiers who had children of their own in the Fatherland, and with characteristic German sentiment felt deeply their privation. On the whole the sentries were simple, ignorant men, anxious to please, and mystified by the elaborate orders they had to execute. Usually they were much astonished to learn my nationality. Once when a sentry had carefully studied my passport, he said in a pleasant tone of astonishment: " Ah, so you are an American!"

"Yes," I answered. Then, thinking the man had been in America, I asked if he had traveled much.

"*Ach, nein,*" he said emphatically, "Belgium is quite far enough from home!"

Brussels, the proud Paris of the north, clung desperately to her self-respect and tried to ignore the Germans. Shutters were up on many of the fashionable shops. The best hotels were full of officers who lived by requisition. General von Lüttwitz, military governor of Brussels, inhabited a beautiful palace on the rue de la Loi,— a magnificent residence with priceless carpets and enormous cloisonné vases on the grand staircase. Such places were hives of soldiers; orderlies rushed to and fro carrying rabbits and pheasants for the general's table, and a persistent smell of soup swam through the mansion. The Germans stinted themselves for nothing.

Beggars wandered about the streets. Women holding

young babies in their arms stood on all the curbs, begging openly, or selling matches and shoestrings. On the street cars, where soldiers rode free, citizens proudly turned their backs, or refused to sit beside the hated uniforms, and in the crowded *cafés* they frequently left the place entirely rather than sip beer or coffee beside the enemy.

It was hard for Belgian pride. There were no flags but German flags; there was very little currency, except German marks and pfennigs, for the people hoarded their Belgian National Bank notes, and silver and copper had ceased to circulate; there was no opera; there were no theaters; there were only a few moving-picture shows, where John Bunny and Lillian Walker smiled on Belgians and Germans alike from the flickering films. The Royal Palace was a Red Cross hospital. On the heights beside the Palais de Justice—the Acropolis of Brussels—German cannon frowned down upon the city. The Grand' Place echoed to soldiers' steps, and the rue de la Loi, beside the Parc, was closed to all but Germans. The splendors of Brussels dripped ooze, her park walks were churned up by the hooves of German war-horses, and even the alleys "reserved for children's games" were appropriated for the drilling of raw cavalrymen. Thousands of Belgians every day besieged the Pass Bureau for permits to travel. The soup kitchens and bread lines were thronged. There was no work to do. The rust of idleness was on everything. An occasional aeroplane from the Allies dropped little celluloid tubes containing encouraging news, but the Germans, waging a successful war, insolently published all the news, even the official reports of the Allies.

Above the prostrate Belgians, like another race or another caste, roared and flashed the brilliant, careless, militaristic Teutons, their lives hedged about with glory and sudden death.

When an officer went to the front, his fellows gave him a huge dinner. They drank much, occasionally they wept a little, but he whose duty it was to go always made the occasion one for congratulations and conviviality. Then in his spickest and spannest new gray-green uniform, with the black-and-white ribbon of the Iron Cross in his buttonhole, he climbed into a waiting automobile and shot noisily down the dark streets on his way to the lines.

For a week the King of Saxony had the rooms directly below our suite in the Hotel Astoria. Governor-General Kolmar von der Goltz ("Goltz Pasha") was a caller at our hotel. I saw him the day he left Belgium for Turkey. He was a big, heavy man, with keen, humorous eyes behind his thick glasses; his left breast smothered in decorations. There was some sort of wen on his left cheek, and he wore two strips of black court-plaster set at right angles across it, looking ludicrously like the Iron Cross. . . . One day there was unusual stir among

THE BREAD LINE
Waiting for the daily ration of bread and soup.

the officers. "Be here at ten o'clock tomorrow morning," they said, "and you will see the Kaiser." But I had business elsewhere, and so missed the golden opportunity to look on the War Lord.

Late one night, Lieutenant Herbster and I were invited to meet some of the officers. It was nearly midnight. The group about the long table in the Hotel Astoria had been drinking, so that our intrusion produced a marked effect. There was much bowing and scraping, clicking of heels, and commenting, the nature of which I did not altogether understand. But I found myself seated at the table, face to face with the aide to a colonel high in command in Brussels, and found to my astonishment that I had known the man as a student in Harvard University.

The colonel—a hard, thin old Prussian, who was partly drunk and genuinely offensive—gave me a taste of what some of the Germans thought of American relief for Belgium. "You Americans are a nation of sentimental fools," he snorted. "You want to feed these *franc-tireurs,* these barbarians of Belgians. If you did the right thing, you would give the German army the food that you are bringing over for these wretches." . . .

Directly across the table was an officer named Coumbus, a fine-looking man of perhaps thirty-five, who had resided for years in England, and was an officer of cavalry. His perfect English and agreeable manners attracted Lieutenant Herbster and me, and after the other officers had withdrawn, the three of us still sat and talked.

"There are a lot of wounded Africans in a hospital here in Brussels," he informed us. "And in one ward the doctor has been clever enough to put a Scotchman along with the niggers. I go up every day to visit him. Do you know, it pleases me to see that Johnnie lying there with his face to the wall, trying to keep out the smell of the blacks. . . . Damn these inferior races!

"The Belgians are the poorest of the lot, though. They do not understand war, and they do not understand the rules of war. I remember once riding into a little town down here in the south of Belgium and finding my four scouts lying dead in the streets. Civilians had butchered horses and men—shot them from behind. I ordered my men to go into the houses and kill every one they found. Then I ordered them to burn the town."

He leaned over the table and concluded quietly, "There once was a nice little town in that place. There is no such town now." . . .

There was a cat-and-mouse air about the occupation. The army seemed to play with the country, and thoroughly to enjoy itself. But with this went also the traditional German enthusiasm for sight-seeing in order to improve the mind. Some of the officers and most of the men were in Belgium for the first time. They felt it was an opportunity not to be lost, and I often saw them with little red-bound Baedekers in their pockets, "doing" the Belgian cities with the thoroughness of holiday tourists.

Herr Baedeker is singularly felicitous in some of his Belgian notes, if read in connection with the war. "Dixmude," he remarks blandly, "is a quiet little town on the Yser!" "Nieuport is a small and quiet place on the Yser, noted for its obstinate resistance to the French in 1489 and for the 'Battle of the Dunes' in July, 1600, in which the Dutch defeated the Spaniards under Archduke Albert." Of Termonde he says, "Louis XIV besieged this place in 1667, but was compelled to retreat, as the besieged, by opening the sluices, laid the whole district under water." Blankenberghe is "a small fishing town with 6,100 inhabitants, visited by 45,000 persons annually, half of whom are Germans!" And of unhappy Ypres the learned author observes, "The siege of the town and burning of the suburbs by the English and the burghers of Ghent in 1383 caused the last of the weavers to migrate!"

German Government

But the Germans were working as well as playing. Their organizing power was amazing. To choose an expert, to put him in charge of a department, to give him a clerk or two, and then to leave him alone, seemed all there is to the modern miracle of German administration.

170 BELGIUM AS A GERMAN PROVINCE

Belgium was not treated as an administrative unit. Governor-General von der Goltz, and later Governor-General von Bissing, controlled only about two-thirds of the territory actually occupied by the German armies. Antwerp, Brussels, Liége, Namur, Dinant, Mons,—all these fell to his share. But Ghent was in a second division, governed by a general of the *Etappen-Inspection*. Bruges constituted still another division, controlled by an admiral of the Imperial navy, where sailors from the fleets in Hamburg, Kiel, and Wilhelmshaven, their ribbons tucked up under their sailor caps and in landsman's uniforms, fought as infantry. And along the fighting lines in Belgium and northern France, each army corps was a separate unit of government, responsible only to the General Staff Headquarters at Charleville, or to the Emperor personally.

"But in Belgium it is like the old religious and secular governments in the Middle Ages," they explained. "We have always a civil and a military arm to our government. In each Belgian province the government is dual. In each military county (*Kreis*) or Belgian arrondissement, we have *Kreischef* and commandant. You have seen it? Even the villages are garrisoned and governed. We do not interfere with the Belgian local self-government or the local courts; but we have our dual government to oversee them. We have soldiers everywhere."

"And spies?"

"Spies, too. The Belgians must be quiet. His Excellency the Governor has promised the armies that Belgium will be kept quiet. That is most important."

"Do you expect outbreaks?"

"We expect—everything and nothing. We anticipate everything. That is the German way. . . . The Belgians will be kept quiet."

The new Governor-General, Baron von Bissing, took office immediately after "Goltz Pasha" left for Turkey. His position carried with it the dignity and authority of royalty. His proclamations were written in the first person: "I command. . . . I ordain. . . . I decree." They say that in his youth Governor-General von Bissing was a chum of the Kaiser's and that the Kaiser used to pay the bills at a time when his friend's personal fortune was too small to permit even of the ordinary expenditures of a dashing young army officer. If that is true General von Bissing has advanced a long way since then. He lives in a Belgian palace, he rules a nation, and he stands on a par, under the War Lord, with the petty monarchs of some of the oldest German states.

Many officers in the Civil Government were Germans who had lived for years in Belgium and had been on excellent terms with the Belgian Government and people. Others had made special studies of Belgian conditions. The German Civil Governor in Brussels, *Excellenz* von Sandt, was formerly president of the Local

Government Board at Aix-la-Chapelle; the head of the Department of Engineering and Public Works, Councilor of Justice Trimborn of Cologne and member of the Reichstag, was formerly German Consul-General in Brussels; the head of the Brussels Pass Bureau, Lieutenant Behrens, was, until the day war broke out, head of a pool of shipping companies in Antwerp and had resided there for years. The Belgains doubtless were right in believing that their conquerors knew where every stick of furniture, every horse and cow, every cart and automobile, every man, every gun, and every franc in Belgium was to be found. . . .

I called one day at the offices of the Civil Government in Brussels, called in German *Zivilverwaltung,* to learn something of Belgian agricultural conditions in normal years. Herr Doktor Frost was introduced to me —a thin, studious young man in lieutenant's uniform, to whom I explained my wants. "How much wheat, how much rye, how much oats, how much barley does Belgium produce in average years?" I asked.

Lieutenant Frost smiled and leaned across his study-desk, pointing to a bulky blue-bound book lying before him. "Look in the book," he said, smiling as if at a joke. "Page 367; paragraph two. You find it? Yes?"

I pored over the concise academic tables with their crisp footnotes in German script. Every bit of information I wanted regarding the crops of Belgium stood on that page. Then I closed the book and scanned the cover. "The Agricultural Resources of Belgium," it read; "by Doctor Walther Frost, Munich, 1913." . . .

The retreat of the Belgian armies and government had removed every trace of national organization. King, Cabinet, and Parliament were lost at a stroke. The Royal Provincial Governors were deprived of their seats, and the nine provinces and their constituent communes were isolated and prostrate.

The only nucleus of a governmental connection between the invaders and the Belgian people was the Belgian Permanent Deputation—a sort of executive committee of the Provincial Councils, which exists whether the councils are sitting or adjourned. Its powers are not important. The Royal Provincial Governor is its president. Now, by military decree, the German Civil Governors assumed the presidency of the nine Permanent Deputations, and the structure of civil government was re-erected. The communal authorities were, for the most part, left in possession of their normal powers and responsibilities, subject always to the military. The Belgian courts were not greatly disturbed, although their decisions were subject to military review. Belgian *agents de police,* in uniform, but deprived of their short cutlasses, kept order in the communes; Belgians manned the fire-departments and kept the prisons; Belgian customs officers served at the frontiers, although their services were largely perfunctory; Belgian employees managed the street- and light railways, although the regular state railways were entirely in the hands of the military and no Belgian could go near them; Belgian *gardes champêtres* continued to serve as rural police; Belgian burgomasters and aldermen went through the motions, at least, of local self-government; and the Belgian relief work, whether feeding and clothing the destitute, or giving money to the needy, remained entirely outside the German sphere of influence, in the hands of the Belgians and the American members of the Commission for Relief in Belgium. The sole exception was the Belgian Red Cross which was taken over bodily by the German authorities and placed under the control of a German administration with Prince Hatzfeldt at its head.

Two things the Germans wanted of the Belgians—quiet and cash. These two things they got.[1]

[1] See Appendix II, page 331.

CHAPTER V

STARVING BELGIUM

The Catastrophe

FEW know in detail the situation in which Belgium found herself in the autumn of 1914. The invasion by the German armies overwhelmed the country almost as completely as an avalanche overwhelms a village lying in its path. The superstructure of civilized society was swept away.

Belgium had been the most highly industrialized country in the world. It imported seventy-eight per cent of its breadstuffs. Its own agricultural products afforded sustenance to the population for only four months out of the year. For the other eight months the country was dependent upon imported foods; much of them quickly perishable. A peaceable interruption of overseas or overland commerce would have brought the whole country into immediate sight of starvation, even without the horrors of invasion.

For weeks following the outbreak of war transatlantic traffic was virtually suspended. American foodstuffs remained in American warehouses while European consumers were in growing need of them. The ship in which I sailed for Europe on August twenty-fourth carried a large cargo of flour, for the distress in neutral Holland was acute even in the first month of the war. Belgium was suffering as much as or more than Holland; but in addition to this the land was overrun by the Germans, and an acute crisis was transformed into an overwhelming disaster.

Forty-nine per cent of the population were salary and wage earners. Almost half the population, then, was dependent on the normal functioning of industry.

Credit, which is the basis of modern industrial activity and the rock-bottom basis of Belgium's national existence, was shattered by the shock of the German armies. Within ten weeks from the fourth of August almost the entire country was in the possession of the enemy. With credit destroyed, production came to an instant standstill. Mines and workshops, factories and mills closed, and panic seized the land. The whole of the working population was plunged into the deepest misery.

The harvest was being gathered as war broke on the country and the ripe crops were left standing in the fields where they were trampled by the armies or left to rot. Belgium on July thirty-first was a land of intense activity. A week later it was a land of the unemployed. July thirty-first found 1,757,489 men, women, and children occupied in upwards of seven hundred industries. 1,204,810 people were tilling the land. August seventh found practically every man, woman, and child on farms,

THE CATASTROPHE 177

in fields, on canals, on railroads, in every village, town, and city, suddenly idle, without work, and without food.

Preceding the westward march of the invaders came a wave of refugees. Uprooted from the soil, flung from villages and cities invaded, often burned and pillaged, they fled westward, carrying with them panic and blind terror. While Belgium's heroic army by its stand at Liége and Namur may have saved Paris and Calais, it could not save its own country. As the Germans advanced they seized every line of communication,—the railroads, street-cars, canals, telegraphs, telephones, and mails. The copper nerves and iron veins which are the life of every modern nation were wrenched from the Belgians. Every village was cut off from its neighbor; every town from the next town. There was no means of transport, except for German troops, so that every commune, from the tiniest village to the greatest city, was suddenly isolated, ignorant of what was happening a few miles off, and unable to ascertain the most vital news, except through a few hasty words that might fall from the shaking lips of fugitives.

Belgium was singular among industrial nations in having a great mass of floating labor. The policy of the Government-owned railway system had been to make transportation for the working classes as reasonable as possible, so that it was the cheapest system of transport in the world. At the same time a system of peasant proprietorship in land had been fostered for many years by the Government, but under it the peasant could barely sustain life. The man of the family often migrated from place to place during the summer months, working in the mines, in the farms and vineyards of France, while his wife and children cultivated his tiny holding. By strict economy he was able to make both ends meet, although, even so, tens of thousands of workers found it necessary during the winter months to make lace; Belgium's great lace-making industry being largely parasitic.

J. DeC. MacDonnel has fitly described the state of these workers.[1] " There are no villages, broadly speaking, that are purely agricultural. Men who labor in the towns continue to reside in the most distant part of the country, rising in the first hours after midnight to tramp miles along dark roads to a railroad station, and travel thence almost incredible distances, day after day, by train to their work. These are the workmen whom astonished tourists see sleeping in doorways and by roadsides in the streets and suburbs of Antwerp, Brussels, Ghent, or any of the Belgian cities during the midday hour of rest, and snoring in the evening, their weary bodies piled on top of each other, on the benches and floors of the waiting-rooms of railway stations and in the third class railway carriages."

Under such conditions, transport facilities, and the

[1] J. DeC. MacDonnel's *Belgium, Her Kings, Kingdom, and People*, published by Little, Brown & Co., is an interesting though biased account of conditions before the war. The author is sometimes a better churchman than historian.

THE CATASTROPHE

railways in particular, were essential to the people; and these were the first of Belgium's necessities upon which the Germans seized. Many of the canals were blocked by the retreating army; barges were sunk, bridges blown up, and dykes cut; and as it was by means of the canals that the bulk of the foodstuffs normally was distributed over the country, the food-supply was automatically cut off.

As the Germans occupied town after town, province after province, they quartered soldiers upon the Belgians, and these hastened the consumption of what little food was available. General von Emmich's proclamation to the Belgians before Liége ran:

> I gave formal guarantee to the Belgian population that it will not have to suffer the horrors of war; that we shall pay in money for the food we must take from the country; that our soldiers will show themselves to be the best friends of a people for whom we entertain the highest esteem, the greatest sympathy.

But the patriotic resistance of the Belgians changed all this. General von Beseler's despatch to the Kaiser following the fall of Antwerp is typical of the psychology of the soldier, and has a curiously medieval ring:

> The war booty taken at Antwerp is enormous: at least 500 cannon and huge quantities of ammunition, sanitation materials, numerous high-power motor-cars, locomotives,

wagons, 4,000,000 kilograms of wheat, large quantities of flour, coal, and flax wool, the value of which is estimated at 10,000,000 marks; copper, silver, one armored-train, several hospital trains, and quantities of fish.

There are few of the raw materials of industry which cannot be put to some military use. A great part of the machinery of peace-time can be converted into machinery with which to manufacture implements of war. Above all soldiers need food and consume it in immense quantities. Finding all these things at hand in Belgium the Germans proceeded to commandeer them right and left. Linseed oil, oil-cakes, nitrates, animal and vegetable oils of all sorts, petroleum and mineral oils, wool, copper, rubber, ivory, cocoa, rice, wine, beer—anything and everything that men could consume or that the German factories could utilize—were seized and transported to the Fatherland. In many cases the goods were confiscated; in others they were requisitioned by the conquerors, a price was decided upon, and payment promised at some convenient time in the future.

Belgium was gutted.

The Cry for Help

From the isolated communes came frantic appeals for help. The Belgians appealed first to the Germans, who in some cases divided their army rations with the people, although this was unsystematic and utterly useless when seven millions were concerned. They appealed to their neighbor Holland, but the Dutch were eating war bread and anxiously hoarding every bit of foodstuff, for they were as yet unable to import enough for their own uses. They appealed to Brussels, sending purchasing agents with dog-carts to buy a little flour and potatoes in the open market; for Brussels was officially the capital, and they were accustomed to turn to Brussels.

But Brussels, like themselves, was isolated and face to face with famine. The sole advantage it possessed over the other communes was a volunteer relief organization, called the Central Relief Committee (*le Comité Central de Secours et d'Alimentation pour l'Agglomeration bruxelloise*), formed on September fifth under the patronage of the American and Spanish Ministers, Mr. Brand Whitlock and the Marquis of Villalobar.

In every little village there was a *Bureau de Bienfaisance;* often there was a Society of Saint Vincent de Paul and a *Comité de Secours*. In the larger cities there were sturdy branches of the Red Cross, with committees of charity, cheap restaurants, committees to take charge of the children of soldiers, to provide proper diet for nursing mothers, and a variety of other relief organizations, secular and religious, such as the Little Sisters of the Poor, mainly under the auspices of the Roman Catholic Church.

But though the local machinery was at hand there were first four general problems to face: the re-establishment of order and credit abroad; the right to transport foodstuffs through the British blockade into territory in the hands of the Germans; the right to use the transport facilities of Belgium in the distribution of such imports; and the securing of a guarantee that the Germans would requisition for themselves nothing thus imported for the Belgian population.

The Central Relief Committee, which had been formed to care for the wants of Brussels, appealed through its American and Spanish Minister-patrons to Governor-General Kolmar von der Goltz to guarantee the safety of any supplies which might be purchased or donated abroad for the benefit of the Belgian civil population. On October sixteenth the Governor-General gave formal assurance that "foodstuffs of all sorts imported by the Committee to assist the civil population shall be reserved exclusively for the nourishment of the civil population of Belgium, and that consequently these foodstuffs shall be exempt from requisition on the part of the military authorities and shall rest exclusively at the disposition of the Committee."

Meanwhile Mr. Whitlock had appealed officially to the United States Government. In the London *Times* for Wednesday, October fourteenth, 1914, is the following telegram:

NEW YORK, October 13.—The Administration cannot permit Mr. Page to have food supplies for the starving population of Brussels shipped in his name to Mr. Whitlock until the German Government sanctions this step. Mr.

THE CRY FOR HELP 183

Page's urgent representations concerning the immediate necessity of relieving the wants of Brussels were communicated to Germany last Wednesday, but no reply has yet been received."

Armed with the assurance given by Governor-General von der Goltz that nothing imported by the committee would be requisitioned by the Germans, Émile Francqui and Baron Lambert of the Central Relief Committee, and Hugh Gibson, secretary of the American Legation, went to London to explain to the British Government the desperate situation of the city of Brussels and to request permission to import food. At the same time they appealed personally to American Ambassador Walter Hines Page and were by him referred to an American mining engineer named Herbert Clark Hoover who had just rendered notable services to the Embassy and to his fellow-countrymen by heading a committee to advance funds to send home to America those of our nationals who had been caught in Europe at the outbreak of war. As a result of conferences between Mr. Hoover and Mr. Francqui a plan was drawn up and submitted to the British Government, which granted permission to Mr. Hoover and to an American Committee which he should organize under the patronage of the Ministers of the United States and of Spain in London, Berlin, The Hague, and Brussels, the right to purchase and transport through the British blockade to Rotterdam, Holland, cargoes of foodstuffs, destined to be trans-shipped into

Belgium, consigned to the American Minister in Brussels, and to be distributed through the Central Relief Committee—now expanded to the Belgian National Relief Committee (*le Comité National de Secours et d'Alimentation*)—under the direction of American citizens, who should certify, as representatives of Mr. Brand Whitlock, that the food was equitably apportioned and consumed only by the Belgian civil population.

This plan was not for the assistance of the city of Brussels alone but was for the whole of Belgium.

The London *Times* of October twenty-fourth, 1914, says:

A Commission has been set up in London under the title of "The American Commission for Relief in Belgium." The Brussels Committee reports feeding 300,000 daily.

On November fourth it states:

The Commission for Relief in Belgium yesterday issued their first weekly report, 3 London Wall Buildings. A cargo was received yesterday at Brussels just in time. Estimated monthly requirements:

> 60,000 tons grain
> 15,000 tons maize
> 3,000 tons rice and peas

Approved by the Spanish and American Ministers, Brussels.[1]

[1] See Appendix III, page 333.

Brand Whitlock

The Spanish Minister—the Marquis of Villalobar y O'Neill—I first met in Brussels in December. He was as Irish as the maternal half of his name, thoroughly *simpatico*, a trained diplomat, keen-eyed, heavy-set, of charming manners and force of character, whose influence with the Belgians was great. He and Mr. Brand Whitlock were the only diplomatic representatives who remained in Brussels after the occupation. Like Mr. Whitlock, the Marquis of Villalobar had been a patron of the Central Relief Committee of Brussels, and when that organism was expanded to take in the whole of Belgium he became, with Mr. Whitlock, Minister-patron of the Belgian National Relief Committee.

Among the remnants of the former diplomatic circle was a delightful Mexican *chargé d'affaires,* destined also to help in Belgian relief work, with the inappropriate name of German Bullé. Waxing and waning revolutions in Mexico had made Señor Bullé careless of his official status, which was, as defined by Hugh Gibson, secretary of the American Legation, "representative of a country without a government to a government without a country."

The American Legation was a busy place, for the interests of half a dozen belligerent nations were in American hands, and the busiest person in it was the secretary. Hugh S. Gibson was an alert, slender young

Hoosier of about thirty, with the hawk-like Yankee look, keen dark eyes, crisp hair always in place, fine firm mouth, slender hands, and few gestures. His wit and fearlessness were the talk of Brussels. He drove into Louvain under fire to report to the Legation on conditions. He rode into Antwerp while the siege was in progress, carrying a Belgian Minister of State to present to King Albert a confidential message from Governor-General von der Goltz. The King repulsed the messenger, and the Minister of State reported afterward that he was coerced into going. But for Gibson the journey was a routine matter of business, even if the hood of his motor-car was shot off *en route*. He had been frequently under fire and he had the happy faculty of telling about his exploits without the taint of boastfulness.

Like most of the Americans in Belgium, Gibson was dogged by spies. One of these hangers-on made himself so conspicuous that Gibson began to take notice of him and to treat him familiarly, much to the spy's disgust. One very rainy day the pet spy was discovered standing under the dripping eaves of a neighboring house. Gibson caught up a raincoat and hurried over to the man.

"Look here, old fellow," he said in German. "I'm going to be in the Legation for three hours. You put on this coat and go home. Come back in three hours and I'll let you watch me for the rest of the day."

Ante-bellum Baedekers have not starred the American

Legation at number 74 rue de Trèves, Brussels. It is no worse and no better than most American legations, but it is not a beauty spot in a Belgian pilgrimage. Straight walls enclose the Whitlock residence, a dingy plaque with the Legation seal leans forward over the door, a flag droops weakly from its staff in the incessant rains, and the dull streets are empty. The house itself is a severe rectangle with a pleasant reception room and dining-room upstairs, but with gloomy offices below, to which one is led by way of a white, sepulchral hall, where a plaster bust of Washington stares undisturbed at eternity.

One usually found Mr. Whitlock sitting before a gas grate in a room where winter and summer the windows were closed. He rarely walked out. Almost the only times he left the Legation were for automobile rides in a closed limousine.

He always looked tired and worn. The academic severity of his face is accentuated by his thinness, and his eyes have the tense look of a man constantly straining to see something too close to him. He is the tall, scholarly, cloistral type of American gentleman, so often sacrificed to practicalities in a work-a-day world; a man happier in libraries than in executive offices; happiest of all, perhaps, in the atmosphere of universities. The dry, mechanical precision of his speech rarely changes pitch or tempo, and he speaks as he writes: academically, in the best sense of the word.

A day or two after the war broke out, a friend of Mr. Whitlock's in America received a letter written from the seclusion of a *château* near Brussels, where the Minister was writing a novel. There was no hint, no thought of war in the letter. The writer whimsically deplored the idle life of an American representative in Europe. " I am afraid, after all, that I am made for a more active existence," was the substance of what he wrote. " There is nothing to do here."

There was something of the same aloofness from contemporary affairs in our first conversation, as if literature and not life had again gained the upper hand.

" How do they make maple sugar back home? " Mr. Whitlock asked.

I described the process as best I could, adding that after a plethora of sugar a bite or two of sour pickle will clear the appetite for more! " But why do you ask me that? "

" I had just reached a ' sugaring off ' episode in my novel when the war began, and I have often wondered since how we used to make maple sugar in Ohio." . . .

The Fates have not been overkind to Mr. Whitlock. Beginning as a newspaper reporter in Chicago—he was born in Urbana, Ohio, on March 4, 1869—he definitely determined to be a man of letters. He studied law, was admitted to the Illinois bar in 1894 and to the bar of the

Photograph by Paul Thompson

BRAND WHITLOCK

State of Ohio in 1897. He was a friend of Governor Altgeld of Illinois, Tom Johnson of Cleveland, and "Golden Rule" Jones of Toledo, Ohio, whom he succeeded as mayor in 1905. He was re-elected in 1907, and again in 1909 and 1911. And all the time he was writing. "The Thirteenth District," "The Turn of the Balance," "The Fall Guy," "Forty Years of It,"—these of his books are widely read; but Mr. Whitlock has never had time to do the writing which he wants most to do.

With the outbreak of the war his placid life as a diplomat, "lying abroad for the good of his country," as Sir Henry Wotton wittily defined the mission of diplomacy, was invaded by a storm of horrors such as the most self-contained could not resist. Mr. Whitlock was the representative of the only great neutral power left in the world and he was at the very center of the cyclone. Waves of refugees, many of them utterly destitute, all of them in a state of abject panic and demoralization, thronged into Brussels as the Germans advanced. Day by day their numbers and their distress increased. Relief measures were imperative unless the fugitives were to starve by the roadside or be driven in desperation to plunder right and left. Mr. Whitlock had lived all his life in the amiable atmosphere of Middle Western liberalism; he was humane and kindly and idealistic. He belonged to the "Free Speech League" and prison reform associations; his impulses and ideals were generous, and now before his eyes a nation was being throttled. It was natural and I think it was typically American for Mr. Whitlock to do what he did. He threw himself at once into the work of relief. The American Legation became the foundation head for all sorts of help and advice. Bread lines were formed and supplied, soup kitchens were opened, and depots where the naked could be clothed; and after the German armies entered Brussels on August twentieth, 1914, the American Legation afforded the one stable point around which the demoralized population could rally.

That is Mr. Whitlock's unforgettable contribution to Belgium and especially to the city of Brussels. He has represented to a people imprisoned and oppressed the ideals of freedom and helpfulness which we like to think are characteristically American.

And that is what the Belgians will never forget. That is why, on Washington's Birthday, they filed before the heavy doors at 74 rue de Trèves—men, women, and children, of all classes; a few in furs, more with shawls over their heads and *sabots* on their feet; professors, noblemen, artisans, shopkeepers, artists, functionaries of the State, slum babies, and peasants—dropping their *cartes de visite*—engraved, printed, or written on slips of stiff cardboard torn from paper boxes—in tribute to Mr. Whitlock and the nation which he represents.

To Belgians and to Americans the Legation was a haven of refuge. A vast weight of suspicion hung upon us all. We almost feared to think; we could never speak out. The American Legation was the only spot in Belgium where one might talk and listen without fear of spies; where even in the midst of war one might share for a while the sheltered, test-tube existence of diplomatic representatives abroad. And for that we were deeply grateful.

To the popularity of the Legation Mrs. Whitlock contributed much. Her tact and sympathy, her charm and good sense were at every one's command. She also took a prominent part in relief work in Brussels. She was president-patroness of the Children's Aid (*Aide et Protection aux Œuvres de l'Enfance*) and of the Committee for the Relief of Lace Workers (*le Comité de la Dentelle*). At her little Friday receptions the women always knitted for the poor.

Herbert C. Hoover

" Who is Hoover? " I asked of every American I met in Brussels.

" Chairman of the Commission for Relief in Belgium —Going to be one of the biggest figures of the war."

" But who is he now? "

" Mining engineer—Californian—Lives in London— Directs a lot of mines all over the world—Employs one hundred and twenty-five thousand men—Annual output of his mines is worth as much as the total annual output of metals of California. He's a consulting engineer and financier and administrator—Interested in everything—Oil fields, half a dozen engineering, construction, and development companies. Everybody in London knows Hoover. If any one on earth can feed Belgium, he can."

Later I knew more of him: that he comes of Quaker stock; was born at West Branch, Iowa, in 1874; graduated from Leland Stanford University, California, taking his degree of B. A. in mining engineering in 1895; spent a year with the United States Geological Survey in the Sierra Nevada Mountains, was assistant manager of the Carlisle mines in New Mexico and the Morning Star mines in California, and at the age of twenty-four went to West Australia as chief of the mining staff of Bewick, Moreing, and Company. He married Miss Lou Henry of Monterey, California in 1899, and with his bride went to China as chief engineer of the Chinese Imperial Bureau of Mines. Next year he took part in the defense of Tientsin during the Boxer disturbances. After that he was engaged in the construction of Ching Wang Tow harbor, and was general manager of the Chinese Engineering and Mining Company; and a year later, in 1902, became a partner in the firm of Bewick, Moreing, and Company, mine operators, of London. He has been consulting engineer for more than fifty mining companies.

It reads like the record of a crowded life, but it is

only a prelude to his real work. By the first of January, 1915, all the world knew of Hoover, knew that to him more than to any one else is due the creation and maintenance of the Commission for Relief in Belgium, the day to day toil on behalf of seven million four hundred thousand non-combatants in Belgium and two million one hundred and forty thousand in northern France caught in the nets of war, the enlisting of the sympathy of the world on their behalf, the organization and successful operation within two or three weeks by a body of volunteers of relief measures involving an annual turnover of almost one hundred million dollars. That, as all the world knows today, is the achievement of Herbert C. Hoover, American.

In appearance he is astonishingly youthful, smooth-shaven, dark haired, with cool, watchful eyes, clear brow, straight nose, and firm, even mouth. His chin is round and hard.

One might not mark him in a crowd. There is nothing theatrical or picturesque in his looks or bearing, for from his Quaker forebears he has inherited a dislike for sham and show of any sort. At work he seems passive and receptive. He stands still or sits still when he talks, perhaps jingling coins in his pocket or playing with a pencil. His repertory of gestures is small. He can be so silent that it hurts.

Being an American he sometimes acts first and explains afterwards. But his explanations, like his actions, are direct and self-sufficient.

In the *Outlook* for September eighth, 1915, Lewis R. Freeman describes Hoover's contempt for precedent, his fondness for the *fait accompli;* for action first and explanation later. He tells how, before the Commission was fairly on its feet, there came a day when it was a case of snarling things in red tape and letting Belgium starve, or getting food shipped and letting governments howl. Hoover naturally chose the latter.

"When the last bag had been stowed and the hatches were battened down," writes Mr. Freeman, "Hoover went in person to the one Cabinet Minister able to arrange for the only things he could not provide himself —clearance papers. 'If I do not get four cargoes of food to Belgium by the end of the week,' he said bluntly, 'thousands are going to die from starvation, and many more may be shot in food riots.'

"'Out of the question,' said the distinguished Minister. 'There is no time, in the first place, and if there was there are no good wagons to be spared by the railways, no dock hands, and no steamers; moreover, the Channel is closed for a week to merchant vessels while troops are being transported to the Continent.'

"'I have managed to get all of these things,' Hoover replied quietly; 'and am now through with them all except the steamers. This wire tells me that these are now

Courtesy of *The Bellman* and *The Northwestern Miller*

HERBERT CLARK HOOVER

loaded and ready to sail, and I have come to have you arrange for their clearance.'

"The great man gasped. 'There have been—there are even now—men in the Tower for less than you have done,' he ejaculated. 'If it was for anything but Belgian Relief—if it was anybody but you, young man—I should hate to think of what might happen. As it is—er—I suppose there is nothing to do but congratulate you on a jolly clever coup. I'll see about the clearance at once.'"

Mr. Freeman quotes a member of the Commission as saying, "You have heard, doubtless, that Lloyd George has the reputation of being the most persuasive man in England. Well, a few months ago, when we were trying to simplify our work by arranging for an extension of exchange facilities on Brussels, the then Chancellor of the Exchequer sent for Hoover. I will tell the story as Lloyd George himself told it to some friends at the Liberal Club a few days later.

"'"Mr. Hoover," I said, "I find I am quite unable to grant your request in the matter of Belgian exchange, and I have asked you to come here that I might explain why." Without waiting for me to go on, my boyish-looking caller began speaking. . . . For fifteen minutes he spoke without a break—just about the clearest expository utterance I have ever heard on any subject. He used not a word too much, nor yet a word too few. By the time he had finished I had come to realize, not only the importance of his contentions, but, what was more to the point, the practicability of granting his request. So I did the only thing possible under the circumstances—told him I had never understood the question before, thanked him for helping me to understand it, and saw to it that things were arranged as he wanted them.'"

On April tenth, 1915, a submarine torpedoed one of the food ships chartered by the Commission; a week later a German hydro-aeroplane tried to drop bombs on the deck of another Commission ship, so Hoover paid a flying visit to Berlin. He was at once assured that no more incidents of the sort would occur.

"Thanks," said Hoover. "Your Excellency, have you heard the story of the man who was nipped by a bad-tempered dog? He went to the owner to have the dog muzzled.

"'But the dog won't bite you,' insisted the owner.

"'You know he won't bite me, and I know he won't bite me,' said the injured party doubtfully, 'but the question is, does the dog know?'" . . .

"Herr Hoover," said the high official, "pardon me if I leave you for a moment. I am going at once to 'let the dog know.'"

Hoover has a habit of going straight to the highest authority with anything he has on hand. He never

HERBERT C. HOOVER

wastes time on the titled office boys who administer so much of the machinery of this world of ours. When he meets a new problem he takes it to an expert. When he wants an obstacle removed from his path he goes to the man who can remove it, or he removes it himself. He gives no small coin of flattery or favors to figurehead officials.

Of course he makes enemies. The wonder is that they are so few. He uses men, throws them aside and forgets them, as every world architect must, for he has, along with his amazing diplomatic skill, as frank a way in dealing with men as with conditions. I have known a word or a phrase of his to reveal a man to himself as naked and as startled as a patient under psychoanalysis. Hoover is a diplomat in the high, not in the trivial sense of the word; a constructive artist in human destiny; a leader who is too busy to waste time flattering the petty pride of those he leads.

He appeals to the imagination and the dreams of men. But he too is a slave to dreams. Today the Commission for Relief in Belgium—the " C. R. B." as the Belgians have nicknamed it—is his great dream. He wants the names of all who serve in it to be swallowed up in the organization, to be forgotten in service to Belgium. He would like his own name to be forgotten in the same way; but that is not to be. I am not a prophet or the son of a prophet, but I know that the public service of Herbert C. Hoover has just begun. He belongs not only to Belgium but to America, and as soon as the war is over and Belgium is free, his own country will have need of him.

THE COMMISSION FOR RELIEF IN BELGIUM

In October, as Chairman of the Commission for Relief in Belgium, Mr. Hoover established his headquarters at 3 London Wall Buildings, London, England. The diplomatic direction of the entire work of Belgian relief, the solicitation or purchase of supplies and their shipment, were governed by this central office. The active members of the Commission, all of them volunteers and most of them American citizens, consisted chiefly of personal friends and business associates of Mr. Hoover; almost all of them engineers, or men of careful technical training.

The Commission in London was modestly housed and modestly manned. The general direction was in the hands of Mr. Hoover; Colonel Millard Hunsiker was director for Great Britain; John Beaver White was purchasing agent and manager of shipping; and Edgar Rickard, editor of a mining journal, was manager of publicity.[1]

The Brussels office, which was headquarters for all of Belgium, at first was divided between the American Legation and number 48 rue de Naples—the latter a typical Brussels office building with unnecessary marble, paneled oak cubby-holes for private offices, oak ceilings, oak-

[1] See Appendix IV, page 334.

wainscot, and big mirrors. There was an oak mantel with carven, well-fed cupids on it, American telephone instruments on green baize tables, electric lights, and deep comfortable chairs. Later the headquarters were transferred to a rambling suite at number 66 rue des Colonies. The first director was Daniel Heinemann of Brussels, and following him, Captain J. F. Lucey, Albert N. Connett, Oscar T. Crosby, Professor Vernon L. Kellogg, and W. B. Poland.

Rotterdam, the port of entry for all Belgian supplies, was the principal shipping point, so that a trans-shipping office for Commission goods was opened at 98 Haringvliet, on a tree-bordered Dutch lane lying beside a busy canal where the schools of herring used to run, and where nowadays market carts and fisherwomen, motor-cars, delivery wagons, and peasant farmers in whitewashed wooden shoes clatter leisurely by. A century ago 98 Haringvliet was the residence of a Dutch merchant prince. The ceilings bear allegorical figures. Some of the walls are paneled. In the waiting-room, which used to be the dining-room of the mansion, is a massive fireplace, with long vertical Dutch mirrors and wall paintings in the style of 1750, showing quiet landscapes, Ruskin's "fat cattle and ditch-water," or violent storms at sea.

Stolid Dutch and Flemish barge captains and dock laborers stood in line below stairs. Captain J. F. Lucey, the first Rotterdam director, sat in a roomy office on the second floor overlooking the Meuse—the river which flows from Verdun, Dinant, Namur, and Liége, thence through Holland to Rotterdam. From his windows he could see the Commission barges as they left for Belgium, their pilot houses decorated with huge canvas flags bearing the protective inscription, "Belgian Relief Commission." He was a nervous, big, beardless American, a volunteer, like all the rest, who left his business of manufacturing oil-well supplies to organize and direct a great trans-shipping office in an alien land for an alien people. Out of nothing he created a large staff of clerks—American, Dutch, and Belgian—secured special permits from the Dutch Government, even wrung from them permission to break the laws whenever necessity dictated; received the immense cargoes necessary to stave off Belgian starvation; loaded them into canal boats; got from the German Consul-General in Rotterdam passports for cargoes and crews; and shipped the foodstuffs consigned personally to Mr. Brand Whitlock.[1]

A fleet of three hundred canal boats was engaged exclusively for the Commission's work. By means of floating elevators a nine thousand ton ship loaded with bulk wheat could be unloaded in thirty-six hours and sent on its way through the rivers and canals into Belgium. All Dutch records for speedy freight handling were broken, and still Belgium cried for food.[2]

[1] See Appendix V, page 335.
[2] See Appendix VI, page 335.

THE COMMISSION FOR RELIEF IN BELGIUM 201

By mid-November gift ships from the United States were *en route* for Rotterdam, but the Canadian Province of Nova Scotia was first in the translantic race. The steamer "Tremorvah," out of Halifax, brought one hundred and seventy-six tons of flour, forty-nine tons of meat and bacon, and two thousand three hundred and thirty-eight tons miscellaneous,—everything edible which could be got on short notice by the generous Nova Scotians and thrust into a ship. The "Tremorvah" reached Rotterdam on November fifteenth.[1]

As an American citizen I was deeply interested in the budding work of the Commission for Relief in Belgium. Through Dr. Henry van Dyke, American Minister in The Hague and an honorary chairman of the Commission, and through Captain Lucey, the Rotterdam director, I learned that Americans were urgently needed in Belgium to oversee the distribution of food in each of the provinces and to certify that all of it went to the Belgians. Men were wanted who knew both French and German and who had business training, and they were wanted at once. It was suggested that I go into Belgium and help in whatever way I could.

The suggestion was made to me at four o'clock in the afternoon of November twenty-third. I left for Brussels next morning at eight o'clock, by way of Bergen op Zoom and Antwerp.

[1] See Appendix VII, page 336.

On December eleventh I was again in Antwerp, this time holding Mr. Brand Whitlock's power-of-attorney as chief delegate of the Commission for Relief in Belgium in charge of the fortress and province—a territory as large as the State of Rhode Island, and with a population of more than a million.

A 'Dead City

It was the season of Saint Nicholas, with Christmas only a fortnight away; a time when all the world has a right to be merry. But it seemed as if there could be no real Christmas in 1914; food and clothing would be blessing enough for the Belgians. At the office of the Red Cross, at number 30 Place de Meir, hung a pathetic notice:

"This year Saint Nicholas cannot make a proper distribution of presents to the poor children of Belgium. Therefore it will be necessary to have useful things to give to the little ones:—a pair of slippers, a warm dress, or something of the sort—for distribution through the hospitals, children's refuges, and *crèches.*"

A few shops exhibited the customary Christmas cakes, gingerbreads, and candies, although the stock was strictly limited on account of the lack of milk and eggs, and in a department-store on the Place de Meir stood a ruddy lay figure of Saint Nicholas in a bishop's golden mitre and chasuble, white lace cotta and black cassock, mittens, and gold crosier,—a touch at least of the Christmas season, although the good bishop did not resemble our jolly, homely Santa Claus. . . .

The silence of the dead metropolis was shrilly broken by old women, screaming "*Handelsblad! La Presse!*" to people too poor to buy newspapers. The hum and throb of industry were gone; the quays were empty; factories were shut; acres of rusting wagons and rotting ships lined the northern basins; the warehouses were sealed and guarded by German soldiers; labor was dispersed, and the very air was idle and noisome.

There was nothing to do but to promenade, so the streets were thronged with women in mourning and idle men who passed aimlessly up and down, or studied the pillar-posts where the German Government posted its regulations in the German, Flemish, and French languages. Barricades of sandbags and a row of ugly rapid-fire guns pointed down the avenue de Keyzer from the Central Railway Station. Few beggars were abroad: the crowds were not mendicants. But they walked aimlessly and indifferently, and their faces were inexpressibly sad. Refugees were drifting back from Holland: thirty thousand were lodged in the city. Many of them were without homes, most were without money, all were without work.

Long lines of people stood every day at the Pass Bureau to petition for passes to Brussels or the suburbs of Antwerp, for three lines of German sentries girdled the fortress and permitted no one to go or come without the magic script furnished by the Pass Bureau, "for a consideration." Passes were costly articles. Peasants coming to town on market days to sell their scanty stock of vegetables and milk paid sometimes as high as three marks for the privilege. Draft animals were few, because of the requisitions, so one frequently saw dogs, and sometimes men and women, pulling the heaviest carts over the cobble-stones.

Out of the crowding impressions of my first week's stay in Antwerp as delegate for the Commission for Relief in Belgium, comes a composite picture of helplessness and hopelessness, lightened by the incorrigible optimism of one man. That man was Louis Franck, president of the Provincial Relief Committee. On the day of my arrival in Antwerp I went at once to the beautiful Town Hall, a structure famous before the "Spanish Terror," —a Flemish gem in old gold and ivory, set in a Flemish square, all ringed about with guild halls and medieval shops. At the door stood German sentries and a stench of cabbage soup swam out of the open doors, for most of the guard was at mess, laughing and eating below stairs.

In the office of the Burgomaster of Antwerp, Jan de Vos, I found Mynheer Louis Franck, president of the Inter-communal Commission and the provincial branch of the National Relief Committee (*le Comité Provincial de Secours et d'Alimentation*). Through a clear pane in the stained-glass windows behind him, I caught a glimpse of the cathedral tower, with the German flag flaunting at its top; but the appearance and surroundings of Mr. Franck filled the eye completely. He sat in a paneled room of Flemish oak and gold, behind a massive oaken desk, facing a magnificent marble chimney-piece from the old abbey of Tongerloo; his bold head framed with a cascade of curly, jet-black hair and black Assyrian beard. He was forty-seven years old, in the prime of his strength, with an optimistic faith in the future of Belgium which was contagious. Later I was to learn more of him; to recognize in him one of the keenest intelligences in Belgium, a famous maritime lawyer, the legal-minded type of adroit politician, and a born leader of men. I learned to know him as a Fleming from a Flemish Province, a leader in the Flemish Movement, but as a cosmopolitan as well, and an admirable orator in five languages beside his native Flemish.[1]

We walked together into the Marriage Hall to open the first sitting of the Provincial Relief Committee. Down upon us from the walls smiled paintings of marriage ceremonies, Gaulish, Roman, Old Flemish, of the time of Rubens, and of the period of the French Revolution. It was the hall where the civil ceremony preceding all Antwerp marriages must take place, and where, if the persons be prominent, the Burgomaster himself gives the

[1] See Appendix VIII, page 337.

bride the famous white and red rose which is the emblem of Antwerp. But our assembly was neither gay nor festive. It was a confused vision of bearded gentlemen, grave as prophets, in long black coats and stiff collars, whom later I was to know as loyal co-workers and patriots. They were aldermen and notable citizens of the city, country burgomasters and provincial deputies; representatives of all three political parties—Catholic, Liberal, Socialist; of all three classes of society—noble, *bourgeois,* and proletarian; and of a variety of professions and callings. They served without pay.

Up to that time no American foodstuffs had been received or distributed in Antwerp.[1]

AMERICAN DELEGATE FOR ANTWERP

I left the meeting of the Committee and walked to 74 rue du Péage. On my way I stopped at the cathedral. Workmen were rapidly removing all trace of the damage caused by the bombardment; the stone rail had been repaired with cement, leaving a strange leprous patch, and

---

[1] Our first circular letter to the one hundred and sixty-five communes belonging to the province of Antwerp, bore date of December eleventh, the day of my arrival. It asked: 1. the total population of the commune; 2. financial resources; 3. immediate financial needs; 4. inventory of existing foodstuffs of every sort; 5. estimated daily necessities in foodstuffs,—the basis for flour being not more than 250 grams per day per person; 6. estimated daily necessities in fodder for the cattle; 7. if a building were ready to serve as communal food depot; 8. if medicine were needed in the commune. The answers to these inquiries were to be attested by the burgomasters and sealed with the communal seal.

Louis Franck

I was amused to see the stall formerly lettered "English Confessor," now covered with a card in German script bearing the words, "Field Preacher Confessor Doctor Braun."

Through seared and smashed byways I went to the familiar street, past the ruins of houses, their windows barred with wood or blocked with canvas, and on the door at number 74 I found Donald Thompson's name and address branded for posterity with indelible pencil.

There were two candles in the hallway, and a box of matches, just as we had left them. It was still and dark as a tomb. Down in the kitchen was the familiar clutter of bottles and pans; in the cyclone cellar where we had weathered the bombardment were the names of the four of us—Thompson, Weigle, de Meester, and me—just as they had been written for the eyes of our heirs on the night the shelling began. Upstairs in what had been my bedroom I found the pile of French books which had amused me so, and Ella Wheeler Wilcox's "Poems of Passion" lying safe on top of the heap. ... On the third floor was a mountain of plaster and I picked up half a pint of lead pellets in the midst of it. On the fourth floor in the *débris* of the walls were a broken couch, a smashed wardrobe, cracked mirrors, and torn chairs, beds and bed linen, all tumbled together by the explosion. The hole where the shell had entered was covered with canvas neatly nailed.

At the American Consulate where Donald Thompson photographed the battalions of Germans tramping along the rue Leys on October tenth, I met the kindly old Consul-General, Henry W. Diederich, and the Vice-Consul, Tuck Sherman. Thanks to them, all over Antwerp were signs, " under the protection of the American Consulate," which may have moderated German thoroughness and which certainly heartened the Belgians. Messrs. Diederich and Sherman granted me office space in the Consulate and after a day or two arranged with an insurance company in the suite below the Consular offices to give me space of my own. In the insurance offices a caretaker and two or three clerks dismally played at business, keeping the long hours of the ordinary Belgian business-day, dusting, sweeping, casting up accounts, and puzzling over cryptic anagrams which prophesied the Kaiser's death or the capture of Berlin. They were delighted to have me near them, for in their eyes I guaranteed protection from the Germans.

My furniture consisted of a modest table, a typewriter, and five chairs.

My duties as American delegate were necessarily ill-defined but capable of almost unlimited extension. Holding the power-of-attorney of the American Minister, I was in theory the owner of all supplies imported into the province of Antwerp by the Commission for Relief in Belgium from the time they reached me on the canal boats from Rotterdam up to the time of their consumption by the Belgians. The Commission's imports were consigned personally to Mr. Whitlock, so that as provincial delegate I acted as consignee for the province in which I served. Once at the wharves the contents of the boats were under my direction, and in theory this applied to the later steps,—to their transference to the docks or the Commission warehouses in Antwerp, Turnhout, Malines, and Tamise; to their transport thence by canals or light railways to the regional warehouses; then to the one hundred and sixty-five communes; and so to the million and more individual consumers. The Americans in Belgium were in honor bound to know what became of every item of supplies, for only on terms like these would Great Britain modify her blockade in favor of Belgium.

It was necessary, then, for the American delegate to be familiar in detail not only with the transportation and distribution of imports, but also with the condition and needs of every commune in his province, and to report on these matters regularly to the headquarters of the Commission for Relief in Belgium and to the American Minister.

The course of the war had abolished the independent, democratic life of the Belgian people. Out of the chaos had emerged the neutral Commission for Relief and the Belgian National Relief Committee pledged to extraordinary caution in handling supplies, so that at times the

American delegate could not help appearing as a sort of Oriental satrap. There were the usual routine problems of insurance, shipping, bills of lading, warehousing, and trans-shipping, the preparation of extensive reports, debits and credits, where the delegate's share tended to become more and more supervisory; but complaints and misunderstandings on the part of the German authorities, inadequate communal reports, or friction of one sort and another, complicated by the political disabilities under which our Belgian coadjutors labored, made it necessary for the delegate to be jack-of-all-trades and all things to all men. In a situation so critical as ours a small matter might easily develop into a crisis threatening the whole.[1]

The plan for the relief work required a highly centralized organization. Instead of the comparatively simple problem of feeding, the work developed, almost in spite of itself, into a comprehensive plan of national preservation; all under the drastic conditions imposed by modern warfare.[2]

Misery in the Campine

The first task was to secure reports from each commune on the amount of destitution, the condition of employment, the prevalence of sickness, the possibility of providing work for the workless, and the need of food;

---
[1] See Appendix IX, page 338.
[2] See Appendix X, page 339.

MISERY IN THE CAMPINE

then from these to reduce to a card-index formula the conditions in the province and ultimately the condition of every individual who required relief.

In a borrowed automobile and with passes which I requested from the German authorities, Messrs. François Franck, A. Palmans, and I visited the village of Boisschot on December sixteenth. The conditions we found there were fairly typical. The town was a bare oasis of wattled or brick cottages in the less prosperous part of the province, on the edge of what Belgians call the "Campine"—a country district, Oligocene in geological formation, supporting scrub evergreens and purple heather more readily than any other growing thing, and cut by a few slim watercourses lined with pollard willows.

Wayside shrines of Our Lady of Sorrows were decorated with fluttering strips of white paper, but otherwise one saw few signs of life. Almost every village through which we passed had been hammered with shells. Chickens and live-stock were rarities. Fear of the Germans was universal.

The Town House of Boisschot was a small, ugly building, not much superior to the old-fashioned Little Red School House of American pioneering days. The Burgomaster's office was a cold, bare rectangle, with sanded floors, a few thin chairs, and a long table piled with papers. A cheap lithograph of King Albert and Queen Elizabeth hung on the whitewashed walls of the room, and a framed proclamation printed in German,

Flemish, and French, signed by the commandant of the district.

Our borrowed Minerva limousine puffed stertorously at the door in the midst of a crowd of wooden-shoed villagers—the first automobile they had seen in four months; while inside I found myself vigorously shaken by the hand and on friendly terms with a big blond Burgomaster named Baron de Gruben and a thin, bearded spectre who was the communal secretary.

Our questionnaire was written in Flemish, but out of deference for my ignorance the questions were asked and answered in French.

"Monsieur le Bourgmestre le Baron de Gruben, it is a gentleman very excellent," whispered Messrs. Franck and Palmans before we began. "Most of our burgomasters ask for more than they have a right to. He is not so. He is a fine man, that Baron de Gruben. You must always be on your guard with the Belgian burgomaster, Monsieur le Délégué. The Belgian is a man who always complains—*qui toujours se plaint*. And he is stubborn, too. Always tell him what he must *not* do, then he will do what you wish. He is a man who goes in the door marked 'Exit' and comes out the door marked 'Entrance'!" . . .

Burgomaster? "Baron de Gruben, present," we wrote the answer.

Police or guard? "Monsieur Jean van Caster is about

to return. He has been replaced provisionally by a private guard."

Doctors? "Messieurs Dens and Goossens, present."

Instructors? "Two under-instructors are prisoners of war; one at Munster, the other at Sennewald, in Germany."

Clergy? "Monsieur le Curé and Monsieur le Vicaire were made prisoners with many curés of neighboring towns. Twenty priests are interned at Munster."

Notables? "The Germans arrested two hundred civilians and transported them to Germany. Since then one hundred have been released; those over forty-five or under sixteen years old. The others are interned at Paderborn in Westphalia. Among the prisoners in Germany are thirty fathers of families."

Population? "Three thousand three hundred, of whom nine hundred have to be supported by charity.

"The town was never bombarded and therefore no houses have been destroyed, but twice the whole population fled and twice the town was pillaged,—private houses and public buildings."

Is there work? "There is no work of any sort."

Is there a relief committee? "A small volunteer committee is struggling to give soup and bread."

What money is on hand? "The treasury has two thousand francs, to which three thousand francs is about to be added which the Burgomaster has secured as a loan from the *Comité d'Assistance* of Antwerp."

Maladies? "None."

What things are lacking? "The commune suffers especially for lack of flour, peas, beans, rice, bacon, herring, petroleum, and coal."

Monthly budget? "For the clergy, fifty francs; police, ninety francs; personnel, which includes the school, still open in spite of the terrible condition of the times, one thousand one hundred francs; electric light, one hundred francs; cost of communal administration, three hundred and ten francs; and cost of maintaining nine hundred persons in distress, five thousand four hundred and sixty francs. Total, seven thousand one hundred and ten francs."

"Now, Monsieur Burgomaster, you can persuade the communal officers to reduce their own salaries from patriotic motives?"

"Yes, I think so."

"They have done so in many communes already,—reduced their salaries one-half or one-third or two-thirds."

"That is excellent. They are true patriots!"

"And the Committee will allow you one thousand francs a month."

"Ah, messieurs, thank you! thank you! We shall do our best. But we must have clothes, too. We must have blankets and clothes—anything. Send us anything. We have been twice pillaged. We have nothing. We still eat, but we have no clothes."

MISERY IN THE CAMPINE

On our return we passed through Heyst op den Berg, and my heart thrilled at the climb out of the flat Belgian plain, although the Berg is only a little hill. One could imagine oneself for a moment on the roof of the world, after the incessant monotony of Flemish polders and Campine. From the Berg on a clear day one can see Brussels and the outlines of Antwerp. From that hill, too, the Germans had battered the forts of Lierre on their final thrust into Antwerp.

In Koningshoyckt, a town of three thousand inhabitants, ninety-eight houses had been completely destroyed, and twenty-seven partially destroyed. In so small a village the ruin was enormous. The church was annihilated, but a pert statue of Leopold First stood in the public square, unharmed by the shells.

The beautiful old town of Lierre had suffered dreadfully from bombardment. It had been mercilessly hammered and then burned, and lay in a confused pile, smashed, scorched, and outraged. But peasants and burghers were cleaning and piling bricks in the yawning window openings, and with the incorrigible art-instinct of the Belgians were arranging them in crosses and diamonds instead of plain, mathematical courses. A few frame shelters were appearing in the ruins. Typhoid raged. Fire, storm, and disease had been loosed on the unhappy people.

The town of Duffel, too, had suffered terribly. It lay in a country of kitchen gardens and numbered eight thousand people. It had been drowned out by the opening of the dykes and then shot to pieces. Three thousand one hundred and eighty persons were being fed at the public expense, and the town had literally nothing. Two hundred and fifty houses were completely demolished; all the others had suffered more or less. The commune got a few francs every day for relief work by taxing all, except Germans, who crossed the bridge over the little river Nèthe.

COMMUNICATIONS

Working with a people who had no telegraph, no telephone, no railways, no post office, and no freedom of movement, my first effort was to establish regular communications with Rotterdam and Brussels.

Commission telegrams, written in German and sent through the German Civil Government to our headquarters, took not less than a day and a half in transit. We could not use the military telephone.

To go from Antwerp to Brussels by train, a journey which by *rapide* in peace time requires about thirty-five minutes, now took two and a quarter hours. A pass for this journey cost three marks, and the railway tariff was twice as high as in peace time.[1] There were few trains and these were uncertain.

[1] An old Flemish peasant applied for a pass at Antwerp.
"How long is this pass to be good for?" growled the German clerk.
"How long are you Germans going to stay in Belgium, mynheer?" countered the peasant.

COMMUNICATIONS

A tugboat captain advertised cheap and rapid transportation from Brussels to Antwerp by way of the Scheldt and the canals, but this trip required more than half a day and seemed a curious reversion to the facilities of the 'forties. The only other way was to go by cart or on foot, and the Antwerp-Brussels highway was filled daily with nondescript carryalls or little jaunting carts drawn by pitiful horses, donkeys, and dingo dogs.

To go to Rotterdam was, of course, much more difficult.

Edward D. Curtis, courier of the Commission, or, as he preferred to be called, its "traveling secretary," was the sole reliable means of communication between the Brussels headquarters, Antwerp, and the Rotterdam office.

Curtis was twenty-four years old, a graduate of Harvard, class of 1914, but already a veteran in the service. Twice or even three times a week he motored from Brussels to Rotterdam, carrying the Legation mailbags for Mr. Whitlock, the Consular mail for Consul-General Henry W. Diederich, and the Commission mails for Brussels, Antwerp, Rotterdam, London, and New York; he imported new members of the Commission and their baggage; and at odd times of the day or night he turned up in every German *Kommandantur en route,* usually under arrest, but always imperturbable. He throve on silence and relished rules.

He drove in a long, low, rakish automobile, given him

by Mr. Ernest Solvay, of the famous Solvay Process Company, president of the National Committee; his sole companion a smart Belgian chauffeur. In mud-colored raincoat with thick fur padding, slouch hat, soft shirt, and high boots, Curtis turned up always unexpectedly at Antwerp, his admirably insolent face as nearly like a Japanese mask as he could make it, spattered with bits from the surface of Flemish and Dutch highways. His trips were not regularized until January. Then a system of Commission couriers was arranged for all Belgium, and Curtis went thrice each week from Brussels through Antwerp to Bergen op Zoom, where he met a special messenger who came and went from Rotterdam by train.

About ten days after my installation at Antwerp, Curtis came in covered with mud and smiles and informed me that three new Americans delegates and three Overland automobiles were on their way from Rotterdam to Brussels.

"One of those automobiles is mine; *n'est-ce pas?*" I asked, speaking the dialect of the Commission—a strange hodge-podge of English and French with an occasional spice of Flemish.

"Brussels say they intend to supply themselves, and afterwards the provinces."

"Tell them two automobiles are coming. This office has a motto,—it's 'Antwerp first!'"

An unexpected move by the German police made my

highwayman's task easy. The new delegates and their cars were arrested in Antwerp, and kept three hours at the *Kommandantur,* so that it was not difficult for me to confiscate the car I wanted. . . .

There is historical precedent for my conduct. Once on a time there lived a giant named Druon Antigon in a lowering castle where Antwerp now stands. Shipmasters who rowed up the Scheldt to trade with the ancient *Belgae,* or sailed down river to carry civilization and liqueurs to the painted Picts and the naked Frisians, were obliged to pay toll to the giant. If any refused, old Antigon cut off the customs-dodger's right hand and threw it into the Scheldt; and from this highhanded procedure on the part of the first *douanier,* the Flemish name, *Antwerpen,*—from *hand,* " hand "; and *werfen,* " to throw,"—is supposed to be derived.

The legend tells further of a young hero named Brabo, an ardent free-trader, it seems, who objected to Antigon's tariff restrictions, fought and conquered him, and then cut off the giant's hand and flung it into the river.

Hence my seizure of the automobile had excellent, if perilous, precedent. . . .

A few days after the automobile incident, Curtis brought me two aides, Bennett H. Branscomb and Oliver C. Carmichael, American Rhodes Scholars from Oxford University, slangily called " Rhodesters," who had volunteered their services for the work of Belgian relief. They were the first of a flood of young Americans eager to help the Commission and Belgium in any way they could.

A Visit from Hoover

The canals and light railways [1] are the life of Belgium. No other country has so perfect a transport system. In Belgium, as in Holland, one can reach almost every point by water. The valleys of the Scheldt and the Meuse spring like the sticks of a fan from an imaginary center at Rotterdam, and from these in turn in all directions radiate navigable waterways. The light railways, too, are models of their kind in cheapness and accessibility, but many light railways were blocked, or had suspended operations; much of their rolling-stock had been destroyed, or taken into Holland before the German advance. As for the canals, some of the dykes had been cut and were not yet repaired; bridges had been blown up for military reasons; barges had been sunk; and at important points the Belgians were not permitted to approach the canal embankments for fear they might attempt to damage the system to the detriment of the German armies.

On December seventeenth Captain Sunderland, U. S. A., attached to the American Legation in The Hague, visited me in Antwerp and brought an urgent request

[1] Narrow-gauge steam railways, called in French, *vicinaux*, or neighborhood railways.

A VISIT FROM HOOVER

from Captain J. F. Lucey at Rotterdam for information regarding the Belgian canals. The Rotterdam office had been in operation for eight weeks, yet in that time it had secured practically no information regarding the condition of the Belgian waterways. In sheer desperation Captain Lucey had dispatched canal-boats of flour, rice, peas, and beans, without knowing whether the canals were navigable or blocked.[1]

On a matter so vital as this I could get no data for more than a week, and then I secured it from a Dutch spy who was in cahoots with the Germans, and so was able to travel through the *Etappen* district and along the canals.

A stream of supplies glided by and was warehoused, milled, distributed, baked, and consumed. Lighters daily floated up the Scheldt bearing romantic names such as " Marie Germaine," " Louisa," " Ariel," " Deo Gloria," " Helene," " Rosalia," " Dorothea," " Maria Cecelia," " Josephina," " Madonna," " Maria Amelberga," " Fred-

---

[1] In the province of Antwerp the canals were clear, except at one point. Our distribution was dependent almost exclusively on the waterways—a troublesome state of affairs if these ways should freeze. The center of distribution was the city of Antwerp; subcenters—all reached by canals—were at Turnhout, Malines, and Tamise. Under Antwerp we established sixteen cantonal or regional centers; under Turnhout, six; under Malines, two; and under Tamise, two. From each of these centers, food was shipped once a week by wagon, light railway, or canal-boat. In every commune there was a distributing center, usually in the schoolhouse or Town House, where the supplies were weighed out in scales verified by the American delegate or his inspector, and delivered to rich and poor alike on presentation of a food-card.

erika." A system of control was necessary, so that we might report to Rotterdam and Brussels on the passage of lighters not destined for Antwerp, for sometimes we spent days patrolling the canals in search of a lighter which had dropped from sight almost as if swallowed by Father Scheldt himself.

I appealed to Brussels for another assistant, especially for this work, and they sent us W. W. Flint, another of the indispensable "Rhodesters." He set out on a river boat and disappeared for five days. Then he returned to Antwerp with a tale of great adventures, arrests, detentions, conferences, and agreements. He had done his work well. Lillo, the frontier post on the Scheldt, was obviously the spot for our control station to report on the passage of Commission lighters.

Fort Lillo was a high, old-fashioned earthwork on the Scheldt: a few trees, a few small Flemish houses in orderly rows, a single customs house overlooking the river —that was all. When we motored out to the customs post, our limousine completely blocked the narrow lane before the customs house and drew all the civil and military population about us. Several *Landsturm* soldiers strolled up, puffing away at their pipes and staring. The Belgian population ranged itself silently about the car. The dead silence, the dropped jaws, the fixed eyes of such crowds were always disconcerting to us, but our Belgian chauffeur seemed as indifferent as a good actor before a crowded house.

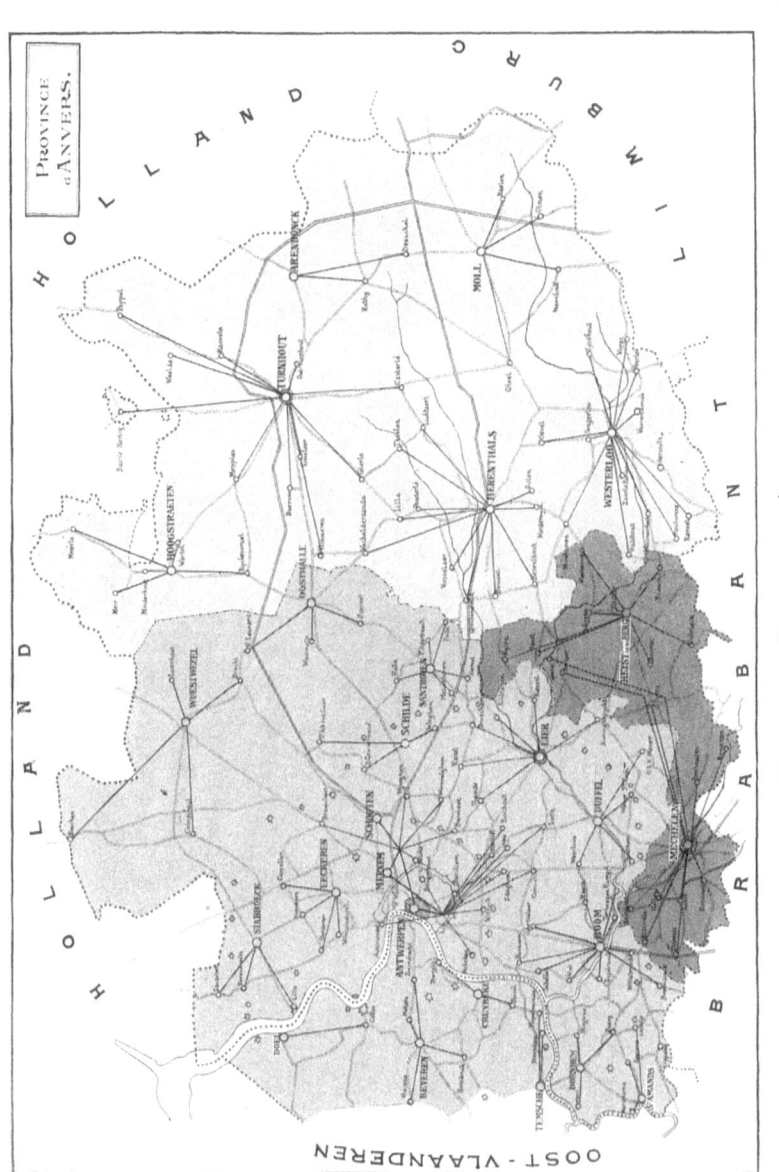

Map of the Province of Antwerp

Showing the three arrondissements of Antwerp, Malines, and Turnhout and the system of regional distribution.

Two Belgian customs officers in faded green uniforms and box caps came out, touched their foreheads, and bowed gravely. We explained our wants. Ah, we were the American Commission, then? They would take delight in giving us the names of all Commission lighters passing Lillo. Name and shipment numbers, then? Perhaps the German officer would telegraph this information to Mr. Hunt through the Civil Government at Antwerp, for the officer was obliging. They, the Belgians, would be most happy to furnish the information regularly. We, the Americans, were saving their lives. They were infinitely grateful.

We lifted our hats, shook hands all round, and motored to a small bar-room,—the office of the commandant. He was a lonely young under-officer who greeted us with obvious pleasure because we broke the monotony of his exile. We explained our business.

"Certainly, certainly," he said. "I am pleased to help. I will telephone every day what lighters pass Lillo. It is a pleasure to help."

A day or two before Christmas, 1914, Curtis arrived from Rotterdam and there preceded him into the Antwerp office a man in a raincoat and automobile cap, his serious, boyish face splashed with mud.

"Mr. Hoover," explained Curtis, by way of introduction.

It was the founder and Chairman of the Commission for Relief in Belgium.

My guest quietly took a chair in a dark corner and required no further attention from me, although I thought he listened carefully to the word Curtis brought me from Rotterdam, and to the messages I sent by him to Brussels.

"You deserve better quarters," he said as he was leaving.

"I have them already," I answered. "Mr. Edouard Bunge, vice-president of our Belgian Committee, has donated an excellent suite of offices in his bank for the Commission's work."

"Um. . . . Good-by," he said. . . .

That was my first encounter with Herbert Clark Hoover.

The Christmas Ship

One of the thrilling experiences of the first month's work was the coming of the "Christmas Ship,"—the steamer full of Christmas gifts presented by the children of America to the children of war-ridden Belgium. I was amazed to find that before the ship docked in Rotterdam the Belgian children knew all about it. By some occult means of communication, such as the Sudanese are reputed to employ, they had heard of the ship and understood its meaning. Saint Nicholas's day had brought them few presents. They were hungry for friendliness, and the thought of getting gifts from children across the sea meant unspeakable joy to them.

We planned to distribute the presents on Christmas Day, but difficulties arose. The German authorities decreed that every package should be opened in Rotterdam and every scrap of writing taken out before the presents were sent into Belgium. It was a tremendous task to search the gifts. Notes written by the American children to the Belgians were tucked away in all sorts of places: in the bottoms of bags of candy, in the backs of fairy books, in dolls, in pairs of shoes, in babies' dresses, —in every likely and unlikely spot which a child's imagination could think of as a convenient receptacle for writing. And all the charming, naïve little notes, painfully copied by childish hands, had to be removed before the presents could go forward.

It was too late to get them into Belgium by Christmas Day, but three big motor-boats made the attempt. One went to Brussels, one to Liége, and one came to Antwerp. It brought boxes of clothing, outfits for babies, blankets, caps, bonnets, cloaks, shoes of every description, babies' boots, candy fish, striped candy canes, chocolates, and mountains of nuts—nuts such as the Belgians had never seen in their lives before—pecans, hickory nuts, American walnuts, and peanuts galore.

In one of the boxes of peanuts was a note which had escaped the vigilance of the searchers at Rotterdam. It was from Caleb Moss, of Texarkana, and he wrote in perfect certainty that the Belgian child who got the peanuts could read what was so carefully spelled in painful English.

"I dug these peanuts myself for you," the letter ran. "Please write me that you got them and what the Germans did to you and all." . . .

There were scores of dolls, French bisques smiling pleasantly, pop-eyed rag dolls, old darky mammy dolls, and Santa Clauses; picture books, fairy books, and story books. One child had written in the cover of her book, "Father says I ought to send you my best picture book but I think that this one will do."

I remember six linsey-woolsey dresses of a sort worn only in the Kentucky and Tennessee mountains, pitifully ugly and cheap, but symbolizing as fine charity as anything among the gifts. And there were bunched ears of corn tied with twine, given by Americans as poor as the Belgians for whom they were intended. These things made American sympathy more real to me than all the rest. My countrymen had "given what they could."

As a direct result of these gifts, all Belgium learned the meaning of America's aid. Hitherto the people had known us officially through our Minister and through those of us who were beginning our service as delegates of the Commission for Relief in Belgium. The gifts made us and our country the personal givers of what Belgium was to eat and to wear through the months or years of war. Never after that was American help thought of in terms other than those of burning gratitude.

Replicas of the American flag were scattered among the Christmas gifts, and through them our flag became familiar to all Belgium. Its sensational and violent symbolism must have seemed strange in a land accustomed for the most part to tri-colors, vertically or horizontally striped, but the Belgians loved our flag. At first we bore it on all Commission automobiles, and our trips frequently caused delightful demonstrations. The children, especially, were sure to recognize the red-white-and-blue and to wave and cheer as we darted by, although I think there was a shade of disappointment when they first learned that "the Americans" were not red-skins, that they did not wear feathers in their hair, and that in many respects they resembled the familiar Belgian type of bifurcated human animal. Later they thought of Americans as only a little lower than the angels.

A beautiful letter of gratitude for the Christmas gifts was printed by the children of Antwerp to send to their American friends. The presses and even the type used, were made by the famous printer, Christopher Plantin, who lived in Antwerp three hundred and fifty years ago, and the impressions were struck off in the press-rooms of the Plantin-Moretus Museum, where Plantin printed and Rubens chatted with him at his work. The seal of the city of Antwerp, with the towers and roses and the severed hands of Druon Antigon, were set on the letter, together with the seal of Christopher Plantin and the round signatures of the children.

Belgian Gratitude

There followed lighter after lighter of gifts; food which meant to the Belgian people not only health and life, but sympathy and support; gifts which were touching evidence that their fate had not been forgotten in the free world beyond the lines of barbed-wire and bayonets. In the half year to come, all or part of the cargoes of one hundred and two ships was gift goods, and included in the number were entire gift-ships: five from Canada, three from the Rockefeller Foundation in New York, two from the New York Belgian Relief Fund, two from Philadelphia and the State of Pennsylvania, one from "the Northwestern Miller" group of Minneapolis,[1] and one from California. Publications such as the *Literary Digest* and *Christian Herald* of New York, solicited funds for the purchase of flour, Governors and Premiers issued appeals, and Belgian relief committees spontaneously organized in every state of the American Union, Hawaii, all parts of the United Kingdom, New South Wales, Canada, Victoria, India, New Zealand, Australia, Queensland, Tasmania, South Africa, the Argentine, China, Italy, Holland, and Spain.

[1] See Appendix XI, page 341.

Christmas MCMXIV
Belgian War Souvenir

With the cordial thanks of the poor children of Antwerp to their kind-hearted comrades of the United States for their nice Christmas presents.

René Van den Eynde,
Jozef Van Steen
Jan Struijf

Lodewyk Van der Wyngaert
Laurent De Waele.
Karel De Pooter

zullen U eeuwig gedenken
7e klas Jongensschool 23,
Antwerpen.

Antwerp

25 Dec. 1914.

Printed with the old original types of

Christophorus Plantinus
(1514-1589).

CHRISTMAS 1914
Souvenir made by the children of Antwerp to send to the children of America.

BELGIAN GRATITUDE

About one-half of the total contributions came from the United States.

A flood of Belgian acknowledgments greeted these gifts. The provincial offices of the Commission in Belgium were stacked with beautiful souvenirs for the American people. Silk banners, wrought metal boxes, leather work, a magnificent carpet woven on the famous looms at Westerloo and intended for the White House in Washington, lace souvenirs of great value and rare beauty, medallions symbolizing America's benevolent protection, picture post-cards, and etchings were among the gifts.

But the most touching and the most original souvenirs were made of American flour sacks. No one knows who first planned these gifts. They seemed to spring up spontaneously in all parts of Belgium as the simplest expression of the feelings of the people. To take the sacks, emptied of their precious flour, and turn them into souvenirs for the American donors was an inspiration, and some of the results have been very beautiful. Most of them are embroidered with designs in finest needlework, and lettered "Homage to America," "Thanks to America," "Out of Gratitude to America," "Grateful Belgium to Kind America," "To the Saviour of Belgium," or in simplest Flemish or French, "Thanks." One of them shows Lady Columbia with a Belgian baby in her lap and is inscribed, "The Protecting Mother of Belgium."

For to the Belgian people one thing seems very clear: that they would have starved without the intervention of America.

Their gratitude also is poured out to Canada, and to Great Britain as a whole. The Belgians are intensely loyal to their allies. Little British flags decorate many of the souvenirs, and in one of the naïve attempts to bracket Canada and the United States as benefactors of Belgium, a map has been drawn showing North America, which is lettered "the United States," and South America, which is lettered "Canada."

Charming gifts came to the delegates as unofficial representatives of the American people. On the morning of New Year's Day our butler presented us with a pot of beautiful cyclamen and made us a little speech explaining that the blossoms were not his gift only; "they are from all the Belgian people to *messieurs les américains.*"

There was a sacramental blessing in such gifts, and even when we laughed, as sometimes we did at the quaintness or the crudeness of some of the offerings, our laughter was never far from tears.

Some of the most touching remembrances came from children in all parts of the province. Every child in the town of Tamise, for example, wrote a letter to America and deposited it with me for transmission. All are in

Flemish, and the handwriting gives a fair indication of the age of the authors. This one is by a little boy about nine years old.

Good People of America:
If I had a flying machine I would fly to America to thank the brave people there. I haven't one, so I write a little letter, and I tell you that I shall pray very much for you and never forget you.
JOZEF SEGLERAS.

This is by a boy of ten:

To Our Friends in America:
How glad I am that I can thank you out of my whole heart, brave people of America, for all the things to eat and the warm clothing that you sent us, for without it we should certainly have died of hunger and cold. I want to come to America myself to thank all the brave people.
GERALD VAN LANDEGHEM.

This is by a still younger child:

Dear America:
I thank you because you sent great big boats over the great sea—eat-boats—rice, corn, bacon, stockings, clothing, and shoes. I know that you like the little Belgians, and I like you, too. ACHIEL MAES.
Saint Jozef School, Cauwerburg, Tamise.

The letters are always childishly specific. A little boy of ten or eleven writes:

Dear Americans:
It is war here. We have known hunger and need. We have been fugitives. But, thank God, America helped us

out of need by sending us clothing, beans, bacon, and bread. We thank America and the Americans also, and every day we pray Our Father for brave America.

ALFONS JANSSENS.

Here is another:

Brave People of America:
It is now war with us, and starvation has stood before the door. Our friends of America sent us meal, flour, bacon, and clothing, and we were freed from hunger and cold. Brave people of America, be therefore a thousand times thanked.

FRANS REYNIERS.

Letters from the little girls are equally charming and naïve. One of them runs:

Oh, dear Americans, I am still small. My words cannot tell you very well how I want to thank you, but, dear Americans, you must feel my heart.

I pray every day to the good God that He shall bless your lives and that He shall spare you from war, hunger, and all other horrors.

Take, then, loving and noble gentlemen, with my deepest feelings, the thanksgiving of my elder brothers and sisters.

'A thankful heart,
GERARDINA VAN DER VOORDT.

The next child is about twelve, and has decorated her letter with a very attractive border in the Belgian national colors. "*Ik ben de kleinste van ons huis,*" she writes, " *en kan de meeste boterhammen eten* "—

I am the littlest one in our house and can eat the most bread-and-butter, and now that our bread is made of such good flour I can hardly leave a piece of it alone. It is thanks to you that I can eat so well, for your flour is delicious, and in order to thank you I pray the Giver of All Good that He will bless you. Your faithful,
PHILOTHEE SPEELMAN.

Another little girl about ten years old writes:

I often saw Mother weep when we came downstairs in the morning, because she could not give us the bread we asked for, because there was no flour. But you have dried her tears with the good flour which you have sent.

"Drying tears with flour" may sound amusing, but Julia Soevenirs was expressing a very serious feeling.

The next letter, from Jennie Ketels, speaks of the method by which food imported by the Commission for Relief in Belgium is sold to those able to pay for it, the profit going to relieve the destitute.

It was so sad here. There was almost nothing more to eat, but dear America has come to our help. You sent us flour, rice, maize, and clothing, and in Tamise now there is also a little shop where one can buy things to eat at the usual prices, and that also is thanks to you, O good Americans. What would have become of our dear Belgian land without you!

The following refers to the same little shop:

Business lies all still here, and so Father is without work. And we should certainly have had to eat up the very last penny we had, if it were not that gracious America came to our help. Thanks, good gentlemen, for the shop opened here in Tamise, where we can buy our food at the usual prices. I shall pray the Lord that He will bless you.

Your thankful,

CAROLINE BUMMEGHEN.

The next letter is a charming tribute:

I have often heard a little girl friend of mine speak of an uncle who sent her many things from America, and I was jealous. But now I have more than one uncle, and they send me more than my friend's uncle did, for it is thanks to you, dear uncles, that I can have a good slice of bread every day.

MARIE MEERSMAN.

Suzanne de Cubber's letter is philosophical:

I have often heard people speak of great and rich America, but with my childish understanding I could not imagine that it was possible. Yet now that Mother tells us every day, 'This bread, this bacon comes from our friends in America,' I am overjoyed that your land is not only rich, but that its inhabitants are kind-hearted and lovingly disposed toward the tried Belgians.

There is more than a touch of Flemish humor in the next letter:

If you could see me now you would not know me, for I am dressed entirely in a little American suit of clothes. Oh, what a warm, solid suit it is!

And here is a letter intended for the President of the United States:

Highly Honored Mr. President:

Although I am still very young, I feel already that feeling of thankfulness which we as Belgians owe to you, highly honored Mr. President, because you have come to our help in these dreary times. Without your help there would certainly have been thousands of war victims, and so, noble sir, I pray that God will bless you and all the noble American people.

That is the wish of all the Belgian folk.

AUGUSTA VAN RAEMDONCK.

CARDINAL MERCIER'S PASTORAL LETTER

Belgium gave her word of honor to defend her independence. She has kept her word.

The other Powers had agreed to protect and to respect Belgian neutrality: Germany has broken her word; England has been faithful to it.

These are the facts . . .

I consider it an obligation of my pastoral charge to define to you your conscientious duties toward the Power which has invaded our soil, and which, for the moment, occupies the greater part of it.

This Power has no authority, and therefore in the depth of your heart you should render it neither esteem, nor attachment, nor respect.

The only legitimate power in Belgium is that which belongs to our King, to his Government, to the Representatives of the Nation. That alone is authority for us. That alone has a right to our heart's affection, and to our submission.

These are the words I read in a little green-bound booklet called "Patriotism and Endurance," sent me about Christmastime. Inside had been written in English in a firm, delicate hand: "To Mr. Edward Eyre Hunt, Cordial souvenir, ✠ D. J. Card. Mercier, Archbishop of Malines."

It was the famous New Year's pastoral. Its author is the bravest man in Belgium.[1]

The Cardinal-Archbishop is like a Degas painting, if Degas had pictured Cardinals instead of ballet-dancers. He receives in a tiny whitewashed room furnished with horsehair chairs, walnut-wood desk and table, and a small coal stove. On the wall is a beautiful little image of the Virgin, framed in glass. Through the windows one looks into a dead garden where shells have plunged and burst.

From the archiepiscopal closet one may wander through long white halls and cloisters, formerly open to wind and rain, I suspect, now closed and glassed from the elements by a less heroic race. One may see the *salon* which used to be a hall of state, where German shells have torn through the roof and burst, leaving jagged fragments in the tall mirrors, so that the glass is splintered like ice under the hammer and flings grotesque reflections and spars of light into the emptiness overhead. The dais with its crimson hangings drops in shreds; the hardwood floor is plowed and uprooted, and

[1] See Appendix XII, page 341.

CARDINAL MERCIER'S PASTORAL LETTER 237

carven cherubim smile placidly from the wreckage. In still another room huddle paintings of Archbishops of old: saints and politicians, ascetics, and men of the world, long forgotten now in spite of their imposing Louis Quatorze wigs; and among them the familiar faces of the Popes, Pius IX, Leo XIII, and Benedict XV.

The Cardinal seems preternaturally tall; six feet five, I think. His face, thin, scholarly, ascetic, with sparse, grayish-white hair above it, is bloodless, and his forehead so white that one feels one looks on the naked bone. His eyes are deep-set, the eyes of a man who sees a great deal. There is a pleasantly humorous look about the corners of the firm mouth, but the expression of his face in conversation is that of a man who knows what he thinks, measures what he says, and feels in advance the exact effect of every remark he makes and of every look he casts upon one. His black habit with the cardinal-red braid, the heavy gold chain about his neck, and the heavy gold cross at his breast, the wide violet sash and the black-skirted cassock—all serve to emphasize the old ivory whiteness and tooled artistry of the fine face above them.

There is something feminine in the Cardinal's face, a feminine deference and sympathy and comprehension perhaps, but the effect which he makes on a caller is the same as he makes on the world at large—that of a finely poised, keenly intelligent, yet very gentle Prince of the Church and shepherd of a nation.

The beginning of the war found the Catholic Party in Belgium vacillating. Two or three of its leaders in Parliament and at least one in the Cabinet counseled against resistance to the invaders. When the German armies overran eastern Belgium many priests ran away from their flocks. Now religion in certain classes in Belgium is hardly more than skin-deep, and the timid patriotism of some of the Catholic authorities might well have cost the Church its leadership if the Cardinal had not taken his firm stand. The pastoral letter was good politics and it was also a noble assertion of what was in every liberty-loving heart and in the Cardinal's most of all. In him conquered Belgium found a voice. She recovered her pride and something of her old buoyancy and resistance to the Germans became bolder. Belgium had re-discovered her leaders.

On New Year's Sunday, 1915, every priest at the mass read out the Cardinal's ringing challenge to the nation. German soldiers were in the churches, but by some mysterious means the letter had been distributed to the priests without a word of it reaching the ears of the authorities, and the astonished soldiers could only listen in open-mouthed amazement. The Governor-General appears to have been taken completely by surprise. But after the first mass orders came swiftly

DÉSIRÉ JOSEPH CARDINAL MERCIER

from headquarters prohibiting further readings and demanding that every copy of the letter be surrendered to the Germans. Soldiers forced their way into churches and rectories and extorted the letter from the priests at the bayonet's point; the readers were arrested for recalcitrance and haled to *Kommandanturs;* but in spite of these measures, copies of the letter were scattered abroad, and on the second Sunday, in churches in practically every city in Belgium, priests read out the Cardinal's sonorous words.

Meanwhile in Malines a dramatic struggle was on. The archiepiscopal printer, Mr. Charles Dessain, Burgomaster of Malines, was in England. His brother Francis, the acting Burgomaster, an Oxford graduate and a prominent lawyer, printed the letter in his brother's bookshop and had it delivered to the Cardinal's secretary. On New Year's night Mr. Francis Dessain was awakened at midnight by the rattle of gravel against his window. He looked out to see five muffled figures standing in the street below, one of whom asked him in French to come down and open the door. When the bolts had been slipped back in the big Flemish door and an opening appeared, wide enough for a man's arm, Mr. Dessain was suddenly seized, and a voice hissed: "Say a word and you will be shot!"

The door swung wide. In stepped a German in civilian clothes and four others in the uniform of officers. Behind them came a squad of soldiers with fixed bayonets, who stood guard in the halls and courtyard.

Mr. Dessain was taken into his library; there the officers and he sat down, and a long examination began. As it proceeded, Mr. Dessain's eye fell on a printed copy of the proscribed letter lying in plain view on his desk. He felt an insane desire to conceal that particular copy; an insane anxiety for fear the Germans would discover it.

At two o'clock in the morning the examination ended. Mr. Dessain was ordered to prison; but as he stood up to leave the room, he unobtrusively reached for the copy of the pastoral letter, covered it with another book, and then marched off with his mind relieved of a very heavy burden.

In the case of the Cardinal, of course, the problem for the Germans was much more difficult than in the case of the printer. They could not imprison a Prince of the Church for fear of its evil effect on German Catholic opinion; so Governor-General von Bissing adopted the easier plan of sending an emissary to the Cardinal to demand that the letter be suppressed *in toto,* on the ground that it would incite to rebellion. The Cardinal refused to recall the letter. The emissary then submitted a set of propositions for the Cardinal's signature, meanwhile intimating to His Eminence that the Governor-General wished him to remain in his palace for the present. This quasi-confinement lasted only for a day, but it was the foundation for sensational rumors of the Cardinal's imprisonment. Of course the Cardinal signed none of the papers submitted to him.

The net result of this manœuvering was, as I have said, that a few bold priests actually read the letter on two Sundays in succession, that every man, woman, and child in Belgium knew its contents, and that the outside world buzzed with conjectures.

The Cardinal was quickly released, and the printer, after three days in prison, was tried and sentenced to pay a fine of five hundred marks.

Patriotic Clocks

Patriotism was a cult. Symbols were marvelously dear.[1] Puzzles showing when the war would end or prognosticating the date of the Kaiser's death were reverenced to an extraordinary degree. Medallions of King Albert, Queen Elizabeth, Prince Leopold, Duke of Brabant, Prince Charles Theodore, Count of Flanders, and the curly-headed Princess, Marie José, were treasured like sacred relics. The Belgian flag was forbidden, but black-yellow-and-red cord was used in wrapping packages in the shops; blouses were made in the national colors; hats were trimmed with them; and little rosettes of them were worn in all patriotic buttonholes.

[1] See Appendix XII, page 341.

Even the hands of a man's watch were an indication of his patriotism. European Central time—the standard time of the German Empire—was forced upon Belgium by the military in order to avoid conflicts in time with Berlin. The Belgians ordinarily keep Greenwich time—a full hour earlier than German time—and they stubbornly refused to accept the new time, even with the weight of the law behind it. Clocks on church towers and in all public places were obliged to keep German time, or those responsible for their upkeep were fined. It was no excuse to plead that one's clock was an hour slow: the Germans knew better.

The thing was comic—especially if one remembers the time-worn charge against the Germans in 1870-'71: that they always stole French clocks! But it was not so funny when one began to mix engagements. We Americans kept Belgian time. If we arranged for a German to call at one and a Belgian to call at twelve, they arrived at exactly the same moment and glowered at each other in the ante-room. The cathedral clock in Antwerp furnishes time for the whole country-side. The clock was obliged to record German time, of course; but when the city fathers sent out notices of municipal meetings, they avoided the suggestion that the clock kept unpatriotic time by stating that the meeting would be, say, at two o'clock, "hour of the Tower." [1]

---

[1] There was an Antwerp family whose patriotism was under suspicion, because, it was rumored, they kept German time.

PATRIOTIC CLOCKS

Many clocks in public places were allowed to run down as a patriotic protest.

But simple matters like these constantly bordered on tragedy. On the night of December thirty-first at about eleven o'clock Belgian time there was an outbreak of shooting and yelling in the streets of Antwerp. People fled to their cellars as they had done during the bombardment three months before. The big guns in some of the forts began booming and close at hand in the town echoed volleys of musketry and isolated shots. It sounded as if rioting had broken out and as if the Germans were quelling it with tremendous uproar. Then down the streets rolled the sudden blare of a band and a mighty chorus of voices beginning " The Watch on the Rhine." . . . It was midnight, German time, and the soldiers were celebrating the birth of a new year.

The tenacious patriotism which had been awakened by the war is new in Belgian history. Local pride, local traditions, local dialects and manners had been developed at the expense of wider civic loyalties. The Belgian state was not in existence before 1830; but the Belgian commune has been in existence from time immemorial. It had survived under an almost endless trampling of foreign armies. Spaniard, Austrian, French- and Dutchman marched over it with the centuries. So that the commune, not the nation, was the Belgian fatherland.

But war, which translated their parochialism into

patriotism, stole from the people their new-found country and their King, set foreigners to rule over them, and thrust them impotently back again into their narrow communes. The pity of it can never be told: the shame of it, the broken pride, and the baffled longing. Ruined and embittered, they turned for consolation inward upon themselves, or to the Church.

One day, long after the event, there came a big, black-bordered announcement that the nineteen-year-old son of an Antwerp house had been killed at the Yser. Later still his body was brought home for burial through England and Holland—the only instance of the sort which I recall. One of my Belgian friends described the service.

"We are forbidden to have our flag, but a priest brought it and laid it over the coffin, and in that naked church, where we stood about him with our candles, it seemed a sacrament of all the body and blood of Belgium poured out in this war. I am not a believer, but I wept.

"At the last the organ played the 'Brabançonne.' It was heart-rending to hear our national anthem played so and at such a time. I knew abject despair at that moment, and there was not one there who did not weep, except him that was in the coffin."

Always on quiet nights, often in the daytime, we heard the guns. The hard pulse-beat of cannon along the Yser or on the North Sea filled all that one thought or did. Hope flew like wild winds over Belgium if the noise were unusually loud; but it was hope mingled with fear. The people of Antwerp often talked of what seemed to them an inevitable thing—the second bombardment of their city—when their rescuers, the British and French, rolled back the German armies and came pounding at the doors.

The wildest rumors seemed sane. Belgians could not write to the front. They got no word from their army and their loved ones, except such as spies and frontier-runners brought them and spread by word of mouth, or an occasional message dropped in a celluloid tube by an Allied aeroplane, so the words of most encouragement were spoken by the Yser guns.

"Did you hear the cannon last night, sir?" the 'longshoremen often asked me on my visits of inspection to the Commission docks and warehouses. "The Englishmen will be here in a month!" And every one turned to his work more joyfully.

ALARUMS AND EXCURSIONS

Only a common danger of appalling proportions could weld the Belgians into a nation. Other forces than local partiotism fought against national unity. Belgium had been divided to an extent which Americans can hardly credit. "The coming revolution" was in all men's minds and on most men's tongue. Before King Albert's face the Socialists had cried, "Hurrah for the republic!" Parliament and press were battlegrounds where fundamental political principles met and fought: Republicanism against Monarchy, Clericalism against Anti-Clericalism, Flemings against French-speaking Walloons, Socialism against Capitalism. Business, society, every department of life, was divided and subdivided into self-contained cliques. The bitterness of the struggle and the disunion were almost unbelievable.

And even in the midst of war men could not be expected to lay aside fundamental principles. Only an overwhelming calamity could arrest the internal struggle. Not until all—politicians, populace, clergy, republicans, and Clericals—found themselves confronted with the physical problem of mere existence, could they forget their quarrels. Before the necessity for food and clothing; before the naked, elemental needs of life, even primary principles went down.

But the process was not complete. Belgians still feared and distrusted their fellow Belgians. War exaggerated certain of their suspicions, instead of allaying them. In theory the Antwerp Relief Committee represented all classes and all interests, but some one group had to be in control. Monsignor Cleynhens, doyen of the Cathedral of Notre Dame, in his black cassock with purple facings, sat beside Common Counselor Delannoy, once a dock laborer, now a Socialist leader. Edouard Bunge, merchant prince; Senator Alfred Ryk-

ALARUMS AND EXCURSIONS 247

mans, lawyer, Clerical, conservative; Jean Della Faille, proprietor; Alfred Cools, the Socialist Controller of Antwerp (*Échevin des Finances*); Francis Dessain of Malines, Oxford graduate, lawyer, and athletic churchman who made Rugby football popular in Belgium; the great landed proprietor, young Count Charles de Mérode de Westerloo, whose ancestor had been offered the Belgian crown by the top-hatted revolutionaries who freed the land from William Fourth in 1830; octogenarian Dr. Victor Desguin, alderman of Antwerp and dean of Liberal politicians; Walter Blaess, representative of Lloyd's; Emmanuel Montens, member of the Permanent Deputation of the Provincial Council; Jakob Smits, artist, *genre* painter and etcher, with the temperament proper to his high calling,[1]—such men as these were members of the Committee presided over by the Liberal Deputy, Louis Franck.

Such a machine could not run smoothly from the start. There was a period of necessary readjustment and even of revolt, in which the rôle of the Americans was to fight for independence from political influence and for administrative unity.

At the first meeting of the Provincial Committee a list of proposed members, whose names of course meant nothing to me, was submitted and approved. The first circular letter to the communes contained a copy of this

[1] See Appendix XIV, page 342.

list. The nominees were notable citizens of the three arrondissements—Antwerp, Turnhout, and Malines.

A week later four gentlemen from the arrondissement of Turnhout came into my private office to protest against inclusion in the Antwerp provincial organization. They told me that they wished to deal with Brussels and not with Antwerp. They would be delighted to deal with me personally, or through the Brussels Committee; but they did not wish to deal through the Antwerp Committee.

At the second meeting the trouble came to a head. There was an exciting moment when all the Turnhout delegates were on their feet at once, speaking Flemish instead of French, as they usually did when much excited, protesting that they had never seen the circular addressed to the communes, an answer to which was required on the following day, and adding that they were appealing to Brussels for complete separation from Antwerp.

I protested vigorously against division. They patiently explained again that they would be delighted to deal directly with the kind Americans, but that they did not wish to deal with them through the Antwerp Committee. One of the gentlemen wept in the excess of his feelings, and choruses of recriminations, which I could not understand, were exchanged between the groups. When had Antwerp, rich and pious in the Middle Ages —now subject to tradesmen and freemasons—when had it been generous to Turnhout? Or when had Turnhout, rustic, old-fashioned, and Clerical, trusted the merchants of Antwerp?

I count it one of the miracles of our work that on this foundation we built a solid, durable relief organization. Turnhout had not yet received an ounce of American foodstuffs and had not fathomed the purpose of the American Commission. It looked on us as an association of benevolent grain-dealers, selling flour to a body of Antwerp business men, who, in turn, would resell it to the Turnhout delegation, of course at a profit to themselves!

I had not the least intention of permitting a division of the province. But the difficulties of communication were still so great that Brussels ratified the secession of Turnhout before my reports reached them. The division appealed to them as logical, since the agglomeration of Brussels was treated as a separate organism in the relief work; another committee having been created for the remainder of the province of Brabant. But more as a favor to me than for any sounder reason, Brussels consented to reverse this judgment, and on January first they sent me a fourth assistant, Richard Harvey Simpson, "Rhodester" like the rest, especially to take charge of the arrondissement of Turnhout.

The arrondissement of Malines was restive for much the same reasons as Turnhout. The city of Antwerp had shipped them no food from its stores, acting-

Burgomaster Francis Dessain had borrowed food from the German authorities much as the Jews "borrowed" from the Egyptians before the crossing of the Red Sea, and had even appropriated a lighter of commission grain *en route* to Brussels, rather than see his townspeople without bread. Conditions were most unsatisfactory, but for the sake of harmony the Malines delegates pledged themselves to work with the Antwerp organization, and Oliver C. Carmichael was assigned to duty as delegate for the arrondissement committee of Malines.

There was good reason for Antwerp to be in control. The city had been for a month and a half the capital of Belgium after the fall of Brussels. Cash, credit, and food were at her command. She was the sole support of the poorer communities about her, especially the seventy-seven communes lying inside the rings of fortifications. Up to the time that I became delegate for the fortress and province, every bit of relief which had been given out had been due to the generosity of the municipality of Antwerp, and had been apportioned through its municipal organizations.[1]

Relief, then, was a municipal matter from the point of view of the Antwerp authorities. These authorities were party men. They belonged to the Liberal or Socialist party. No Catholics were among them. With a fine spirit of patriotism they had shared with their neigh-

---

[1] See Appendix XV, page 343.

bor communes what food and money the municipality controlled, but they saw no reason why they should not claim credit for their generosity, or why they should surrender their favored position at the center of supplies when food began to come from America instead of the municipal warehouses.

INTERNAL CONFLICTS

As American delegate I was pledged to a different point of view.

The work we were inaugurating touched one million people and one hundred and sixty-five communes. It required a meticulous system of distribution and control, so that there should not be one ounce of waste or misuse. Business men with long experience in handling big business affairs alone could manage such a structure as we planned, so that it was obvious from the start that the Antwerp Provincial Relief Committee must be divorced from the Antwerp Town Hall and the group of party men who had so ably ministered to the wants lying close at hand.

The preliminaries to the divorce were comical. Branscomb, who was just nineteen, had been designated to act as delegate for the city. Almost his first duty was to remonstrate with the local committee regarding their reports. Standing in the midst of half the aldermen and politicians of the greatest of Flemish cities, Branscomb quietly but insistently drawled, " We cannot and we will not send another such report as this to Brussels. Reports must have our signature as American delegates. We will not give our signatures to tardy and un-businesslike reports."

The Controller of Antwerp whimsically remarked to one of his friends, "I have been accustomed to handle millions of francs every day, and now these young Americans come and ask me what became of such-and-such a bag of flour last week!"

None of us was out of his twenties. We were beardless boys in the assemblies of our elders, but young or old we were equal participators in a thrilling undertaking, and we intended to do our part. Our Belgian coworkers were as eager as we to have the work done expeditiously and well, but while they were volunteers, like ourselves, with temporary powers and prerogatives, they were not disinterested aliens but responsible citizens, and they dared not use their authority as if it were permanent. They could not make enemies and sleep sweetly o' nights into the bargain, so we borrowed their worries and took the initiative, even when it seemed rightly to belong to the Belgians and when a count of noses would have given us a Belgian majority.

In this as in other matters our neutrality was no negative thing. It was positive, aggressive, and self-confident.

In an open meeting of the Provincial Committee and with no previous notice to the members, I transferred the work of provisioning for the entire arrondissement of Antwerp from the Town Hall to a suite of rooms in the National Bank, kindly vacated for us by Mr. Ferdinand Carlier, the director of the bank, and I designated a new delegate, Thomas O. Connett, to serve as representative for the arrondissement of Antwerp, with instructions to arrange immediately for a census of all bread and flour consumers in the district. The transfer was completed in four days. Such precipitate action appalled some of our supporters in the Committee, but even at some cost to the pride and prestige of the local managers we were warmly backed, and those who first opposed learned later to applaud. "Time has shown that you were right and that we were wrong," was the generous summary of Mr. Louis Franck, months after our little revolution was accomplished.

Connett was a quiet, unobtrusive young Cambridge student, about twenty-two years old. In three weeks time, with the co-operation of Mr. Ferdinand Carlier and the staff of bank clerks, he had card-indexed the city of Antwerp and reorganized the system of control over food distributions with a saving of about one-fifth of the supplies.

The work of the Commission for Relief in Belgium and the National Relief Committee brought together in a community like Antwerp groups which had never known each other except as the most bitter rivals. This was often called to my attention. It gave me, as time went on and as I saw more deeply into the situation than I could possibly do at the beginning, a chance to understand and to admire the splendid spirit of practically all who worked with us. It was too much to expect men to give up at a stroke the animosities and conflicts of years. Politics was played under our very noses. But, perhaps for the first time in Belgium, there was a definite feeling of the pettiness of politics in the face of national calamity. The best men in every part of the province slaved at the work of relief. Nearly three thousand served on our communal committees in Antwerp, and by the simple rule that all parties and cliques should be actively represented, the Commission and the National Relief Committee managed to bring together and to keep together representatives of the best in all.

Thus the Turnhout revolt was put down without bloodshed, and the gentlemen of the Turnhout arrondissement committee were soon among the most loyal of our coadjutors; the arrondissement of Malines worked splendidly, under the leadership of Cardinal Mercier and Messrs. Francis Dessain and Dr. Paul Lamborelle; the arrondissement of Antwerp was reorganized and galvanized into activity, and, for the Commission, each arrondissement was represented by one or more American delegates.[1]

[1] See Appendix XVI, page 344, and Appendix XVII, page 345.

The Waesland

Brussels now added to our charge a part of the province of East Flanders, called in Flemish *Waesland*, and in French *le pay de Waes*. It was an arrondissement lying on the left bank of the Scheldt northeast of Ghent. Seventy years ago it was a tract of sandy moorland; just before the war it was one of the most productive and most highly cultivated regions in Belgium with an agricultural population of more than five hundred to the square mile. Its capital, Saint Nicolas, had a population of more than thirty-five thousand.

This teritory, belonging to the Provincial Committee at Ghent, was easy of access from Antwerp, but was a burden to the American delegates in Ghent, since their entire attention was directed toward the needy regions nearer the fighting-lines. I offered to assume charge of the Waesland for the Provincial Committee of East Flanders, but without adding it to the administration of the Belgian Committee of Antwerp. There was an excellent mill at Tamise; shipments from Rotterdam could go directly to Tamise, and from there be forwarded by light railway or wagon to Saint Nicolas.

This arrangement our Brussels office and the National Committee ratified, and a fifth delegate to the Antwerp staff, W. W. Stratton—W. W. Flint had returned to Oxford—came to take charge of the Waesland work.

Stratton was a young "Rhodester" from the State of Utah; tirelessly energetic and intelligent.

The Waesland brought with it peculiar difficulties, since it lay in a part of Belgium outside the control of Governor-General von Bissing. It required special passes for travel, special rules for administration, and sometimes special supplies.

The Waesland also brought special thrills. Riding to Ghent from Antwerp was almost as exciting as the famous ride from Ghent to Aix which Browning imagined and sung. Once it brought me the dubious honor of the German "goose-step."

I fancy I am the only civilian, neutral or belligerent, for whom the "goose-step" has been done since the war began. It was a sadly misplaced parade-march. I was returning from Ghent to Antwerp in a closed limousine when an open automobile full of German officers cut across our bows at the outskirts of a Waesland town called Lokeren. My automobile had created a stir in the *Etappen-Inspection,* because it was the only car permitted to a civilian, with the single exception of the car belonging to the American Consul-General and Vice-Consul in Ghent. The officers stared at me in astonishment as they passed. Their car then rolled along about fifty feet ahead, when suddenly up the street appeared a detachment of troops. Far away I heard a gruff, "*Auf!*" as the soldiers came face to face with the car full of officers, and at the command all the troops began the "goose-step," vigorously smacking the cobble-stones as they strode past the car.

Then the officer in command of the detachment caught sight of my car. "A limousine following a large car filled with officers!" he must have thought. "The Kaiser or the Crown Prince, *nicht?*" There came a second "*AUF! ! !*" considerably louder than the first, and the whole company paraded by, with stiff necks, heads at right angles, and the pavement volleying like a storm.

In Ghent, as in Antwerp, few young men were to be seen. Many of those who had stayed until the city was occupied by the Germans had later fled over the frontier, afraid lest they should be impressed into the army and sent to fight the Russians. No part of the city had been harmed; it had never been bombarded, or even besieged, and this in part was due to Burgomaster Braun.

The Burgomaster of Ghent is the son of a German school-teacher, but a thoroughgoing Belgian. When the invaders drew near he marched out in medieval fashion to meet them, and addressed the German general at the head of his troops.

"General," he said, speaking deliberately in French, "I do not come to you, as formerly the Burgomaster of Ghent came to the Emperor Charles Fifth, clad only in a shirt and with a rope about my neck! No, General, I come before you as a Belgian patriot." And the general spared him and his city.

Most of us have read many times in Belgian history of citizens compelled to meet their conquerors, clad only in their shirts and with a halter about their necks. "Only in their shirts" sounds immodest, until you see and wear a Belgian shirt. The garment is especially designed to meet the needs of just such historical occasions as the surrender of Ghent to the Emperor Charles. It has, even today, long skirts which cover everything almost as far down as the ankles, in spite of a tentative slit effect which crawls perhaps as high as the knees. You would feel no hesitation at being presented at court or in conducting divine service in such a modest dress. Nevertheless we Americans sawed off the skirts with knives and scissors, until the happy day when Simpson discovered Leyendecker shirts and Arrow collars in a shop on the Rempart Kipdorp.

A Belgian Co-operative

By February first, the operations of the Commission and the National Relief Committee had grown enormously. Arrivals from Rotterdam amounted to about eight thousand tons a month.[1] If one figures that each province should have local supplies for at least fifteen days in stock or *en route,* this means three thousand to twenty thousand tons of merchandise, which, at an average price of four hundred francs a ton, totals from one million to eight million francs. Thus these sums were im-

---

[1] See Appendix XVIII, page 345.

mobilized, and the National Committee bore the expense. Such a burden had to be adjusted. The financial guarantees covering merchandise for the province of Antwerp had at first been assumed by the city, but that was at the very beginning when arrivals were small. The provinces of Hainaut, Luxembourg, Liége, Namur, East Flanders, and Limbourg, not having city funds available, had formed co-operative societies to fund the work of the Provincial Committees. The National Committee insisted that Antwerp do the same.

Capital was desirable from several points of view. Some of the provinces had stocks of agricultural produce, such as potatoes, which were much needed in other parts of the country. Antwerp possessed certain stores which the Germans might be persuaded to release to the relief committees for Belgian consumption, and for these inter-provincial trades capital was required. The Committees were obliged, also, to buy in the open market salt, fuel, and other things not imported by the Commission for Relief in Belgium.[1]

The Provincial Committee decided to transform its provisioning department into a co-operative society with a minimum capital of twelve million francs.[2]

The subscribers to the new co-operative were the city of Antwerp, the province of Antwerp, and forty-five banks, commercial houses, or individual groups of sub-

[1] See Appendix XIX, page 347.
[2] See Appendix XX, page 347.

scribers. The co-operative had for its principal object "the feeding of the civil population of the province of Antwerp by purchase and sale of cereals, of foodstuffs, and generally of all things necessary or useful to human life.

"It has also for its purpose the feeding of the livestock of the province of Antwerp by the purchase and sale of grain, oil-cakes, and other forage, and generally of all things necessary and useful to animal life."

And included in its charter were the following provisions:

"It shall have a life of five years from the present date, but it may be dissolved before that time by a general assembly of a majority of its associates, but only after the conclusion of peace. A member is not permitted to withdraw before the dissolution of the co-operative. Of the net profits, after the constitution of a reserve, which the council shall determine, there shall be set aside an annual interest of three per cent on the capital to the profit of the associates, and the balance . . . shall be credited to the benevolent department of the Provincial Relief Committee of the province of Antwerp."[1]

Among the individual subscribers to this excellent organization was Cardinal Mercier, whose power of at-

---

[1] Belgian law requires that co-operative societies shall have a capital, shall pay a dividend, and shall be constituted for a limited period of years, not exceeding thirty, with the power, however, of renewal.

torney I held and whom I represented in the articles of incorporation.

The executive committee of the co-operative acted as executive committee of the provisioning department of the Provincial Committee, and they and their staff of clerks were housed in offices adjoining those of the Commission delegates.

By the creation of the co-operative society we saw our labors at provincial headquarters safe on the highway to success. A purely commercial management replaced the quasi-political organization of the earlier days, and the commercial department was definitely separated from the Town Hall and lodged with us in a new bank building at 2 Marché aux Grains, finished just before the outbreak of the war, and given rent-free to the Commission and the Provincial Committee by Mr. Edouard Bunge. We now desired that the benevolent department of the Provincial Committee be housed with us, and after some negotiations, it, too, was transferred from the Town Hall and placed in offices adjacent to ours.

The days of disunion and divided efforts thus passed away from Antwerp. The very name of the bank where we were housed was a good omen for the future. It was "*la banque de l'Union anversoise*"—The Bank of the Union of Antwerp.

Breathing Spells

The conditions of war soon grow to seem normal, but there is an emotional and physical strain about them which eats at one's heart. We Americans were very busy and we were happy. On the Antwerp staff—from time to time the members shifted, some going back to Oxford or to America, others to stations in other parts of Belgium or northern France—were B. H. Branscomb, O. C. Carmichael, R. H. Simpson, W. W. Flint, W. W. Stratton, T. O. Connett, Gardner Richardson, G. H. Stockton, and J. B. Van Schaick. Our normal number was five. We lived in a quiet Antwerp mansion, given us by our friend, Mr. Edouard Bunge, vice-president of the Provincial Committee. From the windows we overlooked a little park, and the capped, thoughtful statue of the artist Quinten Metseys. The lintel of our doorway was gashed, where an incendiary shell, striking in the street, had ricochetted and burst. Until late in the spring, when a special censorship for the Commission members was arranged with the Germans, we received no letters or newspapers from any one outside of Belgium. We had no new books. We knew little about the progress of the war. Home was almost a myth.

We patrolled the province in our automobiles; attended committee meetings—there were one hundred and seventy of these meetings each week, so our range of choice was large—; carried on extensive correspondence

EDOUARD BUNGE

in four languages; compiled exhaustive reports on official matters, and held the scales of justice as level as we could in a country which reeled and slipped in the bloody path of war.

Breathing spells were not many, and we sometimes longed for escape from Belgium as a convict longs to break prison. At last Mr. Hoover arranged a series of vacations for delegates, because the men could not stay long in the work and remain well in body and spirit.

Crossing the border to Holland was like a spiritual experience. The sudden sense of freedom was as strange and real as mountain air after a long stay in the city, and one's heart sang like a lark, merely to be quit of Belgium. On my first visit to Holland a crowd of Dutch children in a frontier village screamed at the motor-car and flung their caps under it, as children do the world over, except in Belgium. It was a bitter reminder of the repression and fear in the little land behind me; a fear and repression which affected even the casual visitor.

For we had visitors in Antwerp—journalists and others—but these visitors invariably hurried over the border at the first opportunity. We laughed about it, but we understood. Belgium was like a military prison and an asylum for the insane, rolled into one. Always, just under the surface of life, one felt the tearless, voiceless, tragic resistance of an unconquerable people.

Yet the *camaraderie* of the Commission supplied many lacks. When we spent the night in Brussels, Amos D. Johnson's house at 12 Galérie de Waterloo roared with our fun and the recitation of each others' Odysseys: how Bowdin and Gaylor refused to salute the German colonel at Longwy and how the colonel almost died of apoplexy in consequence; how Robinson Smith, translator of *Don Quixote,* gently but firmly refused a gold watch tendered him by the Provincial Committee of Hainaut, until the Committee had adopted his scheme of bread *locaux communaux;* how Carstairs was soon to marry a Belgian girl, and how other delegates were suspected of being matrimonially minded; how Curtis cursed the German sentry, never dreaming he knew English, and was answered in perfect Bostonese, "Same to you, old fellow!"; how Señor Bullé burst into inextinguishable laughter at Hugh Gibson's telling of the soda-fountain joke; how somebody tried to ram a Zeppelin shed, and should have been shot in consequence; of Sperry's *bon mot,* "There isn't one of these foreign countries, but what, if you live in it long enough, it'll ' get your goat ' "; of one of our fellow-citizens who said to Cardinal Mercier, "You're a Catholic, ain't you? . . . Well, I'm a Presbyterian myself; but I ain't got no prejudices"; of tugs and lighters, calories, *manquants, bâches, affiches,* rations, *bateliers, connaissements, excédants, chemins de fer vicinaux,* francs, marks, pounds sterling, and florins, the competence or incompetence of our respective chauffeurs and automobiles, and the greatness of Hoover.

It was a time of joy and sorrow. Isolated and brokenhearted, the Belgians were starving for sympathy as well as for food. There was something almost ritualistic in the reiteration of their gratitude. Never once were they a nation of beggars receiving charity; they were self-respecting fellow-beings receiving merited help from friends. There was no mendicant whine in the words, "You have saved our lives. Without you, what would have become of us and our poor Belgium?" They translated our flour and beans and bacon into brotherhood, human solidarity, and mutual helpfulness.

These were the compensations. But the strain of the work endured. I used to go to the magnificent old Premonstratensian Abbey of Tongerloo to try to forget everyday affairs. The avenues of venerable linden trees, the gaunt halls, the white-gowned canons and gray-gowned acolytes and novices, the sanctity and repose of the place, were irresistibly soothing. But I went to Tongerloo really to see Father Pat—another name for Canon Patrick McGuire—a wilderness of soft white beard with twinkling Irish eyes above it, nature's tonsure, and a smile like a saint's. Nine years Father Pat had spent on a mission in the Belgian Congo. "But you get nervous there," he said. "It's terrible nervous work, keeping all the blackies married to their own wives. You get them all straightened out, married off one by one, and then your boys go off with other boys' wives, and you have it all to do over again!

"Now we are here and you are here, working together for Belgium. God's blessing on America for this great work," he said, with the instinctive piety one met with so often in Belgium. "It would be a delight to the Americans to go round the little villages here about Tongerloo, and see every day how every child has his little bowl of soup and a little bit of bread, and no sickness, no starvation—not yet, at any rate. If only you can keep it up; if only you can work, work, work until the war is over! A bowl of soup and a bit of bread, and they'll all be alive when King Albert comes home."

A pleasant feeling of the transitory nature of war always came over me in Tongerloo. When the monks spoke of war they usually referred to the French Revolution, because in the Revolution their monastery had been burned by the iconoclasts and the whole order had been exiled. In August, 1914, the Belgian Prince de Ligne was shot to death near Tongerloo in an armored motorcar; Norbertian monks had been heroic helpers when the villages in their neighborhood were sacked or burned; but their minds lived in great leaps of time, in centuries instead of years, and one shared their immortality when one stopped in the cloisters of Tongerloo and Averbode.

BREATHING SPELLS

It would be too long, though all too short a story, to tell of the hospitality and the idyllic hours at Hoogboom, Cappellen, Calixberghe, Donck, Tongerloo, Averbode, Malines, Saint Leonarts, Tamise, and Braeschat, and the friends who opened their houses and hearts to "the Americans." Work pressed constantly to be done. The war could hardly be forgotten for a moment. The thunder of the guns was always in our ears.

One night at Hoogboom I ran out of the *château* for a lonely, happy, night walk. The cool spring air was marvelously clear and the new beech leaves were like lattice-work against the blue-black sky. Rhododendrons and azaleas were in blossom, hidden in the dusk like tropical birds. The thrilling smells of turned earth and young growing things were in my nostrils. A lake behind the castle lay mirror-still, and I stopped beside it, listening to the guns—the everlasting guns.

Seventy-five miles away, along the Yser, in the spring dusk, men were killing and being killed. Each explosion could be heard: a toneless stab in one's head, not like a sound, but like a wound; a thrust that twisted and tortured into one's consciousness and could not be forgotten.

But from across the lake, from the depths of a little wood came a new sound. Cannon-thunder was a commonplace to us. If nights were quiet we heard it even in the heart of a city like Antwerp; we heard it every Sunday in the country. The new sound was a bird voice. The first nightingale of the year had begun to sing, clamorous and violent and glad. It rioted in music, and then at last the song sank gurgling into silence.

And again came the remorseless drumming of the Yser guns.

CHAPTER VI
THE BELGIAN NATIONAL COMMITTEE

A Great Financier

THE weekly meeting of the members of the National Relief Committee are held in Brussels in a beautiful parlor belonging to the *Société Générale de Belgique pour favoriser l'industrie nationale,* at number 3 Montagne du Parc—a parlor all cream and gold, with an immense glass candelabrum hanging from the ceiling. Below is a T-shaped table covered with green baize. The baize is old and gray, and looks as if it might have a history. Tall, musical rosewood clocks stand on either side of the wide doors. There are large mirrors at the ends of the room, and white marble busts of King Albert and Queen Elizabeth coolly watch the proceedings. On the walls hang paintings of the two former Belgian kings: Leopold First in coronation dress; old Leopold Second in general's uniform with a double tier of orders showing under his white beard.

There is a suggestion of the French Revolutionary period about the room. It is decorated in the style of the Empire, but one feels that *avatars* of *sans-*

culottes may lurk behind the upholstered chairs, and that one breathes an atmosphere of conspiracy and subterranean activity.

The members gather every Thursday. They are the notable citizens of Belgium. With one or two exceptions there are no young men, and graybeards and bald pates are greatly in the majority.

The meetings bring together a strange mixture of classes and physiognomies. Grouped about the long green table are Paul van Hoegaerden, the vigorous, vociferous president of the Liége Provincial Committee, with a trick of pulling at his collar as if its tightness impeded the flow of his harsh, metallic words; his able son Jacques, secretary of the Liége Committee, one of the few younger men in the National Committee; statuesque Baron Albert d'Huart, president of the Namur Committee; Fulgence Masson, vice-president of the Hainaut Committee, wise in counsel, quick in action, his round face humorous as a clown's; Louis Franck, president of the Antwerp Committee, like an etching by Félicien Rops, with black Assyrian beard and sparse hair, piercing eye and clean profile, always smiling his enigmatic, optimistic smile; attenuated Count Jean de Mérode, Grand Marshal of King Albert's Court, vice-president of the Provincial Committee of Brabant; gigantic Constant Heynderyckx, alderman of Ghent; small, pliant Jean de Hemptinne, also of Ghent; Georges Eeckhout, professor at Ghent University; the dark, foreign, languid figure of Raoul

A GREAT FINANCIER

Warocqué, Burgomaster of Morlanwelz, who lives at Mariemont with kangaroos and Buddhas; Emmanuel Janssen, head of the benevolent department for the whole country, gently smiling on all; modest Louis Solvay; the Michel Angelo profile of Michel Levie, president of the light railways of Belgium (*la Société Nationale des Chemins de fer vicinaux*); Senator Emmanuel Tibbaut, head of the agricultural department; quiet, efficient Chevalier de Wouters d'Oplinter; and executive secretary F. van Brée, swarthy as the pirate Black Beard.[1]

Then there enters the crowded room the burly headed, heavy-set chairman of the Committee, Mr. Émile Francqui. He seats himself, raps on the table for quiet, and without waiting for it, begins to chant the order of the day, his heavy Bismarckian head sunk forward, his voice running like a millrace.

"What time is it?" a Belgian friend asked Mr. Francqui near the end of an important business conference.

"Half-past three."

"Francqui, let me see your watch!" . . .

"I knew," the friend explained, laughing, "that if Francqui were getting the better of me he would want to continue the discussion, so he would put the time about a quarter of an hour ahead. If he thought I was

[1] See Apendix XXI, page 348.

getting the better of him, he would have told me it was half an hour later. So I asked to see his watch." . . .

Mr. Francqui is a type familiar to Americans: a big-business man in the prime of life, self-made, brusque, *bourgeois,* sometimes intolerably rude, but always efficient, and the man of the hour in Belgian financial affairs. He resembles an American trust magnate, with more than a spice of Gallic salt in his composition. He has no small ambitions, no cheap ideas of glory, and no sentimentality or cant. As director of the *Société Générale de Belgique* —a great banking institution, founded in 1822 with an original capital of fifty million francs—he is one of the foremost financial figures in Belgium, and his share in the inauguration of the work of the Commission and the National Relief Committee has placed in his hands the intricate operations of financing the Belgian committees. In the composition of the great financial groups which are the backbone of the National Committee, are Mr. Jean Jadot, governor of the *Société Générale,* vice-president of the National Committee, Mr. L. van der Rest, vice-governor of the National Bank of Belgium and vice-president of the Committee, and Mr. Ernest Solvay, president of the famous Solvay Process Company and president of the Committee; but to Mr. Francqui has been left the active charge of the work of erecting a financial substructure for the whole organization of relief.

Great financiers are usually dictators, and Mr. Francqui is no exception to the rule. But the situation seems to call for a dictator. The weekly meetings of the National Committee are stage-plays purely. No Germans are present, but the sense of oppression is always there, and to break it the assembly seems to take on an attitude of mock-seriousness and to shoulder its deliberations lightly.

So Mr. Francqui does his real work alone. The order of the day which he reads at each meeting so swiftly and so humorously, consists of information from the Commission for Relief in Belgium, instructions to the Provincial Committees, notifications of rules imposed through the Minister-patrons by the German authorities, arrivals in Rotterdam and shipments *en route* to the provinces, subsidies allowed to the various charitable departments of the committees, a financial statement for the week, and a report and instructions from the agricultural department. But the real work goes on behind the scenes, and the committeemen are not sorry to have it so.

Hard Cash

Belgian finance presents complex problems. A moratorium was declared at the start of the war. The value of notes held by the National Bank and affected by the moratorium reached one thousand million francs. As late as April first, 1915, only about one-fourth of this sum, or two hundred and fifty million francs, had been paid, and these by the more solvent or less affected debtors, among whom were many Belgian banks.

On top of all this internal insolvency, the Germans on December tenth levied on Belgium a contribution of war of forty million francs per month.[1]

At the outbreak of the war Belgian currency had almost disappeared. Many communes were so harassed that they issued emergency currency of their own, good only in the communal limits. At least seventy per cent of the important towns and villages of Belgium and northern France were forced to this expedient, and struck off on the municipal printing-presses "shin-plaster" bills for one franc, fifty centimes, twenty-five centimes, or ten centimes; and at least one of them, the commune of Saint Nicolas in East Flanders, struck a paper bill for five centimes—about one cent in American money. These bills had nothing but the credit of the municipality to back them, and had no value outside of the commune issuing them. Three months after the end of the war, or on January first, 1915, they were payable at the municipal till. Of course they were valuable only for small retail trade.

Such currency as reappeared after recovery from the first shock of terror at the beginning of the war, disappeared again as the Germans overran Belgium. Silver and small nickel coins, along with the paper issued by the National Bank, were hidden away in safe places;

[1] See Appendix XXII, page 349.

gold had been sent for safe keeping into Holland or England; and the National Bank of Belgium was thus in no position to carry on its normal function of regulating the currency of the country, even if the Germans had been willing to allow it to do so. As it was, the military authorities took from the bank its privilege of issuing paper money, but in other respects interfered with the National Bank no more than with private institutions.

Meanwhile German paper and nickel coins—five mark, two mark, one mark bills, and pfennigs—began to circulate in Belgium, and the tradespeople were compelled by military proclamations to accept the money of the invaders at a fixed ratio to the Belgian franc.

To meet the extraordinary situation of the national currency, the *Société Générale* in March, 1915, six months after the outbreak of war, and with the sanction of the German authorities, resorted to what is probably an unparalleled financial device. It issued a paper currency, backed solely by its private credit and the credit of its associated banks, redeemable three months after peace is signed by an equivalent bill of the Belgian National Bank; and this extraordinary currency was successfully circulated and bears a definite exchange ratio to the German mark and the Belgian franc formerly issued by the National Bank.[1]

[1] To understand the situation one may imagine the United States of America blockaded on both oceans, with a Mexican army in charge of our financial affairs. In such a case, since the invaders

The earlier bills of the *Société Générale,* issued in March, 1915, bore the portrait of Queen Caroline, the wife of Leopold First. Later issues of bills bore the head of Rubens, and it was commonly believed in Belgium that this was because the Germans objected to the picture of a Belgian queen, even if that queen had been dead for half a century.

With these financial steps the National Relief Committee had nothing to do, but the steps themselves were very important in the relief work. In addition to the normal banking facilities, a considerable number of special "loan banks" had been organized at the outbreak of war. These banks now began making chattel loans, lending small sums, payable in the currency of the *Société Générale,* on the security of personal property. At the same time, through the operations of the charitable department of the Belgian National Committee, the flow of currency was aided by the payment of unemployment benefits, old age pensions, and wages for work provided by municipalities.

Large sums were borrowed from the *Société Générale* by the nine provinces, the loans being secured by notes backed by the credit of the province, as well as by the credit of the wealthier citizens. A singular commentary

could not provide a currency for us, the Standard Oil Company or some other big institution might take over the issuance of bills and coin, pledging for their redemption its own financial credit.

on the whole extraordinary situation is found in the fact that part, at least, of the eight million dollars a month which Germany has exacted from Belgium as a war contribution has been paid in the currency of the *Société Générale*.[1]

[1] See Appendix XXIII, page 349.

OMHEINING
VAN
ANTWERPEN

INTERCOMMUNALE COMMISSIE
KABINET
des
VOORZITTERS

Antwerp 4th of July 1915

To Edward Eyre Hunt Esq
Chief Delegate of the Commission for Relief in Belgium
in the Province of Antwerp

Dear Mr Hunt,

On your national festive Day we wish to express once more to you as representing the Commission for Relief amongst us and in your own capacity our feelings of everlasting gratitude towards the United States & the men & women of your great Republic. Your personal efforts lavishly exerted since several months, your tact and courtesy, your fine energy and your open mind, your high intelligence & generous feelings have helped us immensely in the difficult task of distributing food and giving help in this province on which the war has levied such a heavy toll of ruin and misery

JULY 4, 1915.
A Letter from Louis Franck Proposing to Make July Fourth a Belgian National Holiday.

A day will come when all this will be a thing of the past; we hope that life will then be a blessing to you and that to have helped and remedied so much sufferings in such an altruistic way will evermore brighten your days.

I shall be thankful to you to convey the expression of our feelings towards your country & the Commission for Relief to that energical, able & generous Statesman Mr Brand Whitlock, to Mr Crosby, whom we all appreciate above so much for his untiring labour and competent leadership and to all your colleagues of the American Delegation. and especially your assistants, in this province, present & past.

At the next meeting of the Municipal Council, I shall move that the 4th of July be from this year a festive day in Antwerp, pending the time that we may be able to introduce the measure in Parliament for the whole country.

I am, dear Mr Hunt,

Yours faithfully,
Louis Franck

President: Comité prov. de Secours &
d'Alimentation
Antwerp.

CHAPTER VII

SAVING A NATION

Their Daily Bread

ALTHOUGH the Americans in Belgium perform a variety of functions, they are there primarily for two purposes: to see that the Germans strictly observe the guarantee against requisitioning food supplies, and to see that every Belgian man, woman, and child receives his daily bread.[1]

Every Belgian more than two years old is entitled to two hundred and fifty grams of bread per day, and it is the business of the Commission to see that he gets it.

This ration, which, I believe, is considered by experts to be extraordinarily low, was established at the beginning of our work by Dr. Hindhede, then at the Solvay Sociological Institute in Brussels, and Horace Fletcher,

---

[1] During my year's service in Antwerp there was only one case in which German soldiers violated the guarantees of protection granted to Commission food.

Two soldiers stopped a Belgian bread-cart and demanded bread. The delivery-boy stoutly refused. The soldiers then set upon him, grabbed two loaves out of the cart, threw at the boy the money for them, and set off at a run.

Mr. Brand Whitlock writes: "I am glad to be able to say that there is not a single instance in which a pound of food sent under our guarantee has been touched by the German authorities."

the American food expert and father of the verb "to fletcherize."

Of the members of the Commission for Relief in Belgium Mr. Fletcher was dean, and he was one of our most loyal, most enthusiastic, and most inventive workers. He looked like an angelic boy, masquerading with white wool for hair and eyebrows. War found him studying at the Solvay Sociological Institute, but he volunteered at once to help in the relief work, and his tasks have been varied and important. For a while he was "official taster," and it is a tradition amongst us that he half poisoned himself, "trying out" gift goods sent into Belgium by kind America! He prepared a concise and interesting pamphlet on food values, containing delicious recipes for preparing American products till then unknown to the Belgians: "Susie's Spider Corn Cake," *Bouillie de Maïs Frites, ou Hominy Frit, Petit Pains* Berkshire Muffins, and *Petit Pains de Farine de Maïs Indien d'Amérique,* were some of the products of his skill. This pamphlet, in French and Flemish, was spread broadcast, so that the American delegates and Belgian committeemen spoke of "calories" with the same easy familiarity that they had acquired with "bills of lading," "excesses," and "under-weights."

At first some of our imports of high nutritive value were almost useless to the Belgians. I do not refer to delicacies such as sweet potatoes, maple syrup, and real

Southern hominy, but such standard products as corn-meal and oatmeal. Large quantities of both had been given by generous Canadians and Americans. The State of Iowa contributed a ship-load of corn. But very few Belgians knew how to cook our national foods; the Flemish peasants wished to use some of the choicest of them as feed for chickens, so we had hastily to organize committees to begin a propaganda. Teachers of domestic science from the city of Antwerp went through the villages, lecturing before the peasants and showing them how corn-meal should be cooked. The prejudice against maize products as human food was so strong, however, that our wares had to be rechristened, and thus our good old-fashioned American corn-meal and hominy were baptized "cerealine" and "idealine," and other alien and presumably appetizing names.

By Belgian rules of bread-making one hundred and ninety grams of flour will make two hundred and fifty grams of bread. In February, 1915, the ration was raised to two hundred and fifty grams of flour—about three hundred and twenty-five grams of bread—and maintained on that basis except when failing supplies cut the proportions.

Such a simple-looking mathematical rule for rationing would seem to need no qualification, but only those who have attempted to administer with the wisdom of Solomon a trust like ours can understand the difficulties which

THEIR DAILY BREAD

arose. There were probably many peasants in the Campine who had small stores of rye flour which they could mix with the American wheat flour, whereas the unemployed workmen of the towns and cities had no resources of any sort. Should we, then, discriminate against the peasants? . . . The diet of bread for those confined in prisons, hospitals, penal colonies, and asylums is normally very large. Should we cut these rations to our rule? . . . What about growing children in orphanages? . . . What about patients in hospitals, or those being cared for at home? . . . Should all these exceptional classes of persons be fed on gray war bread, and should they receive only two hundred and fifty grams per day, like everybody else?

A most picturesque plea came from a quarter where Americans would never expect it. We were urged to provide dog-bread! The Belgian dog—*le chien de trait*—is a proletarian, not a parlor ornament, and is worthy of his hire. Meat is always costly, so he is practically a vegetarian, and his diet must be carefully looked after. Bread is his staple food. . . . Dogs are absolutely necessary to the peasants, and strange as the request seemed at first, we finally, after careful study, decided to provide a cheap bread for them.

Perhaps the most striking plea for exceptional treatment was made by the director of a large Belgian asylum. He assured us that the health and morale of his institution depended upon an unusually large ration of bread, because, if the diet of the insane were restricted, uproars and disorders would begin.

With the approval of the Brussels office we ruled that the ration of bread must stand uniform throughout the province, but that if in specific cases bread could be proved a medicine, then, on a doctor's certificate, we would allow a larger portion.

At one time we received complaints about the quality of bread served in a city prison, and W. W. Stratton went down to investigate. The manager of the prison flatly contradicted all unfavorable reports, and explained to Stratton, with a wealth of detail, how fine the bread really was.

"How much bread do you give your prisoners now, Monsieur le Directeur?" asked Stratton.

"How much now?—the same as always. And such good bread, monsieur!"

"*Tiens!* And is the quality of the bread the same as always?"

"But yes, monsieur."

"Oh, la, là, la, là! Monsieur le Directeur, then it is bad, very bad, most bad; it cannot be worse. It cannot be eaten, or digested!" Stratton shrugged his shoulders despairingly, as if there were no more words to express the iniquity of the prison bread.

"But, monsieur!" screamed the unfortunate manager. "How can you know that?"

"How can I know, monsieur? Attend! I have been

your guest. In December I was a prisoner in this very prison!"

"Monsieur!"

"I! The Germans did not like me, maybe. I had just come into Belgium. They arrested me; they gave me to you; you placed me in one of your choicest cells, *n'est-ce pas?* I spent a day under your hospitable roof. But you have forgotten, monsieur? *Comme c'est triste; c'est triste, n'est-ce pas?*" ...

There was a very rapid improvement in the quality of the prison fare.

The supply of white flour was strictly limited, so the Commission imported wheat and milled it in Belgium. This wheat, whether from North or South America, was milled at ninety per cent; in other words, it contained all the bran except ten per cent. Such milling was a measure of economy, for only the greatest care enabled us to give the necessary ration of two hundred and fifty grams of bread, and in many of the provinces ten per cent or fifteen per cent of corn-meal was added to the gray flour, reducing the cost by about ten francs per hundred kilograms, and enabling the committees to maintain the price of bread at a minimum. Mills existed in each of the provinces. Ten were employed in the province of Antwerp alone. These were all under the management of the Commission delegates and the Belgian committees, and were required by the terms of their contracts to return to the committees every product and by-product of the milling operations. The mills were also considered Commission warehouses, under the protection of the American flag, and deliveries to the communes were made direct from them.

Thanks to our regulations, the price of bread, white or gray, was always lower in Belgium than in London, Paris, Rotterdam, or New York.[1]

Joyous Entries

Whenever we dealt directly with the Belgian people all went well; when we dealt with middlemen there was apt to be trouble. This was particularly true in the distribution of flour. In the country districts and smaller towns where the people did their own baking, we distributed flour directly to the consumers: in cities, on the other hand, we delivered flour to the bakers, who then supplied their customers with Commission bread.[2]

There is a Bible story which I now read with satisfaction unknown to me before my stay in Belgium. It runs:

When the chief baker saw that the interpretation was good, he said unto Joseph, I also was in my dream, and behold, I had three white baskets on my head:
And in the uppermost basket there was of all manner of

[1] See Appendix XXIV, page 351.
[2] See Appendix XXV, page 352.

JOYOUS ENTRIES

bake-meats for Pharaoh; and the birds did eat them out of the basket upon my head.

And Joseph answered and said, This is the interpretation thereof: The three baskets are three days:

Yet within three days shall Pharaoh lift up thy head from off thee, and shall hang thee on a tree; and the birds shall eat thy flesh from off thee.

And it came to pass the third day, which was Pharaoh's birthday, that he made a feast unto all his servants . . .

But he hanged the chief baker: as Joseph had interpreted to them.

At one time we needed a despot like Pharaoh to deal with the Antwerp bakers, although as a rule we were not gentle toward offenders. In the case in question, however, the offenders were all the bakers of Antwerp, and retaliatory measures were crushed by sheer weight of their numbers.

To insure honest bread at honest weight and an honest per capita distribution, the Commission began to card-index all consumers in Belgium. Theretofore in Antwerp proper we had estimated requirements on the basis of what we knew to be the whole population of the city. Dividing that population among the big and little bakeries, we had a rough-and-ready method for distribution, and we closely followed up complaints from the ultimate consumers.

Card-indexing is slow but sure. Before the end of the investigations I called for a progress report.

"Twelve bakers' lists are complete out of one hundred and eighty-five bakeries and forty-six pastry shops."

"What do they show?"

"Every one of them is fraudulent. They've padded their lists of customers—given names of refugees who are in Holland or England, or purely fictitious names. And we've been furnishing them with flour for three weeks on a basis of lies! It makes me sick."

"What do you want to do? Fine them?"

"We've done it: that is, I've insisted on fining the biggest baker in the lot, but the Belgian committeemen object."

"Why do they object?"

"They say *all* the hundred and eighty-five lists are padded, and they think it's too hard on that one to fine him alone!"

In times of discouragement like these our only comfort was the positive knowledge that in spite of petty fraud, every Belgian was being fed, and second, that Provincial Committeeman J. G. Delannoy would personally assault the baker who had offended.

In a long ministerial frock coat and tall collar, buzzing through his teeth the tune of the Socialist *Internationale,* Mr. Delannoy would burst into the Commission offices, roaring greetings right and left, smacking the desks with his great hands, conquering ears and hearts by his onslaught, and speaking an extraordinary mixture of English, French, and Flemish—a strong, meaty *potpourri* of languages.

He was one of the most valued members of the Provincial Committee, respected and admired, even by his political enemies; a man of little fear and no favor, with a *penchant* for strong-arm methods.

"Look here, Mr. Delannoy! Stop that *kolome-Vendôme-verdoeme* anecdote a moment and listen to this. We're going to fine Ixe for fraud."

"Mynheer 'Unt, I will explicate. It is the charAKter of the Flemish pupils (people) to make *fraudeur* (fraud)."

"Let's not discuss Flemish character."

"No, no, no, no, no, no, no, no! Listen. I, Delannoy, *moi, je, ik,* I have make fraud—not now, no!—but in peace. I make fraud by the *Garde Civique*—Civil Guard—militia! You know what is the *Garde Civique?*"

"Yes. It is like our National Guard."

"*Eh bien!* I desert, I skip drill, I make fraud."

"The deuce! You're one of the 'straightest' men I ever met."

"But no. I make fraud by the *Garde Civique*. It is the charAKter of the pupils. Like you Americans; you pay not the customs moneys in New York; isn't it?"

A long silence!

"It is the charAKter of the Flemish pupils; always they make *fraudeur*. But, Mynheer 'Unt, I will see Ixe; *n'est-ce pas?*"

"Deal gently with him, for Heaven's sake. Don't massacre him. We don't love him, but we don't want him killed."

"I will kick him down the stair."

The splendid gifts of white flour from America were reserved for hospitals and asylums, but enough remained for us to give the whole province an occasional week of white flour, to break the monotony of the gray. These occasions were dubbed "joyous entries" by Mr. Delannoy.

"They eat always with the eyes, the Flemish pupils, Mynheer 'Unt. *Ils mangent toujours avec les yeux; vous comprenez?* You know what is to 'eat with the eyes'? The Flemish pupils look, look first. Then they eat. *La farine grise,* it is joost so good as the white flour; *mais, c'est gris; ce n'est pas blanc. Enfin!* The Flemish pupils make always *kermis*—picnic, good time—for *de witte bloem*—white flour. *C'est une 'joyeuse entrée,' n'est ce pas, Monsieur 'Unt?* You know what is a '*joyeuse entrée*'? I will explicate." And with gusts of laughter he explained the tremendous welcome which always greeted the first official visit of a sovereign monarch to medieval Antwerp; called, by the old chroniclers, the "joyous entry."

"It is the '*joyeuse entrée*' of Emperoor White-Bread, *n'est-ce pas,* Monsieur 'Unt?"

Not the character of the Flemish, but war-time conditions were at fault. The Commission had established a partial monopoly of flour, without at the same time establishing a monopoly of baking. The bakers were in keen competition with each other, under conditions of terrible strain. Many of them were delivering bread to clients who could no longer pay, and the Commission all the while was paring off the profit on bread-making to keep the price as low as possible for the ultimate consumers. At the same time the Dutch were smuggling flour and bread over the Belgian border, and, although its operations were not great, there was a legitimate committee (*le comité limitrophe*), formed under the patronage of Queen Wilhelmina of Holland and the chairmanship of a Dutch member of Parliament, to restore petty commerce between the Dutch and Belgian border communes.

On recommendation of the chairman of the committee, a Mr. Fleskens, the Dutch Minister of Commerce and Labor issued permits of exportation to proper persons. The committee made no profits for itself, but the transaction was wholly commercial, since no attention was paid to the needs of the destitute in Belgium. The most important article in this petty commerce was white bread baked in Holland and sent into Belgium for immediate consumption. There was nothing to prevent the Germans seizing such bread if they liked. The complications arising from such transactions in the midst of a work like ours are obvious.

Commerce with Holland was not an easy thing. Few could run the border without collusion with the German sentries. Double lanes of barbed-wire stretched from the North Sea almost to Aix-la-Chapelle, in Germany, and these lanes were guarded by mounted patrols. The geographical frontier is tortuous and not easily watched. The first barrier, therefore, was a simple barbed-wire fence. But well within the Belgian border was a second line. Two closely knit, wickedly barbed fences, about eight feet apart, were reinforced by a third barrier which consisted of strands of wire electrically charged with a high current and strung on posts some seven feet high. Except at the highways, which were closely guarded, this formidable barrier was continuous, and land mines reinforced the barbed-wire lanes at several points.

Yet some daring individuals managed to get through. Barrels with men inside could be worked through the wires, and step-ladders or vaulting poles were used to surmount the entanglements, but the commonest way seemed to be to sneak down the river courses or through the swamps, and chance a drowning or the bullet from a sentry's rifle.

Commerce under such conditions was romantic rather than profitable.

BREAD LINES AND SOUP KITCHENS

One difficulty we encountered in our conflict with the bakers was lack of support on the part of the committeemen of the arrondissement of Antwerp. There was a reason for this. Many of them felt that the war would shortly be over and that a makeshift organization was sufficient for the interim. To some of our best friends we must have seemed incorrigible pessimists in our everlasting insistence on a permanent relief structure.

Once when Stratton, as arrondissement delegate for Antwerp, disagreed with his Belgian committee, the committee suggested that we appeal the case to the headquarters of the Commission in Brussels. To this I gladly assented, and the committee, including Stratton, took the next train.

They returned in a day or two, well satisfied. The Brussels director had ruled in accordance with our wishes, and the Belgian committee was now unanimous for war on the wicked.

"Monsieur le Directeur Crosby agrees with Monsieur Hunt and Monsieur Stratton. It is all arranged. We will fine that bad baker five thousand francs and suspend his flour for two weeks."

Stratton winked at me broadly over the head of the speaker. "All is arranged," he echoed.

"But how did you do it?" I asked, when the committeemen had gone. "The courier was in town today, and he says Mr. Crosby is in the north of France."

"He is. But it seemed too bad to spoil our visit to Brussels just for that, so I talked it all over with somebody in the Brussels office and brought him in to talk to the committee."

"You did not introduce him as Mr. Crosby!"

"Of course I'll answer if you insist." . . . Stratton whistled a bar of the *Brabançonne*. . . . "But what's a name between friends?"

In pleasing contrast to the unsatisfactory state of the distribution of flour to the bakers was the distribution of bread and soup to the poor from the Antwerp soup kitchens. Since the beginning of the war the number of bread lines and soup kitchens in the greater city had grown to fifteen. In December, 1914, at one station several men in a single week fainted from hunger; but that never afterwards occurred, although we were feeding more than thirty-five thousand daily. At least ten times during the period from December first to mid-January there were days when soup could be had but no bread, although the universal rule of the Commission was first to care for the destitute of all classes.

The ration of soup and bread given at the kitchens cost from ten to twelve centimes per day per person, and was of excellent quality. Every person brought his own spoon, and might carry his bread home to eat there if

BREAD LINES AND SOUP KITCHENS

he wished. Ten of the soup kitchens were in schoolhouses. Before the war the Antwerp schools were equipped to feed a hot soup at mid-day to such of their pupils as needed it, so that a part of the necessary equipment was at hand, and the municipality furnished extra boilers and other utensils.[1]

There were four standard varieties of soups—pea, bean, vegetable, and bouillon—but variations in the amount of rice which might be added gave practically a new soup for each day.

Every person carried a card, stamped with the name of the soup station and the name of the bearer, with blank spaces where the dates of deliveries of soup might be indicated. The kitchens were open only between 11.30 A. M. and 1.15 P. M. They often opened with grace, spoken by a priest.

Discipline was strict, and the people were remarkably clean. They might be poor and hungry, but they were never dirty. The loathsome filth one might expect was not to be seen in Belgium, and this striking evidence of self-respect was the more noteworthy because soap never is furnished *gratis* to the Belgian poor.

The cleanliness of the kitchens, too, was admirable, in spite of the frequent rainy weather and the relays of people. The workers in the kitchens were almost all of them volunteers, among them men and women teachers, nuns, and priests. Every one had work assigned

[1] See Appendix XXVI, page 353.

him: peeling potatoes, serving food, or supervising cooking.

At the suggestion of the Commission, a more careful system of identification cards was installed in the soup stations, and their administrators became a part of our local Antwerp organization.

There were three milk kitchens and three baby clinics maintained in Antwerp by volunteers. Before the war about thirty-five out of every forty mothers nursed their babies. Some idea of the prevalent demoralization may be gathered from the fact that four months after the fall of Antwerp hardly five out of forty mothers were able to do so.

Economic restaurants were available for those whose means allowed a payment of part but not the full price for food. Three such restaurants were founded in Antwerp, and for fifty centimes or less a good meal was provided in dining-rooms which had none of the barrack-room air of bread line and soup kitchen. Wherever a Belgian had money he paid for his food; but the Commission served rich and poor alike.[1]

HEALTH, CLOTHING, AND HOUSING

Belgium needed far more than bread. Thousands had neither clothes nor dwellings; millions had no work; people of all classes were cold and idle and ill. The task

[1] See Appendix XXVII, page 354, and Appendix XXVIII, page 356.

HEALTH, CLOTHING, AND HOUSING 297

of the Commission for Relief in Belgium could not long remain a simple doling out of rations, for food was almost useless without other things as well—clothing, fuel, dwelling houses, money, and good health.

Typhoid and black measles were the first epidemics reported. In the neighborhood of Willebroeck—a town of twelve thousand inhabitants, where dykes had been cut and the district inundated in a vain effort to keep the Germans out of Antwerp—seventy-five cases of typhoid were known and others were suspected.

Ernest P. Bicknell, director of civilian relief for the American Red Cross, Henry James, Jr., and Dr. Wycliffe Rose, all representing the Rockefeller Foundation of New York, visited Belgium in December and prepared a report on conditions in typical communes. Before January first, 1915, the Rockefeller Foundation contributed almost a million dollars to the work of Belgian relief, and established a station in Rotterdam called the Rockefeller Foundation War Relief Commission, to assist the Commission for Relief in Belgium. This station had charge of the sorting and shipping of clothes sent from America for Belgium, and among its volunteer workers were two American women, Dr. Caroline Hedger and Miss Janet A. Hall, who had served on the Chicago Health Department and were in Holland as representatives of the Chicago Woman's Club. At my request these ladies came to the province of Antwerp as volunteer health officers.

The winter was cold and damp as an icy sponge, but Dr. Hedger and Miss Hall set out at once, with a supply of their own vaccine, for the scene of the most important epidemic. At Willebroeck they lived for two weeks in a tiny suite of rooms over a Flemish *estaminet,* were mould was so thick on the walls that one could scrape it off with one's fingers. In two weeks' time they never once were thoroughly warm, although they were admirably dressed; yet Belgians lived through the winter clad only in cotton and wearing carpet-slippers.

The two devoted women went into every house where a typhoid case was known or suspected. A typical visit was to the village of Sauvegard where they found every one of seven members of the van der Zeippen family ill or convalescent from typhoid. As Dr. Hedger tells it, " Their house had been destroyed and they had lost all their farm possessions but one cow. They were living in one side of a dirt-floored barn that belonged to some friend, and some one else had given them a bed. But why this family was living at all, I do not know. They had rushed away ahead of the Germans with one hundred and eighty Belgian soldiers at the time of the retreat toward Antwerp, and of the one hundred and eighty soldiers only twenty got out alive. Yet this family had come out intact, and survived typhoid fever after that. There were tears in the eyes of that mother —almost the only weeping we saw in Belgium."

Strangely enough, they found all the recent cases were

HEALTH, CLOTHING, AND HOUSING

traceable, not to the inundations, but to the congested refugee camps in Holland, especially those in Flushing. It was a sad commentary on the generosity of the Dutch that their Belgian barracks actually spread disease among the inmates. But it was reassuring to find that we had practically no native epidemics near Willebroeck. This was due in part to the able work of local Belgian physicians, for the German military doctors did not take care of Belgian civilians.

In addition to tracing the source of the Willebroeck infection and inoculating the people against typhoid, Dr. Hedger and Miss Hall presented to the Commission about three thousand dollars' worth of anti-typhoid vaccine, originally the gift of Dr. Mary T. Lincoln of the Chicago Woman's Club, and with this we stamped out the cases of typhoid in other centers of infection.

Dr. Hedger's own words should tell of the conclusion of her stay in Willebroeck.

"We were invited to a Sunday dinner at the house of the acting-Burgomaster, Dr. Persoons. All the blinds were down, so we ate by artificial light. It was a small and simple party. Each gentleman had an American button in the lapel of his coat, and the ladies wore the Belgian and American colors. After dinner we were invited into the parlor for coffee, as the custom is, and there, hung from the ceiling, was a great silk American flag, with President Wilson's picture on the wall beneath it. How they got this flag and picture in that little town I do not know, but there they were!

"As soon as we had had our coffee, the door into the hall opened, and there came in a procession headed by four little children, two boys and two girls; two carrying flowers in their hands, and two with their silk school-flags—their Belgian flags. Then I understood why the blinds had been drawn. Belgians are not allowed to display their flag in public in any way, so they had been obliged to bring them in in the night.

"The little children advanced and read a Flemish address, thanking America for the Christmas Ship and presenting us with their flowers. I replied through the interpreter, and supposed that was all. But the children fell back after presenting the flowers, and then the secretary of the Town Council read a letter of thanks that was one of the most exquisite bits of English I ever heard. It was not absolutely neutral, so you will have to wait until the war is over before you can get the exact wording of those thanks. After this reading wine was brought, and each gentleman came forward, touched glasses, bowed, and gave his thanks individually to America. . . . They apologized because those beautifully arranged flowers were artificial. They said their greenhouses had all been broken in the bombardment, and they could not express in beautiful flowers, as they might do in days of peace, their gratitude to America."

HEALTH, CLOTHING, AND HOUSING 301

In the work at Willebroeck Dr. Hedger and Miss Hall came into intimate contact with all the needs of the people. The lack of proper clothing, for example, was pitiable. For three months some of the children of Willebroeck had stayed away from school, literally because they had no clothing to go in. In every household the brightest child was selected to wear what clothes were available. Little boys appeared in their sisters' dresses and little girls in boy's clothes.

This situation was a commonplace. Appeals for clothing came to Antwerp from all parts of the province. The war had come at harvest time, when clothes are a secondary consideration, and the people had never had an opportunity to provide themselves for the winter. We never had enough to supply them. It was only when the generous gifts of clothing began to come from America through the Rockefeller Foundation War Relief Commission, that the situation improved at all.[1]

Temporary houses, too, had to be constructed for the returning refugees and the peasants in the ruined villages. The building of these was one of the most interesting and able works of our excellent Belgian committees.[2]

[1] See Appendix XXIX, page 357.
[2] See Appendix XXX, age 359.

Plan N° 5.

Abri collectif pour quatre ménages. (Ouvriers).

16 à 24 personnes (8 à 12 lits) — 4 à 8 têtes de bétail.

1° Composition par abri. — *Habitation.*

Au rez-de-chaussée	Cuisine	3,50 à 4,00 × 5,40 m.
	Chambre à coucher	2,40 × 2,50
A l'étage	Grenier	Mêmes dimensions
	Etable	2,50 × 1,65

2° Surface bâtie pour le groupe.

4 habitations . . 20,60 × 5,80 m. = 119,48 m^{tres} c^{rés}
4 étables . . 5,50 × 3,60 m. = 19,80
$\qquad\qquad\qquad\qquad\qquad\qquad\qquad$ 139,28 m^{tres} c^{rés}

3° Devis pour le groupe.

Matériaux :
- Chaux . . . . Fr. 90.—
- Bois (charpente) . . . » 700.—
- Portes et fenêtres . . . . » 245.—
- Carton bitumé . . . . . » 85.—
- Vitrerie et peinture . . . » 65.—
- Ancrages . . . . » 36.—
- Pavement monolithe en ciment » 36.—
- Cuves en ciment pour fosse d'aisance et puits . . . » 81.—
- Pate de papier et imprévus . » 60.—

Intervention totale du Comité Provincial Fr. 1398.—
Briques de remploi fournies par la commune. Evaluées à Fr. 250.—
$\qquad\qquad\qquad\qquad\qquad\qquad\qquad$ Fr. 1648.—

Main-d'œuvre (chômeurs) . . . . » 350.—
$\qquad\qquad\qquad\qquad$ Total par groupe Fr. 1998.—

4° Prix par mètre carré de surface bâtie . . . . Fr. 14.35
    » par tête d'habitant { pour 16 personnes . . . . . » 125.—
                                » 24 » . . . . . . » 83.—

ESTIMATED COST OF TEMPORARY HOUSE FOR FOUR WORKINGMEN'S FAMILIES.

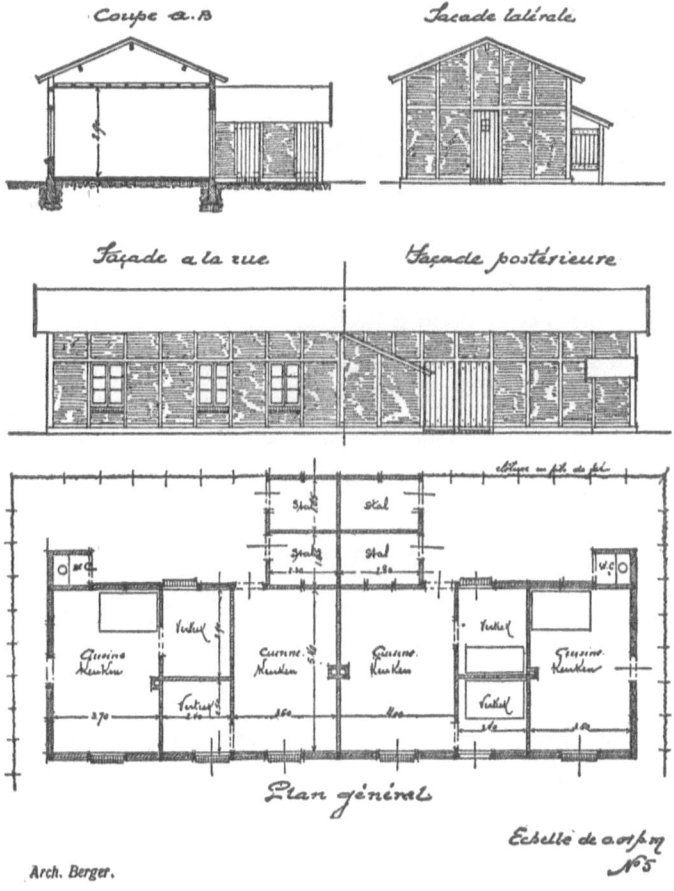

PLAN OF TEMPORARY HOUSE FOR FOUR WORKINGMEN'S FAMILIES.

Unemployment

Normally 1,757,489 persons are engaged in Belgian commerce and industry, and the state of many of these was desperate. In January, 1915, Mr. Michel Levie, president of the Board of Directors of the National Association of Light Railways, drew up for the National Committee an extensive plan for unemployment relief. Excluding agricultural laborers, the entire body of artisans and employees of industry and commerce of both sexes, more than sixteen years old, who, living on the product of their work, had been deprived of this work because of the war, and who were actually at the moment in want, were embraced in the plan. These *chômeurs,* as the unemployed are called in French, were to be utilized by the communal organizations in public works, such as draining, ditching, constructing embankments, and building sewers. The communal authorities having such employment in charge were especially recommended to work through the Labor Exchanges, Unemployment Benefit Associations, Trades Unions, and other similar bodies. The relief was to be distributed in food or other supplies, in money, or in the form of relief coupons or salary checks.

To carry out this plan the National Committee, through the Provincial Committees, subsidized the communal organizations up to nine-tenths of the assistance

UNEMPLOYMENT

to be allowed to the unemployed, the commune to furnish the other one-tenth.

The basis was interesting. If the unemployed were a bachelor, he received three francs per week; if the head of a family, three francs for himself, plus one and one-half francs for his wife or housekeeper, and fifty centimes for each child less than sixteen years old, living with the parents and not working. A woman in industry received the same sum as a man.

The communes were obliged to furnish to the Provincial Committees, for transmission to the National Committee, certified lists of their unemployed, and rigid rules with frequent examinations of the lists were provided to prevent frauds. Invalids, the infirm, victims of accidents who were receiving other assistance, wives and children benefitting by the relief allowed to families of soldiers, or men without employment who refused to accept the work provided for them by the communes, were excluded from the lists of *chômeurs*.

The first enrolment of the classified unemployed in Belgium amounted to more than seven hundred and sixty thousand names. Including those dependent upon them the number was one million three hundred and forty-seven thousand nine hundred and twenty-two persons. In the province of Antwerp out of a total population of one million eighty-seven thousand five hundred the number of unemployed was two hundred and thirteen thousand three hundred and ninety-seven, and this number steadily increased.[1]

The first purpose of unemployment relief was to provide a certain minimum of assistance which would include food, clothing, shelter, fuel, and other things necessary to maintain the family life of the workers. Its second purpose was to provide employment, and so to combat the growing demoralization of the country. From an administrative point of view, however, it brought complications.

Up to this time the Germans had secured a certain amount of labor from the Belgians, and would probably have secured more had the unemployment relief remained unorganized. They could of course provide employment for only a few classes of Belgian workmen, but the system of communal relief for the unemployed practically closed all doors against them. Thereafter Belgians could work without working for the Germans.

The Commission was thoroughly alive to the danger. The plan of relief for the unemployed was a Belgian plan, the administrators were Belgians, and the recipients of course were Belgians. We were neutrals; Belgians were belligerents. We needed constantly to be on our guard against unscrupulous patriots who might use us to club the Germans. From Minister Brand Whit-

[1] See Appendix XXXI, page 361, and Appendix XXXII, page 362.

lock down to the humblest worker in the Commission, we were overwhelmed with appeals for protection which we had no right to hear and with which we had no power to deal. This was awkward for the Commission and irritating to the Germans. Neither we nor the Belgians were wholly to blame, but the situation did not flatter German pride and undoubtedly aroused their suspicions.

In the plans for *chômeur* relief, then, the Commission was not involved, but as a matter of administrative fact the Commission and the National Relief Committee were married partners, and neither could act without involving the other.

CHAPTER VIII

DIPLOMATIC CONQUESTS

HAULING DOWN THE FLAG

A CHANGE had come about in the attitude of the German authorities toward the Commission for Relief in Belgium and the National Committee. The Germans, like every one else, had expected a short war. Belgian relief was a temporary measure. But with every month of lengthened warfare the work of relief and the work of government in Belgium became more definite and inclusive and the occasions for misunderstandings increased.

On October sixteenth, 1914, Governor-General von de Goltz had written with the utmost cordiality to the Central Relief Committee. "I approve with lively satisfaction the work of the Central Relief Committee," his letter runs, "and I do not hesitate formally and expressly to give by this letter assurance that foodstuffs of all sorts imported by the Committee to feed the civil population are reserved exclusively for the needs of the population of Belgium, that consequently these foodstuffs are exempt from requisition on the part of the military authorities, and that they remain exclusively at the disposition of the Committee." Eight months later, on

HAULING DOWN THE FLAG

June twenty-sixth, 1915, Governor-General von Bissing wrote to the Minister-patrons of the Committee in a very different strain. "Having myself made an estimate of the damages occasioned by the war," announced the Governor-General, "no inquiries on the subject of requisitions by the German troops will be permitted.

"The inspectors of the committees and the Commission for Relief in Belgium have the right to make statements of abuses committed by millers, and so forth, but their right is confined to making these statements. It is then permitted them to communicate to the competent authorities (the German Government), with a request to them to give the complaints the attention they deserve."

Until July the committees and the Commission had punished infractions of rules either by fining the recalcitrants or withdrawing supplies for brief periods. If a baker gave short weight or bad bread and was convicted of it, we were able either to drive him out of business or to put him in a temper to play fair with us in future. The two or three instances of communes where burgomasters or other officers were unfair, who exploited either the money or the food which we gave them, were met in a similar way. Now, on proclamation of the Governor-General, this power was taken from us, and we were reduced to the slow processes of Belgian law under the auspices of the German military authorities.

Such a restriction was inevitable in time. But the temper, if not the ruling itself, seemed hostile. The first evidences of German irritation had been shown long before. Officers in Pass Bureaus and at sentry-posts argued with the Commission delegates the morality of American shipments of arms to the Allies. Our monthly passes for automobiles became more difficult to get. Twice or thrice we were forced to lie idle for a day or two on account of the failure of Pass Bureaus to provide our passes promptly.

The inexhaustible kindness which the Belgians showed us seemed to irritate some of the Germans. On one occasion Provincial Committeeman Delannoy applied to General von Bodenhausen, Governor of the city of Antwerp, for permission to show "*les américains*" through the vast sewer system underlying the streets—a system comparable to the Parisian system described by Victor Hugo in *Les Misérables*.

"Permission to boat through the passageways to show the Americans the sewers of Antwerp?"

"Yes, General."

"Certainly not. I will do nothing for the Americans."

Next the authorities objected to the American flag on automobiles and warehouses of the Commission. German officers stopped Commission cars and warned us that there was but one flag in Belgium and that was the German flag. We had flown our flag over our warehouses and storehouses in every city and village in Belgium. It gave the Belgian people a feeling of security to see the stars-and-stripes in their midst. It made them feel that the weight of the United States was behind their bread supply.

At least one German officer, Major-General von Longchamp, stationed at Namur, was a pleasant exception to the circle of objectors. He insisted that the delegates fly the flag on their automobiles, and suggested that they wear American rosettes in their buttonholes, " Because," he said, " it makes the Belgian people more confident and happy."

But the American Minister did not see things as we did. He dreaded hostile demonstrations and deprecated any use of the American flag by the Belgians. At last he ordered us to remove the flag from our automobiles. He then negotiated with the Governor-General who decreed that the Commission must haul down the flag from all warehouses except the principal warehouse in cities where a German Governor had his residence, and that we might hoist in the Flemish provinces a white ensign on which was lettered, " *Nationaal Hulp- en Voedings-Komiteit* "—and in the French-speaking provinces, " *Comité National de Secours et d'Alimentation.*"

Great Britain Takes a Hand

The Governor-General specifically took from the benevolent department of the National Relief Committee privileges which it had hitherto exercised—such as the use of the Commission courier service and the transmission of uncensored instructions to the communal organizations—and abrogated its right to discipline its agents. In cases of fraud the committees were instructed to appeal either to local Belgian police courts, whose decisions were subject to military review, or to the German Civil Government.

In his letter of June twenty-sixth to the Minister-patrons the Governor-General included this ominous paragraph: "All tendency on the part of the National Committee to monopolize the distribution of charitable assistance in Belgium must be stopped. The principle must be maintained that all other charitable organizations, above all, the Belgian Red Cross, have the right to act side by side with, and outside of, the National Committee."

The National Relief Committee had never claimed, nor could it claim, a monopoly of Belgian relief work. Its policy was federal, not monopolistic. Its aim was relief in Belgium and nothing else. Scores of existing relief organizations had been patronized and subsidized by the Committee, but all were engaged in work which was humanitarian and at bottom neutral. Any other basis was impossible. Mr. Brand Whitlock, the Marquis of Villalobar, and their colleague and new Minister-patron, Jonkheer de Weede, Dutch Minister at Havre, could not have lent their names to any other program.

But on the other hand the Belgian Red Cross was no longer Belgian. The German authorities, for reasons

An "American Shop" in Antwerp

which have not been made clear, had taken charge of it, and Prince Hatzfeldt was its head.

Then as always when we were in great difficulty in Belgium came Herbert C. Hoover.

A letter preceded him from the Marquess of Crewe, Lord President of the British Council, demanding that the German Government hand over to the Commission for Relief in Belgium and the National Relief Committee, for distribution to the Belgians, the whole of the indigenous cereal crop for 1915, and add to this the usual guarantees against military requisition.

All small matters under negotiation faded before this fundamental demand. We were informed by the British Admirality that shipments into Belgium must cease on August fifteenth, unless the demand were complied with before that date.

Exactly what followed is known only to a few men. Berlin, not Brussels, took the helm. There came a sudden reversal of policies. Embarrassing orders which had previously been given were tacitly ignored and the entire cereal crop of Belgium was reserved for the Belgians on the terms insisted upon by Great Britain. From the harvests of 1915 the Commission for Relief in Belgium received as steward for the Belgian people fifteen thousand tons of wheat per month, and imported from abroad a supplemental fifty-five thousand tons per month.

To requisition the crop the German General Government constituted an interesting bit of machinery called the Central Crop Commission on which there were five Germans, one Belgian, and one American. A maximum price was decreed at which the crop was to be purchased of the farmer and a maximum price at which flour was to be sold throughout Belgium. Barley was requisitioned for the Belgian breweries; rye was apportioned between human and animal consumers; and traffic in cereals outside of the channels of the Commission was absolutely prohibited.

The function of the Central Crop Commission was to requisition the crop under such circumstances as made it easy for the Belgian National Committee and the Commission for Relief in Belgium to purchase and distribute it to the ultimate consumers. Provincial co-operative societies were instituted with sufficient capital available to buy one-twelfth of the crop each month, and it was then turned over to the committees, and by them distributed as if it were imported grain.[1]

The tension at headquarters relaxed abruptly and a fairer and franker attitude toward the Commission and the National Committee took the place of the earlier distrust. It is safe to infer that much of this was due to Herbert C. Hoover.

[1] See Appendix XXXIII, page 365, and Appendix XXXIV, page 366.

FEEDING THE NORTH OF FRANCE

The work of the Commission now touched a much larger number of people than at first. Its more than seven million four hundred thousand clients had grown to nearly ten million. On April nineteenth, 1915, the Commission, represented by its Brussels director, Oscar T. Crosby, and the Quartermaster Department of the German General Staff Headquarters in the north of France, represented by Major von Kessler, signed an agreement extending the American relief work into those departments of the north of France within the German zone of occupation, and affecting a population of two million one hundred and forty thousand. Five autonomous districts were created: Lille, with a population of six hundred and seventy thousand; Valenciennes, with six hundred and twenty thousand; Saint Quentin, with three hundred and thirty thousand; Vervins, with two hundred and eighty thousand; Réthel-Charleville, with one hundred and fifty thousand; and Longwy, with ninety thousand. Maubeuge, with one hundred thousand, and Givet-Fumay, with thirty thousand inhabitants, had already been annexed for purposes of the relief work to the Belgian province of Namur.[1]

For each of these districts two American delegates were appointed, and a German officer who spoke both French and English was especially assigned to co-op-

[1] See Appendix XXXV, page 367.

erate with the Americans, to accompany them everywhere, and to censor all their telegrams or letters. In theory, the German "nurse" and the American delegates were inseparable. The Americans rode in military automobiles, and they could be provided with free lodgings and the food and service belonging to a German officer, if they so desired.

The same guarantees covered Commission supplies in the north of France as in Belgium.

The spirit of the work in France differed from that in most of Belgium. The misery was as great, or even greater when the work began, but the people seemed less energetic, less resistant than the Belgian populations. Commission delegates often remarked that the conquered French seemed to feel less outraged by the war. "If the Germans were not here, our armies might be in their country. It is war," an old man once said to me sadly.

But the cause lay deeper than philosophy. It lay to some extent in the lack of leaders and a lack of organization. Most of the notables were gone. The young men were in the French army; the older and more important citizens were also beyond the German lines. There were no such men as Cardinal Mercier, Émile Francqui, Louis Solvay, or Jean Jadot in the north of France. The land was a vast concentration camp guarded at every point. But another reason for the listlessness lay in the fact that in northern France there lives a disspirited, exhausted, worked-out racial stock. Hunchbacks, cripples, and other deformities are common; for it is the industrial and unromantic portion, the Pittsburgh district of France, which the German armies hold, and modern industry had taken its toll of the inhabitants long before militarism laid its hand upon them.[1]

[1] See Appendix XXXVI, page 368.

CHAPTER IX

AMERICA AND BELGIUM

THE GOLDEN LEGEND

"'How America saved Belgium' would make a fine title for a book on the relief work," suggested a friend.

"But it wouldn't be true."

"Wouldn't be true?"

"No. Not yet, at any rate. The Belgians aren't saved yet. Saving them is a day to day work until the end of the war. Besides that, America hasn't done the bulk of it so far."

"Hasn't? Why, what is all this Belgian gratitude for? You say America hasn't done the work? Who has?"

"Let me ask you a question first. Do you know how much it costs per month to feed Belgium and northern France?"

"I haven't the ghost of an idea."

"Approximately $7,500,000 for Belgium, and $4,400,000 for France. And do you know how much cash America has contributed up to May thirty-first, 1916? Approximately $1,147,600. . . . And how much food? Approximately $4,809,100 worth. . . . And how much clothing? Most of $4,500,000 worth. . . . Add them

THE GOLDEN LEGEND 319

all together and count them all as food, and you have $10,456,700. Divide that by the monthly requirement, $7,500,000—notice that I omit the north of France altogether—and you have food for Belgium for one and two-fifths months, or about forty-three days.

"Take the two million five hundred thousand destitute who are our special wards. They are about one-third of the total population of Belgium. Multiply forty-three days by three, and you have one hundred and twenty-nine days, or about four months' life for the destitute, if they alone are considered.

"That is not the whole story, of course. The operating expenses of the Commission have been less than one per cent of its expenditures, largely because of the volunteer services given by its members, most of whom are Americans. Hoover time and again has mentioned this in his reports as a contribution amounting to millions and millions of dollars. As long ago as June thirtieth, 1915, he estimated it at $4,800,000.

"And that is not all. Hoover says in one of his reports: 'One feature of publicity has been of the utmost importance to this work. The Commission felt that with the tendency to toss the ball of responsibility for feeding the civil population between the belligerents, the greatest hope of maintaining the open door for the importation of foodstuffs into Belgium and the retention of native food, was to create the widest possible public opinion on the subject. We believed that if the rights of the civil population in the matter of food could be made a question of public interest second to the war itself, then the strongest bulwark in support of the Commission would have been created. Public opinion in this matter has been developed to a remarkable degree, and has yielded results which cannot now well be discussed at the length the subject warrants, but they have been of transcendent importance in the solution of the whole problem.'

"These things are big. The trouble is people think the work is done and so tie Hoover's hands while they pride themselves on his achievement. They can hardly realize that the Belgian Government is straining every nerve to help, that a group of French banks has stood manfully by the work in the north of France, and yet that more money must be had.[1] They surely do not realize that charitable people in the British Empire are giving more to Belgian relief than Americans are this minute. Their contribution was more than $12,000,000 up to May thirty-first, 1916, and still goes on. Small but steady contributions do the most good."

"But America is so big, and there are so many other things to think about," my friend said fretfully. "Aren't we Americans a little tired of Belgium?" . . .

We were sitting in the hall of the Hôtel des Indes in the Hague—a gilded nest of international spies, where

[1] See Appendix XXXVIII, page 372.

secret service agents of half a dozen countries wear the livery of porters, chauffeurs, maidservants, and waiters, or cultivate the languor and Parisian grace of guests. It was a nauseating atmosphere in which to discuss the Belgian work; an atmosphere of intrigue and cynicism and brutality.

My thoughts jumped back into Belgium, and I had sight again of the marvelous vision of America which Belgians believe in as they believe in God—the America which, my friend said, had grown a little tired of Belgium. It was a vision of a new Atlantis, rich, kind, secure from the dangers of war; a land where there is no oppression, a land of toleration and understanding, where every man, woman, and child is a democrat, where there are no classes and no masses, where there is no conflict between parties, or between Church and State, where every one is a friend to those who are suffering in this war from no fault of their own; a mighty land which can afford to be generous to its neighbors, near and far; a land where there is one language, one spirit, and one flag.

Of course the picture is overdrawn. Of course we are not much different from Belgians, or any other people in this tired world. Chapters of our national history, such as our dealings with the Indians, the Mexican War, or the way we deal with industrial disputes, are fortunately unknown to our friends across the sea. But it seemed to me this Golden Legend might be made in part a fact if America were to understand, humbly and humanly to understand, and to support in every way—with money, and service, and national pride in a great achievement—the work of the Commission for Relief in Belgium and of Herbert Clark Hoover.

That is one reason why this book is written.

LA BELLE BELGIQUE

The day came when I left Belgium to go to America with Herbert C. Hoover, who had crossed the frontier a few days before. A thick mist clung to the landscape; the cold, drenching mist which often hid the Belgian soil like a shroud. And a mist of tears flooded my eyes. Leaving Belgium for America was like leaving home to go home.

At the first frontier post an officer whom I had often seen on my trips to and from Holland stepped out and took the passports and inspected the luggage piled high in the automobile. A lancer rode by in the half-light. Ghostly gray sentries stole out with lanterns to the barbed-wire entanglements and high-tension power station for charging electric cables which kill those who try to cross the No Man's Land between Belgium and the outer world. Other soldiers who had been loafing in the sentry house came out to stare in silence at the motor-car.

The officer reappeared and handed me the viséd passports.

"*Bitte sehr,* Herr Hunt," he said. "It is for the last time, *nicht wahr?* May I speak to you frankly? Yes? . . . The Americans are not our friends. Tell them the truth when you get to America, *nicht wahr?* Only the truth."

"I will tell them only the truth," I answered soberly. "But, Herr Officer, in time to come, when you and I see more clearly, in fifty years from now——"

"In fifty years!" he repeated bitterly. "Maybe we shall all be dead in fifty minutes. You Americans furnish ammunition——"

"And bread," I interrupted. "Never forget that. When you think of the ammunition we sell, think of the bread we give to Belgium. Good-by, Herr Officer, and a safe return to Germany. *Auf Wiederseh'n in Deutschland,* when the war is over."

"*Auf Wiederseh'n,* when there is peace. *Gute Reise*—good journey," he said.

The red lantern in the sentry's hand dropped from sight, and my automobile sprang forward. "*Gute Reise,*" a voice called from the dark. Mist rolled down like a sea, the lamps of the car were blinded with moisture, and the road swam beneath. . . . I thought and thought of the ravished land which I was leaving: a land almost as dear to me as home; a place of multitudes of friendships, of countless kindnesses which I had received, not for myself but for the American people.

The trunks piled in my automobile held hundreds of souvenirs: flour sacks embroidered by friends, medallions, lace, paintings, etchings, silk banners, books, parchment rolls, and other intimate reminders of the work and the war.[1] But memories more precious even than these were written in my mind and heart: the loyalty of friends, the hardships and triumphs of the task of relief, the spirit of the men who had served with me in Antwerp, the finished organization which we, Americans and Belgians alike, had at last achieved; the personal knowledge that more than a million people had for one year at any rate received their food, had been kept in good health, and had risen from the pit of despair into self-respect and confidence and hope. It was a work which must go on day by day to the end of the war.

And what splendid people these Belgians are! I had not seen much of the Walloons, but American delegates from the southern provinces were loud in praise of them. The Flemings I knew and loved. A proud, stiff-necked, stoutly independent people; insubordinate, tenacious, clever—they are a stock which will not die; a fine element in European history in the past, and with great promise for the future.

The automobile sped on into Esschen—the frontier town where on my first visit to Belgium I had seen refugees flying from the Germans. Now, in the bleak

[1] See Appendix XXXIX, page 372.

FLOUR SACKS
Embroidered and painted by the Belgians as souvenirs for the Americans.

rooms of the Town Hall sat a relief committee
—reliable, hard-working, conscientious volunteers—
providing daily rations of war bread and other food,
clothing, money, and work for the people of their commune. It was a vast change from the chaos of the year
before. The rebirth of Belgium had begun. . . .

"You are going to America, Herr Hunt?" the Germans asked at the last sentry post. "*Gute Reise, glückliche Reise, auf Wiederseh'n!*"

The car moved forward again. At the back of a little
Flemish church, surrounded with graveyard crosses
swimming in murk and mist, I caught sight of a greater
cross and an image of the agonized Christ—the familiar
symbol of our common humanity. On that dark day
it seemed peculiarly the symbol of Belgium—the little
land which has suffered so much, but whose moral
triumph is sure; the land which has been crucified, dead,
and buried, but from which a free and united people must
rise, or else life is a mockery. . . . The vague shape
of the shrine faded in the dusk as the last sentries opened
the frontier barriers and stepped aside to let me into free
and neutral Holland.

"Good evening, mynheer," called a Dutch officer in
the quaint, sing-song dialect of North Brabant. "Have
you something to show to the customs inspector this
evening?"

And as Pierre de Weert, prince of chauffeurs, fumbled

with numbed fingers at the straps of my luggage, he lifted his face, and gazing through the dusk toward the country we had just left, sadly spoke my valedictory: " *Monsieur, vous avez quitté la belle Belgique*—you have left our beautiful Belgium!"

APPENDIX I

THREE FAMOUS SOCIALISTS

This account was published in the Outlook *of January 26, 1916, after later utterances of Liebknecht had gone far beyond the words here recorded. The following is reprinted from the* Outlook *of Wednesday, April 12, 1916.*

IN its issue of February 17, 1916, *La Bataille*, the syndicalist Paris daily, published a translation of the article which appeared in the *Outlook* of January 26, 1916, on Liebknecht, Kautsky, and Bernstein. The French paper justly said that these were "the three German Socialists best authorized to express opinions on the general situation in Germany and on the attitude of German workmen in the world conflict."

In its issue of March 2 *La Bataille* states that it has learned that Bernstein and Kautsky published in the Berlin *Vorwärts* of February 27 a strong protest, categorically denying the affirmations of the *Outlook's* representative, as follows:

We have never seen the *Outlook's* representative and have expressed ourselves in such terms to no one, for we have been made to say the contrary to what seems to us just and necessary to say.

We have searched our file of *Vorwärts*, and especially the issue of February 27, without discovering the above denial. Again in its issue of March 12 *La Bataille* quotes the Brunswick Socialist organ, *Volksfreund*, as printing the following letter, dated February 27, from Dr. Liebknecht:

I have never been interviewed by a representative of the *Outlook*. My opinions are known and decided opinions. That which the *Outlook's* correspondent makes me to say is contrary to these opinions and—on certain points—to the facts.

La Bataille is mystified. In its issues of March 2 and 12 it discusses editorially the controversy between the *Outlook* and the three German Socialists. From these editorials we translate and combine the following paragraphs which give a fair representation of the not unnatural mystification of *La Bataille:*

The *Outlook* of New York has a reputation for accuracy. As an indication of this we need only to remind our readers of the interview it obtained and published with Sazonoff [the Russian Minister of Foreign Affairs]. That interview has received the seal of approval from the most competent critics. Moreover, the opinions which Liebknecht, Kautsky, and Bernstein expressed, according to the anonymous correspondent of the *Outlook,* are so plausible and reasonable, according to our view, *that they form the only explanation which can serve as an excuse for the conduct of the German Socialists* [the italics are *La Bataille's*]. . . . We propose to send the present issue of *La Bataille* to the Editors of the *Outlook,* inviting them by letter to give us the reply of their correspondent [to the alleged denial of Dr. Liebknecht and his colleagues]. . . . When we have received a reply from New York, we shall be able to tell our readers whether the correspondent of the *Outlook* has indulged in a hoax, or whether there is some misunderstanding regarding the meaning of the word interview. . . . We published the three interviews because they seemed to us to exactly coincide with the actual facts. Investigation confirms us in our belief that in several respects the language attributed to Karl Liebknecht by the American journalist corresponds, word for word, with statements which we have read in other places from the pen of Liebknecht himself. . . . We cannot at present regard as satisfactory the meager statement of Karl Liebknecht that the *Outlook* interview is contrary to his opinions and— on certain points—to the facts.

These denials of the three German Socialists raise issues far more interesting than that of veracity. The issue of veracity, however, we are ready to meet. The *Outlook* stands squarely behind the correspondent responsible for its account of the interview with the three German Socialists.

From this correspondent we have received the following statement:

"The interview with Liebknecht, Kautsky, and Bernstein, published in your issue of January 26, 1916, took place as described. Liebknecht I saw in the private office in which he does his work as a member of the Reichstag. Kautsky and Bernstein I interviewed in a private apartment-house in Berlin. The gentlemen have a right to change their minds, and of course they may say that the interviews misrepresent them. At the time I wrote the article I believed, and I still believe, that it is an accurate account of what took place."

The *Outlook* withheld the name of its correspondent for two good and sufficient reasons. The first had reference to the welfare of the three Socialists interviewed; the second cannot be explained until after the termination of the war. It should be said here that the interviews were not published in the *Outlook* until Dr. Liebknecht's reported utterances in the Reichstag went so far beyond those given in the text of our interview with him that we felt that its publication would not in any way jeopardize his safety. That we did not overestimate the possibility of personal danger to Dr. Liebknecht arising from the publication of his views may be judged by the remarks which Dr. Liebknecht himself made to an American university professor of high standing. We reported these remarks as follows in our issue of March 29:

Dr. Liebknecht said that the position which he had taken in opposition to Germany's action had put him in personal danger, so much so that it was not beyond the bounds of possibility that he might at any time disappear and never be heard of again. As he said this he significantly drew his hand across his neck, and then added that the fortunes of an individual were of no consequence.

The more interesting issues raised by the denials of Liebknecht, Kautsky, and Bernstein are clearly indicated by the following quotation from *La Bataille:*

One thing is certain: German Socialists of the Opposition have not taken into account the interest with which the entire world awaits what they decide to say frankly and without reservation on questions of principle and tactics, and they should not leave their comrades in other countries in doubt as to their attitude regarding the German Government and the Social Democratic majority.

Although the German Socialists failed to make themselves felt on August 1, 1914, is it still " just and necessary " (to use the words attributed to Kautsky and Bernstein by *La Bataille*) that their leaders fail to express themselves frankly until the end of the war? Is it "just and necessary" for their leaders to say one thing in their studies and another thing in their despatches relayed to us by the Wolff Telegraphic Bureau?

Is it "just and necessary" that they allow themselves to be pictured as loyal supporters of the Government, or, at worst, as harmless members of a purely vocal Opposition? Is it "just and necessary" for them to dodge what *La Bataille* indicates is the world-wide interest in their attitude regarding the German Government and the Social Democratic majority?

The *Outlook* agrees with *La Bataille* that the next word on these subjects belongs to Kautsky, Bernstein, and Liebknecht, and wishes that it might have a frank, direct, and uncensored expression of their views. We content ourselves with adding that our correspondent, whose interviews with the three influential German Socialists have become the subject of an international discussion, is a highly educated and thoroughly trustworthy American who has lived in Europe and is in sincere sympathy with international Socialism.

APPENDIX II

PRESS AND POST

IN many of their official dealings with the Belgians the Germans insisted on speaking the German language, although many Belgians cannot understand a word of German, while the officers concerned practically all know French.

Belgians could send no telegrams; they could use no telephones; they could mail no letters, and they could not travel without buying a pass at the German Pass Bureaus. Belgian newspapers were managed by German agents, or else were heavily censored.

In Antwerp as a means of restoring order and confidence after the fall of the city, the German authorities wisely agreed with the municipality that if the local newspapers would resume publication they should be permitted to print uncensored the official despatches of all the belligerents, and that the censor might excise but would not add to editorial or news matter. Five newspapers then appeared. At first they were allowed to print references to King Albert, Queen Elizabeth, and the Belgian army and government; and the Reuter official despatches regularly appeared side by side with those of the Wolff Bureau.

After about a month, however, the censor began to tamper with the Reuter despatches. Later he demanded that articles dictated by the German authorities appear without comment in the Antwerp press, and when the five newspapers drew up a formal complaint which they submitted to the censor and which he in turn forwarded to Brussels, he punished them by suspending them for one week. The memorandum requested that the German authorities observe the conditions under which the Antwerp papers had resumed publication, but the request was refused, and the five newspapers ceased publication.

The most interesting newspaper in Belgium is published without the permission of the Germans, and has puzzled and exasperated them to this day. It is called *La Libre Belgique,* and is printed and distributed to its subscribers in spite of a price of fifty thousand francs set upon the head of its editor or editors, and in spite of unusually severe sentences imposed upon several of its vendors who have been caught in the act of distributing it. Rumor says that the paper is printed in an obscure garage by means of an automobile motor; its price is "elastic—from zero to infinity," and with delicious audacity it declares its telegraphic address to be "Kommandantur, Brussels." It appears at irregular intervals, but usually once every week or fortnight.

In the Wiertz Museum in Brussels there is a horrible painting called "Napoleon in Hell," showing the Corsican haunted by the spirits of those he had slain. After the execution of Miss Edith Cavell, *La Libre Belgique* printed a travesty of this painting in which the Kaiser's face was shown instead of Napoleon's, and among the spirits haunting him the figure of Miss Cavell.

Another issue of *La Libre Belgique* reproduced a cleverly patched photograph of Governor-General von Bissing sitting in his private office, reading the proscribed journal. Beneath the picture was a note, "Our dear Governor, disheartened by reading the lies of the censored newspapers, seeks for truth in *La Libre Belgique*."

APPENDIX III

PUBLIC CHARITY AND EXCHANGE

Reprinted from the first Annual Report of the Commission for Relief in Belgium, October 31, 1915.

It appeared at the outset of relief measures that not only would the destitute of Belgium have to be regarded as a ward of the world's charity, but that even much of the food for the well-to-do, owing to the complete breakdown of Belgian internal finance, would have to be provided from external charity. . . . The first financial activity of the Relief Directors was therefore to set up various economic cycles whereby food sold to those who could pay might be interpreted into gold values abroad. Ultimately, approval was obtained for the Commission to conduct exchange operations through the belligerent lines, and considerable amounts of money owing to Belgium have been collected abroad from individuals, contra-payment being made in Belgium out of paper moneys received from sales of food. These operations relieve the strain on the Commission income and enable the recipient to keep clear of charity. The total of such remittances has been £562,740 9s. 11d. from over 12,000 different persons. The second step of this nature was to borrow certain sums from banks abroad, amounting to £600,000, contra-liability being taken in Belgium. The third step was to undertake the payment of considerable sums in Belgium on behalf of the Belgian Government at Le Havre. At the time of the occupation, certain sums were due from the National Exchequer to various institutions; these sums have now been received by the Commission from the Belgian Government and, in turn, paid to the institutions concerned out of local receipts from food sales.

While the whole of these operations are simply in the nature of commercial exchange, they have an indirect benevolent aspect, for they not only enable a large number of persons to subsist without charity, but also make it possible to reduce the general load upon the Commission by rendering the provisioning of the better-to-do classes a commercial operation affording an incidental profit applicable to benevolence.

APPENDIX IV

INCREDIBLY SMALL EXPENSES

Reprinted from the Report of the Millers' Belgian Relief Movement, conducted by the Northwestern Miller through its editor, William C. Edgar, Minneapolis, Minn., 1915.

OWING to the fact that all officials and directors and a very large proportion of the staff of the Commission serve without pay, the expenses of operation are incredibly small, and probably unparalleled in this respect by any charitable organization in the world.

From October 22nd to March 6th, during which period purchases were effected amounting to £3,000,000, the general expenses of the London office, including cables, postage, salaries, traveling, printing, stationery, accountants' and auditors' fees and sundries, were but £5,200; the expenses of the Rotterdam and Brussels branches were but a trifle more than this amount.

APPENDIX V

GIFTS OF SERVICE

Reprinted from the first Annual Report of the Commission for Relief in Belgium, October 31, 1915.

THE chartering and management of an entire fleet of vessels, together with agency control practically throughout the world, has been carried out for the Commission quite free of the usual charges by large transportation firms who offered these concessions in the cause of humanity. Banks generally have given their exchange services and have paid the full rate of interest on deposits; insurance has been facilitated by the British Government Insurance Commissioners; and the firms who fix the insurance have subscribed the equivalent of their fees. Harbor dues and port charges have been remitted at many points, and stevedoring firms have made important concessions in rates and have afforded other generous services. In Holland exemption from harbor dues and telegraph tolls has been granted, and rail transport into Belgium provided free of charge. The total value of these Dutch concessions is estimated at 147,824 guilders. The German military authorities in Belgium itself have abolished custom and canal dues on all Commission imports, have reduced railway rates one-half, and on canals and railways they give right-of-way to Commission foodstuffs wherever there is need.

APPENDIX VI

THE FIRST SUPPLIES

THE first supplies consisted of 6,000 tons of cereals, 1,000 tons of rice, and 3,000 tons of peas and beans, bought in London by Millard Shaler for the account of the city of Brussels. The next consisted of cargoes of grain, lying in the mouth of the Scheldt at Ter Neuzen and belonging to Belgians. These were appropriated by the Commission and returned to Belgium.

At the same time Brussels secured a lot of 5,000 tons of wheat, belonging to the provisions requisitioned at Antwerp, which the Germans "loaned" to the Belgian Committee for milling and distribution in Brussels, Charleroi, Liége, and Verviers. This was on November 16th. Meanwhile the Belgian appeal was spreading throughout the world.

APPENDIX VII

EARLY FOOD SHIPMENTS

THE report of the Commission for November, 1914, shows the ships "Coblenz" and "Iris" from London, received at Rotterdam on the first and second respectively; five lighters of wheat from Hansweert, received on the second; the ships "Jan Blockx I" and "Tellus" from London, received on the ninth; ten lighters of wheat and flour from Hansweert and three lighters of wheat from Ter Neuzen, received on the ninth; the "Tremorvah" from Halifax on the fifteenth; the "Gramsbergen" from Liverpool on the eighteenth; the "Massapequa" from New York on the twenty-first, and the "Jan Blockx II" from London on the twenty-fourth—a total of 26,470 tons of food for the first month of operations, worth about $1,021,267.

APPENDIX VIII

FLEMISH

EDUCATED Flemings are bilingual, like the Galileans of Christ's day. They speak either French or Flemish with equal fluency, although a guttural quality and local idioms sometimes disfigure the former. For political and cultural reasons many of them cling to their native Flemish. It is the common speech: the language of the people of Flanders. When written, it is practically the same as the Dutch —a low Germanic language—but the spoken language differs from the Dutch in many particulars.

The Flemish Movement is not a separatist movement, as is commonly supposed in America. It is a democratic, and in my opinion a just assertion of the predominant influence of the Flemish stock in Belgium. During the war the Flemish Movement can have no political significance, for the Flemings are as loyal as any other portion of the people to the ideal of a free and united Belgium.

To an American ear the language of Flanders is like Old English resurrected from the tomes. One seems to hear "Piers Ploughman" all about one. It is a warty, hard-fisted, tough-muscled language which has been out in the weather until it has got well sunburned; a splendid language for oratory—and profanity!

Almost every place and every thing in Flemish Belgium has two or more names. Antwerp is "Antwerpen" in Flemish, "Anvers" (please pronounce the final s) in French. The River Scheldt is "Schelde" in Flemish, "l'Escaut" in French. Mechlin or Malines is "Mechelen" in Flemish, "Malines" in French. Ghent is "Gent" in Flemish, "Gand" in French. "Mons" is French, of course, but its Flemish name is "Bergen."

APPENDIX IX

THE POOR

Reprinted from the Report of the Commission for Relief in Belgium, June 30, 1915.

THE actual work of food distribution and the care of the destitute was done entirely by the Belgians. Twenty-five or thirty thousand men and women volunteers throughout the country were engaged in this splendid task. In each commune there was a local committee, working under the direction of the Commission for Relief in Belgium and the National Relief Committee; there was a Provisioning Department to each of these committees, rationing and selling the imported foodstuffs to the Belgian population, who paid either in money or in food checks given them by the Benevolent Department; and there was the Benevolent Department feeding, clothing, and housing the destitute, providing medical attention, organizing work for the unemployed, paying unemployment benefits, and so keeping alive and as well as possible, 2,750,000 unfortunate men, women, and children.

The total number of persons in Belgium receiving some form of relief it is impossible to determine. The relief afforded through the Financial Relief Department, together with the very large and generous support to workpeople being given by employers in practically gratuitous wage-allowances, and the widespread individual charity throughout Belgium save a great number from falling in the last resort on the Communal Committees. Some insight into the situation is afforded by three examples. In the Capital, and therefore largely residential city of Brussels, prior to the supplemental grants, between 8,000,000 and 9,000,000 rations were served monthly from the Canteens, indicating from 25 per cent to 30 per cent of the population as being thus directly relieved. The numbers who are saved from this form of relief through the operations of the indirect services and the large amount of personal charity, it is impossible to estimate. In the province of Liége, a typical industrial section, out of a population of about 900,000 there are some 450,000 persons, or about 50 per cent, being assisted by some of the above services, and there are estimated to be 40,000 more who receive help through other agencies such as the "Financial Relief Department." A typical agricultural province such as Luxembourg shows only about 20 per cent of the population dependent upon benevolence. A study of the distribution and amount of the "Allowances" described above indicates that about 700,000 families are receiving this form of assistance. Altogether this category, together with those wholly supported on the Canteens, would be estimated on the low side at 2,750,000 persons. To this must be added a further 500,000 who are saved from the care of the Local Committees through the operations of Financial Relief measures. It may be repeated that many of those being assisted still have some resources of their own—for instance, the general operation of the coal mines one day or sometimes two days per week might conceivably enable the worker himself to live, but his dependents would be helpless.

APPENDIX X

BELGIAN COMMITTEES

Reprinted from the Report of the Commission for Relief in Belgium, June 30, 1915.

THE organization by which detailed distribution is accomplished can best be understood if it is conceived that there have been created 2,500 different local committees, one in each principal commune, which will be referred to hereafter as " The Communal Distribution Committees." These committees are in many instances headed by the Burgomaster and embrace other communal officials, as well as volunteers, although in some instances they are entirely composed of non-official volunteers. In order to secure consolidation of control and simplification of relations with these multitudinous committees, a federal system has been set up, by which these Communal Committees are represented in Regional Committees and these Regional Committees, in turn, represented in Provincial Committees. The Provincial Committees are the principal centers of stimulative activity and, while they have decided autonomy in provincial matters, questions which affect the entire country are decided by meetings of delegates from these Provincial Committees, and these delegates, together with a small executive body, comprise the working membership of the Comité National. The Commission for Relief in Belgium forms, jointly with the Comité National, the executive control, and it is also represented by delegates on the Provincial Committees, and the whole structure so interlinks that any separate description of functions would only tend to confuse.

Apart from these executive functions, the Commission is itself charged separately with the international guarantees and the elaborate stipulations contained therein, which necessitate that the foodstuffs shall remain in the possession of the Commission, and the control of the transportation and warehouses thus falls on its members. Furthermore, the Commission is under international obligation to maintain rigid justice in distribution.

APPENDIX XI

THE MILLERS' BELGIAN RELIEF MOVEMENT

The Northwestern Miller, an admirable trade paper, solicited from its clients, through its editor, William C. Edgar, of Minneapolis, a cargo of 275,500 sacks of flour, beans, peas, oatmeal, and barley, valued at about $510,000. Mr. Edgar personally accompanied the Millers' Ship to Rotterdam and then came into Belgium to oversee the distribution of the gifts. He has recorded his satisfaction with the work of the Commission in his report to his clients, entitled "The Millers' Belgian Relief Movement," Minneapolis, 1915.

APPENDIX XII

THE PRIEST

THROUGHOUT Belgium the priest is an important character. A few of the cities and most of the towns are Catholic, and the priest is a political and social as well as a religious director. In the towns and villages he is often more important than the Burgomaster. He is accustomed to relieve distress, and in the volunteer organizations through which the work of the Commission for Relief in Belgium is done the parish priest and the whole Catholic hierarchy, with the Cardinal-Archbishop at their head, are most important elements.

APPENDIX XIII

ANTE-BELLUM BELGIUM

UNDER the symbol lay an ocean of feeling deep as life itself. Belgium had always been hospitable to the Germans. Antwerp before the war might almost have been called a German port. The German school was the best school in the city; German society there was considered as good as Belgian society; the German Lutheran Church was supported by practically all Belgians who were not Roman Catholics; throughout Belgium, German was a legal language, on a par with French and Flemish, and if one desired one could require that a case at law be tried in German. In the eastern parts of Belgium were thousands of Belgian citizens who spoke no language but German. In the province of Antwerp some fifteen thousand residents were recorded as speaking only German. Belgians admired German efficiency. They felt a certain contempt for republican France; they thought her effete and irreligious. The Catholics were especially severe on their republican neighbors to the south, and it should not be forgotten that when the Germans demanded the right to send their armies down the Meuse there were not lacking one or two Catholic politicians who felt that the country should give in and should permit the invasion with a formal protest.

APPENDIX XIV

THE ARTISTIC TEMPERAMENT

ART played a subordinate part in the work of the Antwerp committees, except in the Canton of Moll. There it reigned supreme. The president of the Cantonal Committee—Moll is the largest Canton in Belgium—was Jakob Smits. German generals, who admired Smits as an artist, gave him privileges enjoyed by few other Belgian citizens. At one time he appeared to be free to go and come from Holland when he chose, and in Holland, as in Belgium, he received unusual consideration. At the instance of Mr. Louis Franck, Mr. Smits frequently wrung concessions for imports from the Dutch Foreign Office, such as no one else could obtain.

The Dutch Minister of Commerce and Labor was a friend of Smits. On one occasion, I am told, the artist presented himself before the Minister and demanded the right to buy in Holland a quantity of flour and various cattle foods, the export of which at that time was prohibited by the Dutch. The Minister politely refused. Smits persisted. The Minister was obdurate. Smits argued. The Minister regretted, but could make no exception. Smits stormed. " I will kill myself," he shouted, " if you do not give me that permission at once! I will kill myself here in your private office! My blood will flow on your carpet! Here! Now!" The Minister, knowing that he was dealing with an artist, surrendered, and Smits got the permission.

His returns from Holland were always in the nature of triumphal entries, and the Canton of Moll waxed fat.

APPENDIX XV

FIRST AID

FIFTEEN soup kitchens were feeding the poor from supplies laid up in anticipation of the siege. Ten local committees in the greater city were distributing assistance in kind to necessitous Belgians who had never been inscribed at the official Bureau of Charities (*le Bureau de Bienfaisance*). Private charity had established cheap restaurants, where good food could be got at low prices. There was an incorporated bank for loans with a capital of 250,000 francs, in response to the imperative demands of small tradespeople. The Civil Volunteers, for the assistance of the families of soldiers who had fought and died for the country, had assisted about 5,000 families. Side by side with these newer charities were the older homes, refuges, and hospitals, enlarged to care for the floods of those requiring assistance.

All this work had been in the hands of the local relief committees. Outside of the city proper, the people of the fortress had been supplied with food, as long as it lasted, and with financial assistance.

A special machinery had even been set up by the Belgian Government to provide for the chaos which followed the fall of the city. While King Albert and his ministers were in Antwerp they nominated an Intercommunal Commission, consisting of the most prominent citizens of Antwerp and the communes in the fortress, so that when the city fell there should be a provisional Belgian administration, in addition to the Permanent Deputation of the Provincial Council. Deputy Louis Franck was president of the Intercommunal Commission.

APPENDIX XVI

BAR-LE-DUC

An odd geographical feature of the arrondissement of Turnhout is that it has an enclave in the Dutch province of North Brabant. This enclave, the commune of Bar-le-Duc, is like a Belgian island in a Dutch sea, except that the sea is swampy Campine—a compound of sand and purple heather. The Germans cannot invade it, for to do so would be to violate the neutrality of Holland. So the 2,500 inhabitants of Bar-le-Duc fly the Belgian flag, employ Belgian police and guards, post letters at a Belgian post office, and cheer for King Albert and Queen Elizabeth, with no fear of retaliatory Zeppelin raids or Uhlan visits.

APPENDIX XVII

INTERLOCKING ORGANIZATIONS

Reprinted from the Report of the Commission for Relief in Belgium, June 30, 1915.

WITH the partial recovery from complete prostration, the admirable organizing and administrative powers of the Belgians themselves have recovered to vigorous initiative and executive action. Since October, local relief Committees have been organized in practically every commune, and there has been created over these Committees a federal system of District and Provincial Committees with the Comité National at the apex. The relation of this structure to the Commission *per se* is one of joint endeavor, and the membership of the Americans in all these Committees entirely interlocks the organization.

APPENDIX XVIII

FOOD REQUIREMENTS

Reprinted from the Report of the Commission for Relief in Belgium, June 30, 1915.

THE amount and character of foodstuffs required has altered from time to time, due to the exhaustion of native supplies, or seasonal causes, and the monthly consumption now being provided is as follows:

	Tons
Wheat (or equivalent in flour)	60,000
Maize	20,000
Rice	7,500
Peas and beans	4,000
Bacon and lard	6,000
Sundries	—

The approximate cost is about $7,500,000 per month for Belgium alone.

Reprinted from the first Annual Report of the Commission for Relief in Belgium, October 31, 1915.

The total, in metric tons, of commodities delivered during the year was:

	Purchased	Gifts in Kind	Totals
Wheat	508,112	23,166	531,278
Flour	108,575	45,346	153,921
Maize	110,487	8,744	119,231
Rice	72,594	2,406	75,000
Beans and peas	28,758	3,652	32,410
Bacon, lard, and meat	29,149	837	29,986
Potatoes	14,943	3,415	18,358
Sundries	17,159	8,186	25,345
Clothing and miscellaneous	775	2,548	3,323
Totals	890,552	98,300	988,852

The above contains a total of 121,136 tons shipped to northern France, and stocks in Rotterdam on October 31st.

APPENDIX XIX

COFFEE

An interesting inter-provincial trade was the purchase by Mr. Edouard Bunge, on behalf of the National Relief Committee, of a large stock of valorization coffee lying in warehouses at Antwerp. This coffee was the property of the Brazilian state of São Paulo. Through a representative of the Government of Brazil permission was secured from the German authorities to release the coffee to the Belgian Committees, and accordingly it was apportioned among the nine Provincial Committees.

APPENDIX XX

A CO-OPERATIVE SOCIETY

The idea of a co-operative society is typically Belgian. The Socialist co-operative experiments of a quarter of a century ago, notably " La Maison du Peuple " in Brussels and " Vooruit " in Ghent, have had countless imitators. But political lines of cleavage are always observed, so that in Antwerp, for example, we had Socialist, Liberal, and Catholic co-operative bakeries.

J. Seebohm Rowntree has an interesting chapter on Belgian co-operatives in his book *Land and Labor*, published by Macmillan, London, 1910.

In my opinion this book is the most adequate account in English of Belgian industrial and social conditions before the war.

APPENDIX XXI

THE NATIONAL RELIEF COMMITTEE

ITS first patrons were the American Minister, Mr. Brand Whitlock, and the Spanish Minister, the Marquis of Villalobar. In April, 1915, Jonkheer de Weede, Dutch Minister at Havre, became a patron of the Committee. Its president is Ernest Solvay; vice-presidents, Jean Jadot and L. van der Rest; members, Count Cicogna, Baron Coppée, P. Dansette, Chevalier de Bauer, G. de Laveleye, Count Jean de Mérode, Émile Francqui, Baron A. Goffinet, Baron Janssen, Emmanuel Janssen, Baron Lambert, Alfred Orban, L. Cousin, Louis Solvay, Josse Allard, F. M. Philippson, General Thys; two American citizens resident in Brussels —D. Heineman and W. Hulse; and secretaries E. van Elewyck and F. van Brée. The presidents and vice-presidents of the Provincial Committees make part of the National Committee.

The Executive Committee consists of Émile Francqui, president; Josse Allard, Count Cicogna, L. Cousin, Chevalier de Wouters d'Oplinter, D. Heineman, W. Hulse, Emmanuel Janssen, Michel Levie, Louis Solvay, and secretaries E. van Elewyck and F. van Brée.

The National Committee and the Provincial Committees are divided into two departments, a commercial department (*d'Alimentation*) and a benevolent department (*de Secours*). Under the benevolent department are five important divisions: to provide 1, Money; 2, Food; 3, Clothing and Shoes; 4, Work; 5, Houses and other buildings. There are committees for the Aid and Protection of Refugees, the Aid and Protection of Families of Officers and Under-Officers Deprived of their Income by reason of the War, Aid and Protection of Belgian Doctors and Pharmacists, Aid and Protection of Artists, Aid and Protection of Children and Orphans of War, Aid and Protection of the Homeless, Aid and Protection of Damaged Churches, Aid and Protection of the Unemployed, Aid and Protection of Foreigners, Aid and Protection of Lace Makers, a special Commission for Temporary Houses and the Work of Reconstruction, a Belgian Commission for Information for Prisoners of War and the Interned, a Central Committee for the Aid of Invalids of War, a Canteen for Prisoners of War, and a Belgian National League against Tuberculosis. The Belgian National Committee is patron of all these channels for charity.

APPENDIX XXII

THE CONTRIBUTION OF WAR

THE contribution of war—$96,000,000 per year—is levied on Belgium through the Permanent Deputations of the Provincial Councils. It is not paid in gold, but in paper, for there is no gold.

It is interesting to note in this connection that the total Belgian budget in peace time is from $120,000,000 to $160,000,000 per year.

APPENDIX XXIII

FINANCE

WITH the conclusion of peace, the final adjustment of the foregoing financial operations is fairly simple. The sums borrowed by the provincial authorities from the *Société Générale,* and by the individual municipalities, will be repaid in the restored currency of the National Bank of Belgium, while the Belgian Government will probably take over and redeem the *Société Générale's* currency, since the *Société* will have to be regarded as having acted for the Belgian Government in its absence.

But the fiat money of the *Société Générale* bears no relation to the sums expended abroad each month by the Commission for Relief in Belgium on behalf of the Belgian people. In the report of the Commission for June 30, 1915, Mr. Hoover writes:

" The purchase of foodstuffs abroad must necessarily be made with gold, or gold value, and these foodstuffs when re-sold in Belgium are paid for in local paper money. All metallic money and gold reserves have disappeared in Belgium, and these local emergency currencies issued by banking houses, municipalities, &c., are obviously inconvertible into gold. Moreover, the import of these notes through the Allied lines is prohibited, and the export of any form of securities from Belgium is also prohibited. If there were no economic or legal restrictions on exchange, the Provisioning Department, with a moderate working capital, would revolve upon itself. As it stands, however, not only has the currency received in Belgium to be interpreted into gold, but also it must be returned to circulation in Belgium, otherwise a large part of the circulating media would be absorbed by the Provisioning Department, and a further cause of distress added to the many already existing. From the outset, the organization has accepted all forms of currency at the gold value of the Belgian franc, interpreted into dollars or sterling. These various paper moneys are therefore given stability and circulation throughout the country. The rate of exchange fixed has been at Frs. 25.40 to the £ sterling. Belgian exchange is to-day quoted in the neutral markets of Holland at a ratio which would be equivalent to about 25 per cent depreciation of Belgian money. The Commission, however, has believed that if they were to follow any other course than to maintain the gold value it would again add infinitely to the misery in the country, because it would be necessary to advance the price of foodstuffs as the exchange rose, and there is no corresponding amelioration in wages, income, or other economic balances in Belgium."

APPENDIX XXIV

WHEAT AND FLOUR

Reprinted from the Report of the Commission for Relief in Belgium, June 30, 1915.

THE bulk of the Commission's imports of breadstuffs have been in the form of wheat and maize. Considerable latitude is exercised by the Provincial Committees in the manner in which flour is prepared in the mills. Until recently it has been the general practice to mill wheat into flour containing 90 per cent of the whole, the remaining 10 per cent of bran being sold for fodder. Gradually the various Provincial Committees are adopting the Commission's recommendation of 80 per cent milling, and some Provincial Committees have milled from 10 to 12 per cent of maize with the wheat, or have availed themselves of supplies of American corn-meal to produce such a mixture. In certain cases the pure wheat flour imported has been mixed with the flour produced as above. Much discussion has taken place as to the effect upon the population of bread produced by this high percentage of milling, but a careful study fails to detect any deleterious results. Wide differences of opinion have existed in Belgium as well as abroad as to the economics of importing wheat flour as distinguished from wheat. In certain sections milling facilities have not been available, and there has therefore been no question as to the necessity of importing white flour. Furthermore, certain sections are destitute of foodstuff for cattle, and prefer to receive wheat in order that they may have the by-product. The difference in food-value in bread from wheat milled to 90 per cent, as distinguished from the ordinary milling of about 70 per cent to 75 per cent, does not seem to have been sufficient to warrant the difference in the cost of the two products. The occupation given to Belgian mills and their workmen and the useful production of fodder are all factors which have to be weighed. Moreover, experience in baking has enabled an improvement to be made in the quality of the bread, and there is now a general consensus of opinion in Belgium that the import of wheat is more economical and advisable than that of flour.

APPENDIX XXV

DISTRIBUTION

Reprinted from the Report of the Commission for Relief in Belgium, June 30, 1915.

THE method of the detailed distribution of breadstuffs varies in different provinces. Originally the Communal Committees issued the flour from their communal warehouses to accredited bakers, and these bakers were required to submit lists of customers for approval to the Communal Committee, who then issued supplies on a ratio *per capita* of the bakers' customers. The *per capita* allowance of flour has usually been at the rate of 250 grammes per customer, and from this amount a baker in turn normally produces 325 grammes of bread, a differential being made to the baker between the charge made to him for the flour and the price at which he sells the bread, sufficient to cover the necessary cost of his subsidiary constituents and the employment of his labor. Latterly a system has been proposed by the Commission, and is now in use in several Belgium provinces, by which the local Committees deliver the flour to bakers under contracts which provide that 1.35 kilos of good bread must be produced from 1 kilo of flour, the baker being paid 8 centimes per kilo for baking the flour. The bakers, in this case, deliver the bread to an established depôt, and each family must secure their bread from the nearest sectional depôt. There is thus a better check on the baker as to quantity delivered, and a better guarantee of quality. The adult ration is, as before, 325 grammes of bread *per diem*.

APPENDIX XXVI

SOUP RECIPES

THE soup was made from recipes furnished by the city, with the following as a standard base, for 2,000 persons:

100 kilograms		peas or beans
7½	"	bacon
5	"	leeks
150	"	potatoes
5	"	onions

APPENDIX XXVII

SELLING GIFT GOODS

Reprinted from the Report of the Commission for Relief in Belgium, June 30, 1915.

As described under the Provisioning Department it became necessary, as an administrative measure, to sell all gift food, which thus falls into the general stream of supplies to the Provisioning Department. The moneys realized therefor are handed over to the Benevolent Department, and from that department are given out to the Local Committees in the form of cash subsidies, to enable them to purchase foodstuffs from the general stream for supply to the local destitute. Initially, upon the formation of the Commission, it was intended, and an effort was made, to distribute the actual food so generously contributed into the hands of these Communal Committees throughout Belgium, in order that they might in turn distribute the actual gifts direct to the destitute. It was quickly found that, from the enormous size of the problem, this was wholly impracticable as a matter of administration. The gifts in actual food were of irregular character and irregular arrival, and any given canteen dependent on this source might be supplied with an ample amount of flour one week and the next week have to subsist on beans. Furthermore, the distribution of an actual gift cargo throughout some 2,500 different communes would involve a complete duplication of the system of transportation alongside the distribution of foods provided for sale to those who had means to pay. In any event, these irregular gifts must be supplemented by purchases, and innumerable difficulties arose over the inability to adjust gifts to actual and particular necessities. Furthermore, large quantities

APPENDIX 355

of the material given was of the order of luxuries from a Belgian point of view and had less food value than its realization by sale to the wealthier classes would produce in other commodities. With the confrontation of all these difficulties the direct delivery of such charity could only be done either by a radical change in policy or a very extended and costly administration. It was therefore determined that all gift food should, as stated above, be turned into cash and the cash given to the Communal Relief Committees as subsidies. The prices at which this food has been purchased by the Provisioning Department have been determined on the basis of the replacement value of such foodstuffs at the time they were given to the Commission. No deduction for administration or expenses are made from any gifts. This operation can be expressed from an economic point of view as follows:—All sections of the population must be fed, and as it is socially wrong to give food to any who can pay, therefore, if one hundred sacks of flour are a gift to the Commission, then roughly, as 25 per cent of the population is destitute, twenty-five of these sacks will be consumed by the destitute. Seventy-five will be sold at a profit and more than seventy-five sacks bought, of which in turn the same proportion will be consumed by the destitute and the balance will be sold, and the gift continues to revolve, with accretions from the more well-to-do, until it is all absorbed by the destitute.

It has been believed by the Commission that an understanding of this arrangement by intelligent people could not give rise to any remarks other than those of commendation.

APPENDIX XXVIII

"AMERICAN SHOPS"

EARLY in the spring we opened an "American Shop" for the sale of Commission merchandise, at number 51 rue du Jardin des Arbalétriers. Miscellaneous products had accumulated in our warehouses, and we had no adequate means for distributing them. Some of them were staples, such as oatmeal, but most of them were luxuries, fine canned goods, candies, chocolate, crackers, cakes, and other things which we could sell at a good price and the profits from which we could turn into the benevolent department.

The opening of the shop was made a formal event, solemnized with toasts drunk in wine and with kindly addresses in Flemish and in English by the Burgomaster of the city of Antwerp. The little shop was overcrowded from its beginning. Two kinds of goods were sold there: a few staples, such as rice, corn-meal and oatmeal, and the *de luxe* products which I have mentioned. Only limited quantities of staple articles could be purchased by any one buyer; sales to any but Belgian civilians were prohibited, and a private detective ran down suspicious cases. The personnel of the shop was part paid and part volunteer, so that little expense was attached to it, and the things sold were practically all to the profit of the benevolent department. On the first day they amounted to 600 francs, the second day 800, the third day 1,400, and from that they climbed to a sum between 3,000 and 4,000 francs daily.

A second shop was opened in the rue Albert Grisar for the sale of meat and lard imported by the Commission. This was a greater success even than the first, but long crowds stood waiting their turn day after day, until we were compelled to rearrange our distribution and to ask the city authorities to distribute both meat and groceries through little neighborhood shops and to check all sales by a card system similar to that employed in our distribution of flour and bread.

APPENDIX XXIX

THE CLOTHING WORKSHOP

A COMMITTEE of Belgian ladies, under the able direction of Madame Alphonse de Montigny de Wael, Madame Robert Osterrieth-Lippens, and Countess van de Werve de Vorsselaere, had bought up the dry-goods supplies still in Antwerp and opened a workshop in the theater *Folies Bergères* where clothing might be made and repaired. This *ouvoir* became a Commission station, and the gift clothing was sent directly from the docks to the workshop.

The city of Antwerp at first granted the *ouvoir* a monthly subsidy of 50,000 francs. Later the National Committee assumed charge of its finances, and the workshop was transferred from the theater to the magnificent symphony hall on the rue d'Arenberg, belonging to the *Société royale d'Harmonie*. There was a similar but larger *ouvoir* in Brussels at the *Pôle Nord*, under direction of Madame F. M. Philippson.

The stage of the Antwerp *Harmonie* was piled with boxes of goods. Galleries and pit were spread with rows of sewing machines and work tables, and the cloak room was transformed into a steam and sulphur disinfecting bath, where all materials, new and old, were taken apart and thoroughly cleansed. Nine hundred girls and young women worked under supervision in the warm, well-lighted hall, while about three thousand older women were given sewing to do at home. A group of cobblers in the hall made and repaired shoes. All these workers were paid.

From the central workshop, made goods and unmade materials were sent throughout the Province; the latter to sewing circles in the villages and towns.

In the *Harmonie* the girls were encouraged to sing at their work. One afternoon each week a singing teacher came and gave them lessons in the songs of their country. On the occasions of our inspection trips, the great organ behind the piles of boxes on the stage pealed a sonorous welcome, and the sempstresses sang us the thrilling " Lion of Flanders," the " Brabançonne," and once they greeted us with a verse of the " Star Spangled Banner."

Except for this there was no singing in public. Belgian anthems were under the German ban, and war songs especially were proscribed. Children alone, being privileged characters, chirruped about as they pleased, and occasionally one caught a strange reminiscent echo of a familiar chant.

Once it was the tune of " Tipperary," but the words were new. A child, who had learned them from the British Tommies in Antwerp during the siege, wrote them down for me. At first I could make nothing of them, but careful study and enunciation *à la flamande,* and one has the famous chorus beginning, " It's a long way to Tipperary ":

'Ts se lom wee ti parerie,
'Ts se lom wee du koo,
'Ts se lom wee tu parries,
Tot te zwede ke reino.
Dubei pikatilie, waarrie leskwee.
'Ts se lom lom wee peti parè,
Het myn sklatel.

Antwerp's Clothing Workshop

APPENDIX XXX

TEMPORARY HOUSES

As early as January, 1915, the National Relief Committee began an investigation of the damage to Belgian property caused by the invasion of the Germans, but the work was abruptly stopped by the military authorities, and the Committee was informed that such an investigation lay solely in the province of the occupying power.

Shelters, however, had to be built, even if there could be no general investigation of the extent of the damage. Belgian military engineers had done vast damage in putting the land in a condition for defense. This was particularly the case about the fortress of Antwerp, where before the siege began, two wide belts of country were cleared of forests, bushes, and dwellings, and where the dykes had been cut to flood the low lands. Magnificent castles and country houses were made heaps of ruins; barbed wire entanglements and trenches cut through the sites of hundreds of farm-houses, and in springtime bloody waves of poppies, mixed with blue corn-flowers, flowed over and under the abandoned defenses, or littered with beauty what once were shaven lawns.

The ruin caused by German artillery and incendiaries still further intensified the problem of housing. Hundreds of towns in Belgium and thousands of isolated homesteads all over the land had been burned and battered by the invaders. In the villages and towns of the province of Antwerp—not counting the cities of Antwerp and Malines—4,456 houses were completely destroyed, and 1,938 were greatly damaged, so that at least 18,000 villagers were homeless.

The communes most affected were those along the outer ring of fortifications, such as Cruybeke, Tamise, Bornhem,

Puers, Liezele, Breendonck, Thisselt, Willebroeck, Blaesvelt, Waelhem, Duffel, Wavre-Sainte-Catherine, Koningshoyckt, Lierre, Kessel, and Schilde. Some villages had been annihilated. Not even a cat remained.

By springtime the need was intense. In defiance of all the laws of hygiene, and in most dangerous promiscuity, returning refugees housed themselves in stables with the animals, in cellar pits, or in the lee of old walls.

The Provincial Committee, therefore, set aside funds for the repair or reconstruction of such houses as could be rendered habitable, in whole or in part, and the construction of temporary houses. Requests for such constructions were received through the local relief committees, and if approved, a commission consisting of three architects and a sanitary engineer planned the house and provided the estimates. The structures were single or group houses, or communal barracks. In a few towns and vilages the commission approved the construction of small shops for retail marketing.

Brick for the walls and thick paper for the partitions were the materials commonly used, since both could be employed after the war in the construction of the permanent building. Often it was possible to use part of the bricks from the original building, and sometimes the old foundations and cellar.

Labor and oversight were provided by the local relief committee. The terrible state of unemployment made such labor as this a veritable godsend.

The use of the ground was given to the Provincial Committee by the proprietor or the communal authorities. The temporary house remained the legal property of the Committee, and was liable to destruction on orders of the military authorities, the State, or the province. The occupant paid the Committee a rental of five per cent. of the cost, or, if indigent, he paid nothing. After the war, when the permanent structure is begun, the proprietor has the right to buy of the Committee all the materials used in the temporary structure, and the materials on the ground are the property of the proprietor and not of the Committee.

The cost of these temporary houses is remarkably low. Single structures run from 500 to 600 francs; groups of houses, from 1,200 to 1,705 francs. Repairs of damaged houses are made, as a rule, at a cost of less than 250 francs, on a basis of 40 francs per person.

APPENDIX XXXI

UNEMPLOYMENT RELIEF

MUCH was left to the initiative of the communal committees, and sometimes this brought admirable results. In the industrial commune of Willebroeck there were about 1,400 unemployed workmen out of a total population of 12,000. There was not enough work for all, so that the number of working days during which a man had a right to be employed varied according to the size of his family. The men were then divided into shifts. It is an old Belgian custom for groups of transient laborers to march about the country under a leader who acts as spokesman for the men and overseer for the employer, so the Willebroeck shifts of *chômeurs* had designated leaders who put them to work or enrolled the men on the register of the unemployed on days when the shift was obliged to be idle. The distribution of food and money was made in the same systematic manner. Each shift presented itself with its leader; packages of food were prepared in advance; the booklets identifying the applicants and the amount due them were verified; and in less than four hours there was delivered to the 1,400 unemployed all the assistance in kind or in money to which they were entitled.

APPENDIX XXXII

BRICKS AND LACES

BOTH the Commission for Relief in Belgium and the Provincial Committees were large employers of labor. A fleet of more than three hundred lighters and their crews were engaged in the transport of merchandise from Rotterdam into Belgium. Every province employed hundreds of dockers, shippers, warehousemen, and clerks. In Antwerp we engaged one of the remarkable groups of freight handlers called the "Antwerp Nations": organizations which date from the earliest commercial prosperity of the metropolis, which work co-operatively, declaring monthly dividends and poor relief benefits, hold in common their capital of horses, carts, and houses, obey an elected dean and sub-dean, and have from twenty to sixty members each. We had under contract in the province ten steam mills; one for maize belonging to the National Committee and milled for the whole of Belgium; one working on wheat for the account of the Provincial Committee of Limbourg; one for the Waesland, and seven for the account of the Provincial Committee of Antwerp. We employed clerks and accountants to apportion supplies to the 165 communes in the province, and flour to the 185 bakeries in the city of Antwerp. We engaged private detectives to smell out frauds. We paid thousands of women and girls in the clothing workshops, and in the villages we paid day wages to the builders of temporary houses.

But these efforts were as nothing in the face of the all but universal unemployment.

Commerce and industry were practically dead. Of the natural resources of Belgium, only land and minerals were available for an industrial revival. But agriculture was dead until spring, and the coal mines in the region called the *Borinage*, which hold the most important mineral wealth of Belgium, were already opened by the Germans and worked to their profit. In normal years Belgian imports and exports of coal and coke practically balance.

Coal from the Belgian province of Hainaut was shipped in railway cars and canal boats, and sold through a German *Kohlen-Zentrale* in Brussels. With this revival of industry the Commission for Relief in Belgium and the National Committee had nothing to do.

Our interest in Belgian industry was based solely on plans for the relief of the unemployed. A good case was that of the brick industries in the province of Antwerp. These in peace time employ large numbers of people, and as early as December, 1914, the Antwerp Provincial Committee, the city of Antwerp, and the National Bank of Belgium raised 300,000 francs—one-third of which was subscribed by the Provincial Committee—to subsidize the brick works in the neighborhood of Boom, Rumpst, Terhaegen, Niel, Schelle, and Hemixem, where a working population of more than 15,000 brick workers was idle.

The money was advanced to the communes, which in their turn made advances in salary checks to the workers. Special communal storehouses were established, where workmen and their families could exchange the checks for food and other commodities. Salaries were payable up to eighty per cent in these checks, and food was furnished at reduced prices. The brick factories were responsible for the value of the checks, and were under obligations to repay the sums advanced them, three months after the conclusion of peace.

The case of the brick industry was relatively simple. Bricks can easily be stored, and will be readily marketable after the war when the period of rebuilding begins. In the case of other important industries more serious problems presented themselves, and one by one they were found practically insurmountable.

Lace, however, belongs to another category. It is one of the few industrial products which has no military value, and the Belgian lace industry employs vast numbers of people. Unfortunately, it has been brutally exploited. In peace time the lace-makers receive practically nothing for their work, and are controlled by patrons so closely organized that improvement is almost impossible. Both men and women engage in lace-making. Farm laborers who spend the summers in southern Belgium and in France, spend the winters in their Flemish homesteads, and occupy their spare time with the making of lace. Many of the convent schools are lace factories under another name. And the summer tourist will remember having seen in almost every Belgian village he visited, lines of women and girls, sitting in the streets before their cottages, with a handful of little bobbins, spinning white spider web over wooden pillows laid across their knees. Such villagers are the makers of the famous Mechlin and Valenciennes laces.

Immediate relief, not social reform, was all that the Commission could undertake. On the first enrollment, 43,328 lace workers applied for assistance, and were helped through a lace committee of which Mrs. Brand Whitlock was honorary-president. An attempt then was made by the Commission for Relief in Belgium to sell Belgian laces in America, but the effort was not a success, and the Commission abandoned on principle attempts to vend abroad the products of Belgian toil.

APPENDIX XXXIII

THE CROP COMMISSION

Reprinted from the Report of the Commission for Relief in Belgium, June 30, 1915.

NEGOTIATIONS were initiated in the month of June looking toward the drastic control of the 1915 harvest of breadstuffs. The total harvest of such materials in the "Occupation" zone (all Belgium except West Flanders and about one-half of East Flanders) will be controlled by a Commission comprising Belgian and American representatives from the Commission for Relief and the Comité National, together with representatives of the German authorities. It has been determined that an appropriate proportion of each peasant's production will be set aside for seed and food for his family through the year and will be left in his possession. The excess will be taken over at fixed prices by our organization and distributed *pari passu* with imported material over the entire twelve months. Drastic penalties have been enacted against any traffic in breadstuffs except by the Commission. By these means speculation will be prevented, even distribution secured, and the destination of the breadstuffs to the civil population will be assured. The amount in excess of the requirements of the agriculturists—about 1,250,000 people—is not likely to be very great, but this class will have been placed in a position of security and removed from the care of the Commission so far as breadstuffs are concerned. The actual effect on wheat imports cannot yet be determined, but it appears that owing to the exhaustion of other reserves a continued import of 50,000 tons per month will be necessary after harvest. The great staple of potatoes promises well and it is hoped will be sufficient to carry through next year without imports.

APPENDIX XXXIV
BELGIAN HARVESTS

AGRICULTURE had been a constant concern of the Commission and the National Committee almost from the beginnings of the work. On my arrival in Antwerp in December, 1914, I found a small volunteer organization, called the Agricultural and Horticultural Committee, under the presidency of Mr. W. A. van der Veen, a tall, slender Dutchman who had come to Antwerp with money raised in Holland for charitable purposes, and who intended especially to help the farmers of the country. He had been in the Boer War, and told exciting and picturesque stories of his adventures. It was hard to believe that such an immaculate, devout, energetic gentleman once was elected colonel of a band of Boers because, as he told it, " he was the best thief in the lot." His wartime foraging had given way long since to constructive statesmanship, and he knew exactly how to deal with the Belgian Farmers' Union, called in Flemish, *Boerenbond*. It was through Mr. van der Veen's committee that the Agricultural Section of the Provincial Committee was developed for Antwerp.

Belgium uses a greater weight of chemical fertilizers per square mile than any other country in the world. Besides, peasant children on hands and knees scrape up dung from the roads and put it on the land. The Committee organized an agricultural co-operative society which purchased supplies, such as seed and fertilizers; the communes assisted by placing waste land and supplies at the disposition of farmers, and the crop was his who grew it. In several communes men were encouraged to dig up vacant lots, and the municipality donated seed potatoes and manures.

The close-cropped lawns about some of the finest castles in Belgium were plowed up, and potatoes planted where flowerbeds had been. In many cases choice estates were given wholly to cultivation, and the proprietors saw nothing but potato tops whichever way they looked.

In normal times 18.79 per cent of the population is employed in agriculture, and of these 42.82 per cent are women.

APPENDIX XXXV

THE NORTH OF FRANCE

Reprinted from the Report of the Commission for Relief of Northern France, June 30, 1915.

THE inadequacy of local production, together with the destruction resulting from military operations, brought about a shortage of food supply which threatened the population with famine in its most acute form. The condition of the people was much akin to that of Belgium, but instead of the first symptoms of famine appearing in November, as in the case of Belgium, it was, even in the most denuded districts, delayed until January, and the situation did not become universal before March. . . . The figures indicate a shrinkage of about one million from the normal population, due to the mobilization, emigration, and other wastages due to the war. Practically the whole of the male population eligible for military service has gone, and in addition, a considerable proportion of the elderly men of commercial experience and superior character were drafted into other sections upon the advance of the German army, so that there is in many localities a distinct shortage of men of the experience and character necessary for leadership. The difficulties of organization have, therefore, been correspondingly increased, the labor of distribution being concentrated upon a smaller body of available men than in Belgium. One concomitant of this situation is the preponderance of helpless women and children.

APPENDIX XXXVI

FRENCH FINANCIAL ORGANIZATION

Reprinted from the Report of the Commission for Relief of Northern France, June 30, 1915.

THE whole of the foodstuffs imported are sold to the District Committees at prices fixed by the Commission. The District Committees, in turn, sell the foodstuffs to the Communal Committees at a small advance, sufficient to cover the local cost of redistribution. The communes, in turn, re-sell the foodstuffs without profit to the population. At this point in the cycle an involved transaction is necessary owing to the absolute disappearance of all normal circulating media throughout the country, and in order to provide for the destitute. To supply the deficiency in currency each commune is now printing its own notes from 2 centimes up to 50 francs. This currency is put into circulation by the communes by:

(*a*) Payment for communal services,

(*b*) Loans to individuals against property,

(*c*) Benevolence to the destitute.

Under the latter two classes sufficient advances are made to enable the population to live. The Communal Committees in turn accept this local currency in payment for the ration of foodstuffs which the people eat daily. Thus, the Communal Committees become possessed of local com-

APPENDIX 369

munal currency representing the value of the foodstuffs which they have issued to the population. The Committee, in turn, surrenders these notes to the Communal Authorities against an obligation of the Commune to pay an equivalent sum after the war is over, and these obligations, together with guarantees by the individual members of the District Committees, form the basis upon which advances are obtained abroad. In order to facilitate matters of accounting, the foodstuffs are debited by the Commission to the Comité National Belge, who, in turn, debit them to the various District Committees and secure the necessary obligations in return, the Comité Belge thus having the responsibility of detailed accounting.

As stated above, the Commission fixes the prices at which foodstuffs are debited to the District Committees, and these prices are fixed at a rate somewhat above the cost. A margin is thus secured by the Commission, which is devoted to three purposes:—

(a) Indemnification of Local Committees in cases of accidental destruction of warehouses, or deterioration.

(b) Unforeseen losses in transportation.

(c) Reserve against fluctuations in exchange and food prices.

If any portion of the margin remains after these services it will be ultimately credited to the communes, as the Commission operates absolutely without profit, and the whole of its direction is carried on by volunteers.

In the matter of the reserve for exchange and food fluctuations; it will be readily appreciated that there are violent fluctuations in exchange between the French franc and the foreign markets in which the foodstuffs must be procured against gold, and this, together with the fluctuations in the prices of foodstuffs and the cost of transportation, would render it wholly impossible to charge these foodstuffs out to the District Committees at actual cost from day to day. It was, therefore, determined by the Commission that the whole operation could be greatly simplified by adjusting prices from time to time at round figures, which leave a small margin to cover eventualities. Despite the inaccessibility of the area and the enormous difficulties of transportation and distribution, the price of bread has been maintained at approximately the price in Paris.

APPENDIX XXXVII

FUNDING THE RELIEF WORK

Reprinted from the Report of the Commission for Relief in Belgium, June 30, 1915.

THE joint organizations have secured advances, from patriotic Belgian Banks and Institutions, of an aggregate sum of $10,000,000 of working capital for the Provisioning Department, and this sum, together with the credits which have been obtained by the Commission, would be sufficient to revolve the Department on itself, were it possible to effect exchange of the receipts from food sales. In fact, aside from the working capital, the whole financial problem of the Provisioning Department is one of exchange, and this problem is surrounded with the greatest of difficulties. These difficulties arise from the fact that the receipts in Belgium are entirely in Belgian paper currency, and that this currency is inconvertible into gold, for legal and economic reasons. . . .

While the work of the Provisioning Department is in the nature of a commercial operation, its inception and administration constitute a humanitarian effort of the first order, these phases being:—

FIRST.—The negotiations which have opened the door through the belligerent lines by which foodstuffs may pass through to the Belgian people, and the constant negotiations necessary to maintain this opening, the import and distribution being surrounded with an extensive series of guarantees which form part of the responsibilities of the Commission.

SECOND.—The Department is restricted in its operations by the belligerent governments as to the character and quantities of commodities it can import and by its available resources, and it is therefore necessary to insist upon a just and equitable division of the whole of the imports over the entire population, and in this phase the department has up to date succeeded in its task of at least providing a sufficiency to preserve life and health as is evidenced by the remarkably healthy condition of the entire population.

THIRD.—The footstuffs are sold at a profit, and the profits thus earned are given absolutely to the Benevolent Department for the support of the destitute. These profits are in the nature of a tax on those people in Belgium who have means, for the benefit of the destitute. Such profits have been made possible solely by the generous volunteer executive, commercial, and transportation services, and the amount of these profits is practically the measure of the value of such volunteer service, because the prices fixed for foodstuffs in Belgium have been no greater than retail prices in London. It is interesting to note that, aside from the savings in cost, owing to many direct concessions, the entire overhead expenditure of the Commission as shown by the annexed accounts amounts to considerably less than one per cent of the value of foodstuffs handled.

APPENDIX XXXVIII

GOVERNMENTAL SUBSIDIES

Reprinted from the first Annual Report of the Commission for Relief in Belgium, October, 1915.

IT was . . . agreed in February, 1915, that the British and French Governments would advance monthly £500,000 and 12,500,000 francs, respectively, to the Belgian Government at Le Havre for the service of the Commission for Relief in Belgium. . . .

APPENDIX XXXIX

BELGIAN GRATITUDE

THROUGHOUT this narrative I have not spared the personal pronoun. A further offence against delicacy may be permitted me, as evidence of the Belgian exaggeration of one individual's personal importance and as another example of their feelings toward America and Americans.

Translation of part of an article which appeared in the Nieuwe Rotterdamsche Courant, *Rotterdam, Holland, on October 18, 1915.*

ANTWERP, October 16.

The simple official demonstration which took place this morning in the beautiful Marriage Hall of the City Hall had a specially touching significance. The Burgomaster and Aldermen, as well as the members of the City Council, stood grouped together there, in order to say a few solemn words of thanks to Mr. Edward Eyre Hunt, the delegate of the Commission for Relief in Belgium to the National Relief Committee in the province of Antwerp. Mr. Hunt is leav-

APPENDIX 373

ing for the United States, and the administration of our town wished to celebrate his departure in a suitable way.

Burgomaster Jan de Vos first spoke, to express how much the Belgian people, and especially the Antwerpians, in these tragic times, have to thank their benefactors; for Mr. Hunt has, by his devotion at all times, carried out his beautiful humane task in an exemplary manner. As a sign of our gratitude, our comfortable old City-Father handed to Mr. Hunt, in the name of the city of Antwerp, a gold medal of honor with a figure of our King, and replicas thereof in silver and bronze. The medal has the following inscription: "The City of Antwerp to Mr. Edward Eyre Hunt, 16th October, 1915." Our municipal Secretary, Hubert Melis, was then requested by the Burgomaster to read an address, wherein the grateful feelings of all were recorded. This address is printed on Plantin's press by the master-printers, the famous firm of J. E. Buschmann. It reads literally as follows:

CITY OF ANTWERP

Today, October 16th, 1915, the City Council of Antwerp has assembled with the Burgomaster and Aldermen, to say farewell to Mr. Edward Eyre Hunt on the occasion of his departure from this City, and to thank him for the devotion and the skill shown by him in carrying out his mission as Delegate of the Commission for Relief in Belgium to the National Relief Committee in the province of Antwerp. The gathering thereby requested Mr. Hunt to express to his chiefs, and especially to his fellow-citizens in the United States, the deeply moved feelings of gratitude which Belgium, sorely tried, but so wonderfully upheld, feels for her kind and noble friends across the sea.

The Burgomaster
(Signed) JAN DE VOS.

Antwerp, October 16th, 1915
By order
The Secretary
(Signed) HUBERT MELIS.

Mr. Hunt, much moved, thanked them for their praise, and assured them that he would long hold in warm remembrance his stay in Antwerp.

Significant of the respect and reverence in which Antwerp has held the Americans who came here to relieve the prevailing need, so far as was in their power, is the following fact which has come to my ears, and which should be made known, although I do not wish thereby in any way to wound the modesty of our worthy fellow townsman. A great Antwerp business man, Mr. Bunge, immediately placed his palatial house at Mr. Hunt's disposal, while Mr. Bunge himself went to his country estate at Hoogboom. The liberality of the Americans here found a counterpart in Antwerp hospitality.

Word for word, the address of the city is given above. It is in Dutch, the official language of the Flemish city of Antwerp. When the municipal Secretary wished to repeat the address in English for the benefit of Mr. Hunt, to the surprise of all present Mr. Hunt replied that he had understood the address, since, during the year he had lived in Antwerp, he had felt bound to make himself familiar with the language of the people.

A declaration which went to the hearts of the representatives of the Antwerpians, and which the whole of our people will know how to appreciate as a proof of respect for our national character. A noble American citizen here gave a fine example to many Belgians.

www.ingramcontent.com/pod-product-compliance
Lightning Source LLC
Chambersburg PA
CBHW030213170426
43201CB00006B/76